TIME TO LISTE:
TO CHILDREN

Children's needs and rights are being given greater importance in modern society through government and media attention, yet what children themselves have to say is not often taken seriously by adults.

The views of young people and respected professionals who work with them in social services and child protection, the law, research and education, hospitals and voluntary organisations, are represented in *Time to Listen to Children*. They share their interactions through the medium of counselling, art, music and play therapy and emphasise the importance of our multi-cultural, religious and spiritual backgrounds. It is possible to put aside authority without abdicating responsibility, claim the authors, in order to recognise and hear children as people with rights, opinions and ideas equal, but different, from those of adults.

Focusing on what is special about listening to children as the core of a skilled, reflective yet active relationship, this collection should prove a valuable resource for social workers, teachers, counsellors, mediators, advocates and parents.

Pat Milner is an experienced teacher and former editor of the BAC journal *Counselling* and co-editor of the *BAC Counselling Reader*. **Birgit Carolin** is a former teacher and student counsellor, currently working mainly in the voluntary sector with children.

For Joanna, age 10, the inspirer who listens acutely.
With love from Pat (PM)

For my first grandchild, Orla (BC)

TIME TO LISTEN TO CHILDREN

Personal and professional communication

*Edited by Pat Milner
and Birgit Carolin*

London and New York

First published 1999 by Routledge
11 New Fetter Lane, London EC4P 4EE

Simultaneously published in the USA and Canada
by Routledge
29 West 35th Street, New York, NY 10001

Reprinted in 2000

Routledge is an imprint of the Taylor & Francis Group

© 1999 Pat Milner, Birgit Carolin, and individual contributions
to their authors.

Typeset in Times by
The Florence Group, Stoodleigh, Devon
Printed and bound in Great Britain by
Creative Print and Design (Wales), Ebbw Vale

British Library Cataloguing in Publication Data
A catalogue record for this book is available from the
British Library

Library of Congress Cataloging in Publication Data
Time to listen to children: personal and professional communication/
edited by Pat Milner and Birgit Carolin.
p.   cm.
Includes bibliographical references and index.
1. Children – Services for – Great Britain.   2. Interpersonal
communication in children – Great Britain.   3. Children and
adults – Great Britain.   4. Listening. I. Milner, Pat, 1933–
II. Carolin, Birgit, 1936–   .
HV751.A6T53   1999
362.7'0941–dc21   98–35444
                                             CIP

ISBN 0–415–17197–0 (hbk)
ISBN 0–415–17198–9 (pbk)

CONTENTS

CONTRIBUTORS

Lynne Blount is a team leader with the Primary Behaviour Support Service, Essex. She focuses on the school environment, and works with teachers and children with special educational needs that highlight an emotional or behavioural difficulty. She listens to children and encourages staff to understand and respond to their behaviour in order to break the often negative cycle of parent and teacher attitude. Publications for Essex Information Services include *Creating a Telling School: Anti-bullying pack for primary schools, Playground Games* and *Promoting Positive Behaviour.*

Madge Bray is co-founder of SACCS (Sexual Abuse Child Consultancy Service), Leaps and Bounds and Findus Keep Us, an integrated project of care, therapy and home finding for abused children based in Shrewsbury, England. In April 1998, she left the project and continues to develop this work in new forms and directions. She is the author of *Susie and the Wise Hedgehog Go to Court* (1989), *Poppies on the Rubbish Heap: Sexual abuse – the child's voice* (1991 Canongate press: 1997 Jessica Kingsley) and has contributed to *Protecting Children: Challenges and changes* (Bates, Pugh and Thompson eds 1997) and *Good Practice in Counselling People Who Have Been Abused* (Bear ed. 1998).

Mary Carnell is an experienced infant teacher and trained counsellor. She is currently a home/school link teacher in Cambridge, using play therapy and counselling skills, individually and in groups, to support children through traumatic periods, in consultation with parents.

Birgit Carolin has worked as a teacher and counsellor in London schools, at ChildLine and at Anglia Polytechnic University, Cambridge. She now works as a BAC accredited counsellor in voluntary and private practice, mainly with children.

Penny Cook is a paediatric nurse, counsellor and counselling supervisor. Her work in Addenbrookes NHS Trust hospital includes offering support and counselling to children and families and also bereavement support.

Margaret Crompton has gained social work experience from working with children (Leeds/Lincolnshire), lecturing (Bradford/Newcastle Universities) and writing. Her publications include *Attending to Children: Direct work in social and health care* (1990); *Children and Counselling* (1992); *Children, Spirituality and Religion: A training pack for Central Council for Education and Training in Social Work* (CCETSW 1996); *Children, Spirituality, Religion and Social Work* (1998). Present activities include writing, adult education and self-employed consultancy/training.

Carol Dasgupta is a Counsellor and therapist working in private practice with children, young people and adults. She also works for the Cambridge Family and Divorce Centre, and has worked as a play therapist for the NHS.

Heather Giles is a psychology graduate with a Diploma in Person-centred Art Therapy. As a teacher she is responsible for education in the Berkshire Adolescent Unit, where she has run a weekly art therapy group for seven years, aiming to empower young people to create positive change in their own lives.

Colleen McLaughlin is a tutor at the University of Cambridge School of Education, where she is involved in the in-service education of teachers in counselling, guidance, pastoral care and personal/social education, plus research and development work into exclusion from school, guidance and drugs education. Publications include *Counselling in Schools* (McLaughlin and Bovair 1993); *Reviewing, Evaluating and Monitoring Teacher Appraisal: A pack for schools* (McLaughlin and Pumfleet 1995); *Counselling and Guidance in Schools: Developing policy and practice* (McLaughlin, Chisholm and Clark 1996).

Micky Mendelson is a Froebel trained infant teacher specialising in art. She trained in person-centred art therapy and counselling and is experienced as an art therapist and counsellor with children and young people in schools, with social services and voluntary agencies. She has also worked for the NHS and voluntary agencies in the field of alcohol dependency, and is currently in private practice as a counsellor and art therapist.

Pat Milner is an experienced teacher and counsellor of children and students. A Fulbright Scholar, she started the Student Counselling service at University College London, was founder chair of the Association for Student Counselling and tutor to counselling courses at South West London College and Goldsmiths College, London University, in addition to practising as a counsellor and supervisor. For three years she was features editor of *Counselling*, the journal of the British Association for Counselling. Her first publication was *Counselling in Education* (1974, 1980). Recent books include *Counselling: The BAC counselling reader*

(Palmer, Dainow and Milner eds 1996); *Help on the Line: Essential skills for listening and communicating by telephone* (Palmer and Milner 1997) and *Integrative Stress Counselling: A humanistic problem focused approach* (Milner and Palmer 1998).

Pat Monro is a London solicitor working at one of the first specialist child care legal practices to be established in the UK. She is a member of the Law Society Children Panel.

Virginia Morrow was formerly at the Centre for Family Research and Faculty of Social and Political Sciences, University of Cambridge, and is now a Research Fellow at the Gender Institute, London School of Economics and Political Science. Her publications include *Understanding Families: Children's Perspectives*, a report for the Joseph Rowntree Foundation (1998).

Amelia Oldfield has worked as a music therapist in Cambridge for seventeen years. She was the joint initiator of the MA in music therapy training at Anglia Polytechnic University, where she is a part-time lecturer. She has researched music therapy for adults with severe learning difficulties (MPhil), and writes and lectures extensively on many aspects of music therapy. She has four young children and plays the clarinet in local orchestras and chamber groups.

Dorothy Eddi Piper is a BAC Accredited counsellor who works at the Trust for the Study of Adolescence as Co-ordinator of Adolescent Mental Health Training Initiative. She manages the Youth Empowerment Project 'Youth Voice', which involves young people in the training of adults and the 'Someone to talk to' project which is developing a range of nationally accredited training for counsellors of young people. She is a course director of the Cascade Associates/University of East London accredited Certificate in Counselling Supervision. Her previous experience includes teaching, residential care, youth work, therapy in child guidance clinic and stage management. She is currently in private practice offering counselling, play therapy, supervision and training.

Barbara Smedley combines her extensive experience in direct work with children and in social services management, and in operating an independent consulting, training and play therapy service in Wales. She is used widely by agencies concerned with providing help for children who suffer emotional and behavioural difficulties. Barbara also undertakes inspections of social service departments and children's homes. She was a contributor to *Protecting Children: A guide for social workers undertaking comprehensive assessment* (DSS 1988).

Lennox K. Thomas had a background in psychiatric social work and probation before training in psychoanalytic psychotherapy. He works as an individual and family therapist, and his current clinical interest is in the psychological development of black children in contemporary British society. He is active in the development of anti-discriminatory practices in psychotherapy and is a member of the Intercultural and Equal Opportunities Committee of the United Kingdom Council for Psychotherapy (UKCP). He is Clinical Director of Nafsiyat, Intercultural Therapy Centre, and joint course director of University College London MSc in Intercultural Psychotherapy. He has published works on the effects of race and ethnicity on the therapeutic process, gender issues, child protection and organisational analysis, and has long-term consultancy and teaching posts in Germany, Denmark and the Caribbean.

Penny Toller worked as a teacher in inner London schools before joining ChildLine, where she was responsible for the training and development of volunteer counsellors. She works as a counsellor and training consultant in London.

FOREWORD

Just as there is no such thing as a perfect childhood, there cannot be a child alive who does not know suffering; the process and progress of life itself integrates both suffering and joy, but often in very differing measure.

Suffering may come with an awesome shock as the babywalker topples and a small head makes its first unexpected contact with a concrete floor, or as the sudden isolation of being small, alone and lost among the supermarket shelves is ended by the terrible relief of being pounced on by a panic-stricken mother and shaken and shouted at for wandering off. Such experiences and others like them combine with childhood's lollipops and ice-cream to become part of the agony–ecstasy rollercoaster of everyday life. There are many children too for whom the slow, gnawing, jagged woundedness of verbal, physical and sexual assaults on minds and bodies, perniciously tearing at the fabric of their well-being, is fearful beyond telling.

Common to all suffering is fear. And fear lives in all of us. Its positive, short-term purpose helps us to deal with danger, but in a concentrated form its effects can be lifelong. It paralyses our thinking. It changes the way our bodies behave. It alters our capacity to trust the world. It causes us to lose trust in ourselves. Its cumulative legacy prevents us from loving fully, from being all that we are.

To be heard and understood without judgement, to have another human being bear witness to both our suffering and our joy, is a basic human need. To share time with a person who, with wisdom and compassion, can see through the smokescreen of our defensiveness and truly hear what is often beyond words – this is the very stuff of healing. Such a gift, when we are still children, is very precious. In this generation, as in those past, many live their whole lives in yearning – never to receive it.

Time to Listen to Children is a pioneering book, sharing with readers the experience of innovative people who have been courageous enough to go beyond their own fears, to step out and place their heads above the parapet in order to challenge our instinctive fear of children. Such people have, on their behalf, confronted the established order of things, which has its roots

xi

in the collective fear of generations past, whose reflex response is to reject and deny those who seek to create change in a society that is often more comfortable with the status quo of not knowing that which concerns children.

In this book we are given an opportunity to listen to people who have worked extensively with children in many settings, to share their wisdom and experience and to learn from them. Within these pages we find unconditional love being lived in thoughts and actions. There is love in the tentativeness of the adults; there is love and infinite encouragement for the task and in the voices of the children. It is the children who will us on. Within them is a universal wisdom that knows that this quality of listening represents hope for their own individual futures, and hope for a collective future that is not dominated by fear.

It is truly a privilege to have been asked to write this foreword.

Madge Bray
April 1998

ACKNOWLEDGEMENTS

Lines from the poem 'A Witness' from *The Brazen Serpent* (1994) by Eiléan Ní Chuilleanáin are reproduced by kind permission of the author and The Gallery Press, County Meath, Ireland.

To Siobhán Carolin for permission to quote from *Goldilocks Goes to Nursery*.

Thank you to Michèle for decoding my longhand; to numerous friends and relations for their encouragement; to Hélène and John, Chloe and Peter for maintaining base camp in Blackheath; to Peter and his department for invaluable technical help (BC).

INTRODUCTION

Our world seems to be one in which people are increasingly conscious of their 'rights' and this has both direct and indirect consequences for children.

Some women whose fertility has been switched off by their biological clocks, decide that they want the 'right' to have a child. Some couples who are infertile want the 'right' to have a child who may be related genetically to both, one or neither of them. Two women who love each other or two men in a homosexual relationship may want the 'right' to have a child.

Changes such as the upholding of the UN Convention on the Rights of the Child (ratified by the UK in 1991) and the passing of the England and Wales Children Act 1989, have produced a set of principles that acknowledge that children have rights, not only supporting their basic need for care and protection, but also rights to be consulted, to have information made available to them, to challenge decisions made on their behalf and generally to participate and have their voice heard in matters that affect them. The 'legalisation' of children's rights in this way was an intended move from parental rights to parental responsibility. In practice it is seen in different and sometimes opposite ways as meaning more rights for professionals such as social workers and therefore fewer rights for parents (or vice versa). For children, it still too often appears to be no change and no gain. To set the record straight, UNICEF has produced a leaflet *Questions Parents Ask*, which deals with the most commonly asked questions about the Convention on the Rights of the Child (UNICEF 1997).

If we are to respect the principles for which our government has legislated, it will clearly affect the way in which we recognise children as active participants in society. To give increased recognition to children's views and perspectives on a range of issues that affect them, we have somehow to learn to hear what they think, feel and need. In short, we have to listen to them. That is what this book is about.

Authors and publishers are amongst the people who recognise this: Bannister *et al.* (1997); Davie *et al.* (1997); John (1997a and b) and Macleod and Morris (1997) all catch the tide of children's rights and give support

1

to the idea that children have something important to say about themselves and their lives.

However, this particular book is not a treatise on children's rights, but rather a cluster of islands of child-centred excellence in practice, which illustrate how our authors use time to listen to children on matters that concern them and decisions that affect them. The outcome of their work is to enable children to learn an understanding, respect and responsibility for themselves, plus a respect and understanding for others. We hope that these contributions from a variety of settings will interest and stimulate readers to reconsider their own listening skills and attitudes.

We are aware that it is difficult to intervene or offer the fruits of experience on behalf of children without being perceived as anti-parent, teacher, social worker or anti- other adults with responsibility or power over children. This is not our intention and we want to make that clear. We are child-friendly, but not, we hope, child ignorant. Our writers treat the difficulties of listening to children with care and humility, and whilst we do not claim to have all the answers, we do offer the benefits of considerable experience.

What makes listening difficult?

Paradoxically, children's voices can be strong and sometimes strident and impossible to ignore, particularly en masse. A public example may be seen when a group of boisterous children share a railway carriage with other passengers, some of whom wince, affect sleep, look away or take other avoiding action by moving seats or changing carriages, whilst others smile and engage one or two children in conversation.

Almost without exception, our authors consider the difficulties of listening to children and describe those aspects of our adult selves that can contribute to these. The dynamic energy of children, whether in a group, or individually, can activate in us a multifaceted fear. Briefly, it is a feeling in which we seem to be wary of several things:

- our own inner child, or memories of our own childhood
- children's power and their taking over, or of our own power
- losing our control, or of children losing theirs
- children's aggression, or of our own
- indulging and therefore 'spoiling' children
- their sexuality and perhaps our own, and, more recently
- possible child-protection litigation

Such fears are sometimes well-grounded: recent gang killings outside schools, or the murder of a toddler by young boys together with the ambiguities arising from accusations of false memory syndrome are more isolated examples of the worst of those fears being realised. These examples, and many less serious ones, illustrate that children do need adults to demonstrate an understanding control, without which some situations can escalate and get devastatingly out of hand.

We are also familiar with the iniquitous influence of individual or group 'pester-power', to which all adults, but parents in particular, are vulnerable. That persistent wheedling, perhaps embarrassingly in a public place, or just when you are at a crucial stage of cooking a meal, mending the car, in the middle of a piece of work, a favourite TV programme, or just desperately tired:

> 'Can I have this video/toy/computer game/latest fashion gear/ trainers/money? Why can't I have it? David/Karen has these . . . if s/he has them why can't I have them?' Escalating to 'Ohhhhh! Mum/Dad you're so mean!!!! Ugggh I hate you!!!'

When they are a little older there is a slightly different scenario:

> 'Can I go to Karen's all-night birthday party on Saturday? I can can't I? Everybody else is going, I'll be the only one not there. How can you put me in this awful position of letting down my friends? If you don't want to worry you can easily take me and pick me up afterwards. Plee-ease don't let me down!'

If they go to the party, parents lie awake all night worrying about alcohol, drugs and sex, or worse. If they don't go, parents are punished with dumb insolence and feel guilty and totally unreasonable. Even more worrying are those young people who avoid the conflict and just go out at night without telling anybody where they will be or when they may be home.

This is 'pester-power', with accompanying non-verbal gestures of pleading, defiance or sulkiness that would put any Victorian melodrama in the shade. These are unreasonable demands. Children know this and they also know, in their hearts, that they are being selfish when they make them. However, they have a driven need to push their boundaries in order to get ready to fly the nest when the time comes.

Parents often insist firmly that they do listen to their children, when what actually happens is that they succumb to the nagging of pester-power. Winning these battles might turn out to be a Pyrrhic victory for children, their practical satisfactions transitory. Defeat leaves parents inwardly resentful, often spending money they would rather put toward something else in an attempt to buy peace, to please, to be 'with it' or simply because they believe that this is what loving, listening parents need to do.

Is it too fanciful to suggest that months and years of the demands of 'pester-power' can cause loving parents to grow to dislike their children and to cease to enjoy living with them, and of course vice versa? Although we do not have research to prove it, we speculate that these kinds of pressures contribute to ruined adult relationships, separation and divorce; put heavy pressure on the careers of women in particular; deeply affect finances and lifestyles and add immeasurable stress to family life. But those who pay the highest emotional price when families disintegrate are children. Set against that kind of background, parents and children have to get enormous emotional satisfaction from one another if the balance of their relationship is to be seen as a positive one.

Children are a special case; they are our society's most vital investment. However, they are a long-term investment costing money and absorbing adult time and sacrifice to support them. The interest on that investment for many adults is the personal fulfilment that growing children can bring. We propose that the interest rate on that investment rises in relation to the time, commitment and skills afforded to child/adult relationships. In our noise-filled world, the art of listening with undivided attention is seriously at risk, the skill of knowing what you want and need to say and communicating it equally so. Children can be seen clamouring to have their material wants indulged and their urgent needs gratified, but they are seldom able to ask for what we all need: a respectfully listening ear.

That is also what this book is about.

Background

The primary task of all our authors is to listen to children, but it is not their sole task; they are also required to respond helpfully. They embrace a range of psychological and creative approaches – cognitive behavioural, person-centred, psychodynamic, art, music and play therapy – and represent a variety of professional areas – child protection, counselling, counselling training and supervision, education, social work, the law, multi-cultural therapy, nursing and research. We have also included some observations of the very important work of voluntary agencies and the spiritual needs of children.

Despite their diversity of approach and setting, our writers are united in having a deep conviction about their work and in sharing the distilled essence of some of that work in listening to children. They were chosen because they have wisdom to share; some have written about their work before, but not all have had the opportunity to publish their views previously.

Theoretical influences

We asked our writers to refer to the theoretical foundations that support their work, and these include a variety of influences and training. Developmental psychology necessarily informs any study of work with children, and

Piaget is cited here. However, Eric Erikson's psychodynamic work includes a strong developmental emphasis, and he is amongst the influences from the psychodynamic tradition. Anna Freud and Melanie Klein; Donald and Clare Winnicott, together with the attachment theory arising from John Bowlby's writings on mothers and babies, are also mentioned, particularly to underpin play therapy.

We include a chapter that specifically focuses on play therapy, but the use of play as therapy is echoed in several other chapters, and it is Virginia Axline, the internationally renowned exponent of person-centred play therapy (who worked with Carl Rogers in Chicago), who has a pivotal influence in several of our contributions.

The reality therapy of William Glasser and other more cognitive behavioural influences that are unspecified are, not surprisingly, to be found in our chapter on education.

An integrative approach

Within the diversity of their background and approach, another common core that unites our contributors is their child-centredness, echoing the person-centred work of Carl Rogers, the American psychologist who blazed a trail in humanising, structuring and researching the helping process called counselling. He integrated the core human-quality skills of genuineness, unconditional positive regard and accurate empathy, claiming that when counsellors offered these and clients experienced them being offered, they would be enabled to understand themselves better, to free their personal resources and to manage their lives in more effective ways.

On Becoming a Person (1961) is Rogers' most popular book, and it is one which speaks to people all over the world, describing his own development and the evolution of person-centred therapy. A later, very readable account of his approach is to be found in *A Way of Being* (1980), for it had by then become a person-centred approach to life. Since Rogers' pioneering work, other psychologists have extended his humanistic experiential approach by focusing in more detail than he did himself on those interpersonal communication skills that support it. Gerard Egan has consistently refined and integrated Rogers' basic work into his own problem management approach in *The Skilled Helper* (1998).

Rogers' core conditions

Genuineness, congruence or realness is fundamental to the best communication. When we are aware of our feelings, thoughts and experiences and when that awareness is present in what we communicate, we are what Rogers would call genuinely or really ourselves. Several of our contributors link genuineness to the development of self-awareness and stress its crucial role in listening to children. Dorothy Eddi Piper points up the care that is needed in our relationships with children because their experience of life is necessarily more limited than that of adults:

> We attempt to be . . . genuinely ourselves and we need to be as open and honest with children as is consistent with our judgement of how such openness would improve the relationship or further the therapeutic activity. . . . We need to be . . . careful with children because they will interpret our actions and words in the light of their previous limited understanding and experience of adults. They may come to unhelpful conclusions, such as that they are themselves the cause of our behaviour or feelings.
>
> (p. 31, this volume)

Unconditional positive regard is a lengthy term for what in everyday language might be called acceptance, caring and respect. It can be described simply as a particular way of seeing ourselves or a child, positively accepting our own, or their, thoughts and feelings – of confusion, anger or fear – without conditions or judgement and responding to them with care and dignity.

Barbara Smedley integrates self-awareness and respect in her chapter on child protection:

> In order to be alongside children . . . [adults] need great sensitivity and self-awareness. They must be aware of their own feelings, not in order to re-work them at the expense of the children they are trying to help, but to have a deep respect for them; because in understanding and valuing our own feelings we begin to unlock the door to a trusting relationship being established with a child.
>
> (p. 115, this volume)

Empathy embraces sensing accurately the feelings and 'personal meanings', as Rogers himself called them, that a child is experiencing and reflecting these back to them for their understanding. Thus empathic understanding is a sensitive, active listening that respects difference, and this is rare. We may think we listen, but we rarely do so with real insight or true empathy, in the way that many of our chapters illustrate. We listen to words rather than to 'meanings', which can clearly put children at a verbal disadvantage, and we are often too busy forming our own response to value what we hear. Amelia Oldfield, a musician, says of her work with Martin that they both learned to trust one another sufficiently to listen before initiating further ideas of their own; whilst Penny Cook says simply that in a hospital setting she is trying to understand how children feel in the situation as they see it.

6

Combining genuineness, respect and empathy in our listening brings us into a relationship with children and it is that, more than any technique we may use, that allows children to take what they need to heal their lives.

The book's pattern

Part 1: Setting the scene

The theme is children's voices and the scene is set in Chapter 1 by a medley of these, beginning with simple observations of the youngest as we listen in on their everyday lives in a playground, nursery school, a primary school and as they eat out. Fairy stories introduce a literary motif, role play, an issue of moral behaviour and illustrate the fear and anxiety that are intrinsic to the everyday lives of children.

Two older children share their experience of the death of a parent and the counselling that followed. Grief is so often wordless, and we thank Tiffany and Elizabeth, as they wish to be known, for their courage in giving sorrow such fresh and authentic words, and their counsellor for giving them time to allow it to happen.

Another part of setting the scene is to give pre-eminence to the part supervision plays in sustaining people who work with children who are troubled. Several of our authors comment that hearing of disaster befalling children or perhaps of their mistreatment, is usually much more distressing than hearing of similar events happening to adults. Supervision is a responsible way of monitoring and understanding our work while taking care of ourselves and thereby the children we help. Penny Toller invites us in Chapter 3 to consider the complexities and perplexities but also the pleasures of supervision.

> That a child is an individual with feelings and wishes that may be different from those of other members of the family or from peers is an attitude that cannot be taken for granted amongst those who have power over children.
>
> (p. 50, this volume)

One way of changing attitudes is through training. An increasing number of statutory and voluntary groups are stepping up training programmes to enable people to do the work legally required by the Children Act 1989. Penny Toller shows in Chapter 3 how training can help adults with power to recognise children as individuals in their own right. In echoing some of the pitfalls included in Chapter 2, she pays attention to the crucial role of self-awareness and the temptation to rush into action on behalf of children, when faced with the pain of their distress. Her chapter illustrates the value of training as a way out of ignorance and possessiveness into understanding and skill.

Part 2: Multicultures, multifaiths

We live in a society of many cultures, which themselves embrace many faiths. We wish to acknowledge the importance of both these facts in working with children, particularly in listening to their experience, since this will enable us to respect and understand both their difference and our difference.

Lennox Thomas, a multicultural therapist, shares his experience in Chapter 4 in suggesting that:

> child development theories have never featured the experience of black children in a white society, nor in a multicultural society. Thus a whole range of diversity and difference is often missed and therapeutic work with these children can sometimes bear poor results.
>
> (p. 66, this volume)

He speaks universally in stressing the key importance of the issue of self-esteem and self-love for children from rejected or discriminated against groups.

Margaret Crompton reminds us in Chapter 5 that the existence of spirituality is assumed in the UN Convention on the Rights of the Child (1989) and that the Education Reform Act (1988) calls for attention to be paid to children's spiritual development. However, the notion of spiritual well-being is a difficult one for us to address, though children seem more comfortable in this realm than most adults. Questions of religion can also be dismissed as difficult or irrelevant:

> when a girl announced that she had become a Christian, a social worker told a colleague (also a Christian) 'I'm glad you were there, I wouldn't have known how to respond.' Yet both professional practice and everyday life require individuals to respond to many matters of which they have no direct experience, or about which they have personally strong feelings.
>
> (p. 86, this volume)

Part 3: At work with children

Whilst our whole book is about working with children, in Part 3 we focus on particular work settings in which children may or do spend time, beginning with the most obvious one, education. Children who attend school regularly spend about 50 per cent of their waking weekdays there, and they are required by law to do this for about 75 per cent of each year between the ages of 5 and 16, spending much more time there than they do with their families. Yet, seeing a child alone in privacy is the most uncommon activity to occur in a school. . . . However what is clear is that children still want to be listened to and value it enormously and many teachers still want to listen primarily to the child's voice.

(p. 98, this volume)

Three teachers illustrate innovations that deserve wider consideration in Chapter 6. Colleen McLaughlin tunes in to the many different voices abroad in education and introduces the teaching of interpersonal skills to teachers; helping children to listen to each other as peer counsellors, and structured listening in groups, such as 'circle time'.

An introduction to Mary Carnell's work as a home/school link teacher in a primary school is illustrated evocatively through play therapy sessions with Jade, Tom and Nick, three of the

many children whose days do not start peacefully and for whom sleep does not come easily . . . [who] arrive at school tired, often late, without breakfast and with a catalogue of domestic disaster to pass on . . . before any learning process can possibly begin.

(p. 102, this volume)

The exclusion of children of all ages from school, usually for behaving unacceptably, is used with the best of utilitarian intentions: 'the greatest good of the greatest number'. As a school governor, one of the editors (PM) finds the increase in exclusions disturbing and sitting on a permanent exclusion panel a most unhappy experience, sometimes made particularly poignant by a desperate parent who thanks you for having 'listened and tried'. It does indeed feel like an irreversible judgement; a child's education is often scrap-heaped, their life wasted, we have failed them and they have failed themselves, they are written off by society at 12 or younger, and their mother says 'thank you' and means it.

The work of behaviour support teachers like Lynne Blount could begin to make a difference to this sorry situation, because they visit schools to provide 'quality interventions' that help both teachers to understand and children to change those behaviours that are troublesome and make them wretched, *before* they lead to exclusion. Cognitive behavioural interventions integrated with humanistic relationships can show children and teachers ways of changing seemingly intractable situations.

ChildLine, the telephone help line, has a decade of primary sources on those life experiences that trouble children, from their own voices. Perhaps their work on 'CHIPS', the newly formed Childline in Partnership with Schools project, together with their support for peer counselling, may in time bring similar benefits to education (ChildLine 1996).

A behaviour support teacher may well have been able to help Adam to avoid permanent exclusion from school. Together with Lisa and Daniel, Adam offers insights and feedback to social workers in child protection, in Barbara Smedley's chapter (7) 'Child Protection: facing up to fear'. We wish them all well and thank them for their enthusiasm and wisdom, in the face of adversity. This chapter focuses on the complex and difficult area of communication with children who may have suffered abuse, and considers some of the dilemmas facing workers and children. It explores the use of non-directive play therapy as a means of enabling children in this precarious situation to express their wishes and feelings in a way that has meaning for them and enables those in the adult world to offer them care and protection. Barbara Smedley is another of our writers to underline the importance of self-awareness in those adults who wish to help neglected and abused children: 'to help . . . we need to face and understand our own fears before we can begin to really understand theirs. Child protection dominated by fear and anxiety becomes risk insurance' (p. 113, this volume). What these children seem to be telling us is that if we wish to enter their world, we need to be emotionally competent. 'The emotionally charged content of child protection and therapy goes to the very heart of the worker's sense of self' (p. 114). We also need some specific training and supervision.

Medicine and the people who work in it can prove intimidating even to many worldly adults, as a glance round a GP's surgery can prove. Penny Cook confirms this in Chapter 8, where she offers simple and practical examples from her experience as a paediatric nurse and counsellor.

> Medical settings present a range of experiences for adults and children alike. Many adults feel afraid, apprehensive, overwhelmed or ill-informed, and it is not surprising that children might feel the same. Empathic understanding from adults goes a considerable way towards helping children; we need to remember the importance of listening to what they are telling us.
>
> (p. 138, this volume)

In life and death, Diana, Princess of Wales, has helped charities and voluntary organisations to promote the welfare of society's youngest and most vulnerable members. She gave of her care and her time, as the volunteers in these organisations do. Birgit Carolin has a long-standing active interest in voluntary groups who listen to children and young people. In Chapter 9 she observes five diverse examples of these, ranging from the Children's Hours Trust, which helps young children to begin 'to grow a happier life'; through counselling for children affected by their parents' divorce; a children's service of Cruse Bereavement Care; an education support centre for school-age mothers and a young people's counselling service. We think these are all examples of work about which others may wish to seek further information.

Part 4: Listening creatively

Creative approaches have particular therapeutic value in work with young children and those for whom verbal communication is a struggle. Because the 'medium is the message' and taps into a different sensing level, it can often reach where other, more word dependent approaches cannot. This is why we have asked three people who work in creative ways with children to give us the benefit of their experience.

'In working with children it seems a delicate balance to achieve a private space for safe, free expression, rather than a collusive experience that burdens and inhibits' (p. 168, this volume). A reliance on predominently verbal communication can burden and inhibit some children. Chapter 10, '"I'm going to do magic . . ." said Tracey', which gives insight into the use of person-centred art therapy in a young person's psychiatric unit and with young children in a primary school, is revealing in the extent to which both authors achieve a private space for safe, free expression. Heather Giles prepares her art therapy group and tells us how she introduces them to the idea of using art. 'We talk about "having a go", being spontaneous and trusting oneself. There is inevitably initial embarrassed sniffing and shuffling as they question my state of mind!' (p. 163). We follow their development and progress in the world of 'images'. Micky Mendelson tells the story of four disquieted small children, Jack, Tracey, Lara and Jason, and their journey through twelve sessions of person-centred art/play therapy. It is a privilege to accompany them.

Although several writers illustrate the use of play as therapy, Carol Dasgupta provides in Chapter 11 a theoretical sketch of the development of play therapy which includes psychodynamic influences and the work of Virginia Axline. Play therapy is commended as an approach in which 'children will experience being accepted as they are and will be given the empathic understanding, warmth and security they are unlikely to experience in other relationships' (p. 179). Philip was referred to Carol because of concerns about his out-of-control behaviour, and we share in their struggles through twenty-two sessions of play therapy.

'I have an interactive approach that involves live and mostly improvised music making. Most of the children I work with (but not the parents) are unaware of the therapy process' (p. 189). Amelia Oldfield combines developmental, behavioural and psychodynamic insights in her interactive music therapy which is used to help both children and families. In Chapter 12 she illustrates how music can be of particular therapeutic help to children for whom words are not a natural means of communication, and how it can provide 'enormous release from pressures of everyday life (for parents and children) particularly in the "parenting project"' (p. 195).

Part 5: Children research and the law

The final section of our book contains two chapters that are really commentaries on two subjects that are not part of everyday life for most children. The first is research into what children in school have to say about family and kinship.

The Economic and Social Research Council (ESRC) are in the middle of an on-going multidisciplinary project, *Children 5–16: Growing into the 21st century*, which will continue into the next millenium. The twenty-two overlapping projects seek to listen to children's own experiences and responses to their social circumstances, including divorce, co-parenting after divorce, young people's values, their moral education and their sense of identity (including their sexuality), how they live with disability and their experience of a computer world. This project sees children's responses as potentially important in developing social policies for improving their quality of life (ESRC 1997).

We do not need to wait until the year 2000, because Virginia Morrow's chapter gives us a current view of research with children in school as she takes us through her work on *Attending to the Child's Voice* for the Joseph Rowntree Foundation (see Morrow 1998). She calls for more creativity from researchers, emphasising the need for a diversity of communication, not a sole reliance on verbal, or one to one, interaction, and gives examples from her project.

> If we are going to listen to children (which is innovative in itself), then we are going to have to be innovative about doing so in a way that is appropriate and satisfactory and, hopefully, meaningful to the [children] themselves.
>
> (p. 214 this volume)

Our final chapter is different. It is a point of reference rather than a narrative account. If medicine is intimidating for children, as we have suggested, then coming into contact with 'the law' can be traumatic beyond belief (and that is just the experience of being a witness in a road traffic case, PM). There is a group of solicitors calling themselves the Association of Lawyers for Children, and Pat Monro, a 'legal humanist', is one of them. She treads the narrow path through what appears to many of us to be the minefield of the law, as it relates to children who may not themselves have broken that law. Her contribution is important because it highlights, in legal language, the reality and the extreme difficulties of actually using legal remedies in the service of children. It is as if she were saying 'If I want to help a child, I must keep in my head all the legal background. In listening to them I have to ascertain the where and the how of this child's circumstances, to be able to lawfully activate legal remedies which will make "good enough" intervention in their life.' We hope it may be a useful reference.

Now let's hear from the children themselves.

References

Bannister, A., Barrett, K. and Shearer, E. (1997) *Listening to Children*. Chichester: Wiley.

ChildLine (1996) ChildLine in Partnership with Schools Project (CHIPS). ChildLine, Royal Mail Building, Studd Street, London N1 0QW

Davie, R., Upton, G. and Varma, V. (1997) *The Voice of the Child*. London: Falmer Press.

Egan, G. (1998) *The Skilled Helper*. Pacific Grove, CA: Brooks Cole (6th edition).

ESRC (1997) *Children 5–16: Growing into the 21st century*. Swindon: Economic and Social Research Council.

John, M. (1997a) *The Child's Right to a Fair Hearing*. London: Jessica Kingsley.

—— (1997b) *The Child's Right to Resources*. London: Jessica Kingsley.

Macleod, M. and Morris, S. (1997) *Why Me?* London: ChildLine.

Rogers, C. R. (1961) *On Becoming a Person*. Boston: Houghton Mifflin.

—— (1980) *A Way of Being*. Boston: Houghton Mifflin.

UNICEF (1997) *Questions Parents Ask*. UNICEF, Unit 3, Rignals Lane, Galleywood, Chelmsford, Essex CM2 8TU.

Part I

SETTING THE SCENE

Why have we for so long neglected one of the most important tools of prevention, namely, listening to the voices of children themselves? Long before they can speak, infants reveal by their behaviour and through their play whether their need for loving, consistent care is being met or not; while older children show even more unmistakably 'early warning' signs and, of course, can express their anxieties verbally, provided there is someone who is perceptive enough and has time enough to listen.

The Needs of Children
(Mia Kelmer Pringle 1980: 161)

1

A MEDLEY OF CHILDREN'S VOICES

Birgit Carolin and Pat Milner

Beyond the walls, I can hear the children playing
In the riverbed. If I could tell what they are crying
It would lighten my darkness like knowing the language of birds.
(Chuilleanain 1994)

Introduction

The word infant means 'wordless', without speech. Yet every infant is born with a voice and the urge, powerful as hunger, to communicate. Long before language can convey their meaning, babies are programmed to communicate emotion and need, insistently, even stridently, in a way no listener can ignore.

Infants are, equally, born listeners. Within the womb they have become attuned to their mother's heartbeat, movements, patterns of rest and activity. As newborn babies they can distinguish the voices of those who care for them and are startled by sudden, loud noises, although they can sleep through thunderstorms and the sound of heavy traffic. Long before they have learned to copy the sounds they hear, they are busy experimenting with their own voices, shaping their own language. When they begin to acquire the vocabulary that names their familiar world, they are actively putting to use all that they hear around them.

If we, as adults were half so attentive, there would be no need for this book to be written. If we still had the capacity, with which we were born, to absorb what we hear and to take seriously what children say (or do not say, because of shyness or fear), there would be less misinformation and suspicion around listening to them.

This chapter contains the voices and words of children of all ages. The written contributions by young people were eagerly and readily given; they gladly chose their pseudonyms – or remained themselves – and are excited about appearing in print. Those who are too young to write have made

17

their own important contribution by demonstrating how, with actions, sounds and words, they express their feelings and communicate their needs in the confident expectation of being heard.

It is time to listen.

We begin by overhearing children in their everyday lives.

In a playground

It is an afternoon in early autumn, warm and bright. The playground is bubbling with the sound of children: an eager noise composed of mingled calls, shouts, cries and laughter. Their play is energetic and purposeful, under the watchful eye of adults, who occasionally come to the rescue of a little one in trouble, or comfort an older one whose sobs rend the air. Here is a toddler on the seesaw, crowing with delight each time he flies up and chortling in happy anticipation of the bump when he comes down to earth. His mother, her eye on the pram that has begun to rock to the rhythm of her awakening baby, cannot persuade him to get off the seesaw when she does. Obstinately he clings on but without her he is grounded. 'More, more, more!' he insists. 'MORE !' She obligingly leans on her end, so that he can once more enjoy the sensation of lift-off, reminding him that it is time to go home for tea. They call to one another across the length of the seesaw between them – he demanding, she demurring – and finally she turns firmly away to attend to the baby, whose cries are becoming persistent. The little boy pushes vigorously upwards as far as his sturdy legs allow, and then climbs off. He has accepted the inevitable with good humour and races to catch up with his mother, who lingers with the pram, waiting for him.

In a Chinese restaurant

Amy, aged 7, and her younger brother Henry, aged 4, both dressed in their best and on best behaviour, are out for a meal with their parents and grand-parents. In this unfamiliar situation, they need the support of their mother and father and also of their toys. Henry is accompanied by his large and floppy puppy with ears well chewed, and Amy has chosen to bring two small creatures: Nibbles the rabbit and Finn the dolphin, who are conveniently portable. She speaks to them softly, encouraging them to 'be good', and reads them the menu, proud of her newly acquired skill. There is nothing on the menu suitable for rabbits or dolphins to eat, so she says soothingly: 'When we get home, you can have some carrot cake, Nibbles. And I'll make you some fish-pie, Finn. Just be patient.'

Henry, in the meantime, has climbed on his father's lap and remarks that he wants his dummy. His father agrees equally to take him to the baby shop tomorrow and buy him a dummy – and maybe a cot? Henry is delighted. 'I want to go back to being a baby and suck my dummy and sleep in my cot.' 'OK,' says his dad, 'and maybe we'll buy you some nappies too?' This, in Henry's opinion, is carrying the joke too far. 'No nappies!' he says firmly, wrinkling his nose and pulling a face in disgust. 'But I do want a dummy.' And he puts his thumb in his mouth as he snuggles down more comfortably on his father's knee.

Normally a confident boy, Henry's security has crumbled in the face of a recent house move, followed by starting school: two severe shocks to his system that make him partly wish he could put the clock back. His father's ability to understand and humour him affectionately is helping him to recover his usual sunny self.

In a nursery

Today is Soshema's birthday. She's not sure how old she is but is wearing a new dress (a little large, for her to grow into) and her fine, black hair is tied on top of her head for this special occasion. She is looking radiant but bewildered and is quite tongue-tied; her badge speaks for her, proudly announcing 'It's my birthday'. When all the children are gathered together for a song and a story, everyone sings 'Happy Birthday' to Soshema and she smiles shyly. Later, at the head of the table with friends on either side, when a cake with three glowing candles appears, she knows exactly what to do.

With the help of her teacher, Gill has made a news booklet which they later share with her mother. 'When I wanted my mummy I went shopping and slipped over', is illustrated by a sad sketch of a solitary little person. One month later, because both her teacher and parents have heard Gill's wish to be taken to school by her mother, rather than her father, the picture changes. It becomes a bold and colourful scene announcing: 'My mummy takes me to school and I was pleased.'

Fact and fiction merge in the news books: 'One day I went to the farm-yard and there I saw some cows. Then I kept falling off the cow sometimes.'

Adult activities are coolly appraised: 'I went to the cinema yesterday and I watched a funny film. A funny slobbery kiss from a boy to a girl . . . and then they danced like they were getting married.'

Important information is conveyed: 'We sorted our toys out – me and Jim but not Joe – Joe he smacks.'

Children and fairy tales

In another nursery school, a trainee teacher describes how in her encounters with 3- to 4-year-old children she is struck by the degree to which they are familiar with the social and moral 'rules' that are explored in the story of Goldilocks. The children's comments highlight their spontaneous and vociferous condemnation of the behaviour of Goldilocks:

Sophie: She's naughty! Naughty girl.
Teacher: Why is she naughty, Sophie?
Sophie: Because she ate all the porridge and she's going to break the
              chair.

Goldilocks is, from the start, seen as the villain and the bear family the
wronged party, who deserve sympathy:

Matthew: The bears are angry. She ate their porridge.
Amy: And they don't even know who did it!
Joshua: Shall we tell them?

The children find Goldilocks' behaviour quite unacceptable. Not only
does she violate the happy home of the archetypal family ('She's broken the
house' and 'She's got muddy shoes on!'), but her entering the bears' cottage
is seen as fundamentally wrong. The children relate this immoral behaviour to their own experience of their social world:

Georgia: We wouldn't do that. . . . We're good girls. And if we went to
              someone else's house we would be lonely.
Peter: She could go away. Or stand there and wait for the persons to
              come back. Cos they might be bothered [if she went in uninvited].

When the children come to role play the story, the nursery teacher tries
to introduce the possibility of a reconciliation between the bears and
Goldilocks, but the children will have none of it. Perceiving Goldilocks as
the villain, they are quite convinced of the need both to punish the 'bad'
and to protect the 'good': 'If I was a bear I'd growl at her, Grrr!' says
Charles, outraged at her anti-social behaviour.

Thus, children have the chance to redress the balance to fit their own
views of punishment. Liberal growling and shaking of paws by the bears
(instantaneously transformed into menacing characters), is common whenever Goldilocks is caught in the cottage.

Alice: Who's been sleeping in my bed?
Bears: GRRRRRRR!
Teacher: [as Goldilocks] I'm very, very, sorry.
Luke: Well now you have to go back. Grrrrr!
Teacher: How about if I made you some porridge and a pot of tea? Would
              that be alright? I think you're friendly bears.
Alice: Well we're not! Grrr!

Having become an apologetic Goldilocks, the teacher was still given short
shrift by the unforgiving bears, convinced of their righteousness in treating
her harshly.

20

Because the story ends without the classic 'happily ever after', it lacks the fairy tale's usual resolution of conflict, and this is unsettling for some of the children:

Teacher: *And they always locked their door. . . .* [reading text]
Ellie: But she could open it.
Teacher: But she couldn't, could she, now they always lock it?
Ellie: Maybe she might bring a knife with her.
Amy: To chop the door down to get in.

Children have a great need for justice, as they see it, to prevail, and the unpunished Goldilocks is a continuing threat to both the bears' and their own well-being (Carolin 1997).

In nursery schools, children can safely explore the world just outside their own families and communicate the excitement of discovery. In primary schools, their horizons expand further still and they are given opportunities for learning, not only in the classroom, but on school visits.

Reception class visit to a museum

Twenty-five children, with their teacher, file into the vast entrance hall of the museum, wide-eyed and excited. This is a grand building, spacious and complex, with a bewildering array of unfamiliar objects. Here is a huge statue of a naked lady with a life-size tortoise at her feet; her bare bottom provokes a knowing nudge from one boy to another in passing, and a reproving look from their teacher, as they hurry to climb the immense stairs. Awed by the lofty room in which they are now seated cross-legged on the fine old carpet, these children have been urged by their parents and teachers to 'be good', but are not yet sure how they will be expected to behave in these unfamiliar surroundings. One little girl confides to the museum teacher that she is feeling 'nervous'; others are showing apprehension or eager anticipation for this adventure. They are to be introduced, at the formative age of 5, to some of the riches of their cultural heritage. Until recently, museums were not inclined to welcome children. Now, thanks to enlightened museum and educational policies, many are opening their doors to younger school-age children in the hope that, by fostering interest at an early age, museums will remain a source of pleasure and learning for a lifetime, and also a source of their own future revenue.

These children will hear a familiar fairy tale, but first, the museum teacher establishes a rapport with them by introducing herself and inviting comments about their past experiences of museums and their observations on this one. Skilfully, she leads them step by step from what they already know towards the new: education in the best sense, a drawing out of the children's knowledge and understanding, memory and imagination. They listen intently to one another and to the teacher, who encourages them to look about as they respond to her questions. She prepares them by showing a picture book without text, which nevertheless tells a story, and invites them to conjure a detailed mental picture of a puppy. Eyes closed, they 'make a puzzle in their heads', as a boy suggests aloud. The jigsaw takes shape in each child's imagination, with accompanying comments. Its ears look 'floppy'; its fur feels 'lovely'; its nose is 'squidgy' and its tail is 'up-and-downy'. Having experienced for themselves the power of picturing, with the aid of memory, a fully realised puppy dog, they look confident and relaxed, yet alert. They are now ready to follow the plot (familiar to some) of the Sleeping Beauty, illustrated by a number of objects carefully selected by the teacher.

As the story unfolds, the children quietly move around the museum. They gaze first of all at the portrait of a gorgeously clad, sad-faced queen (painted, not photographed 'because cameras were not invented then', one child volunteers), who longed for a baby ('to make her happy', the children suggest). Gradually, through close observation of many paintings, a statue, an antique clock (ticking away for 100 years!) and, finally, a knight in full medieval armour, mounted on a caparisoned horse and bearing a magic lance, each child experiences this traditional tale afresh. In addition to its inherent drama and suspense, there is much humour and interest. Birth, marriage and death are touched upon; serious questions honestly answered; misconceptions and confusions clarified − all within the context of a single museum visit, lasting just over one hour. It is a richly enjoyable experience and the children return to school inspired to re-tell the story by drawing their own pictures.

Children's own stories

Some children also use their considerable imagination and their growing word power to create their own stories, such as this one.

The witch and the magic spell by Siobhan, aged 6
I woke up with a very fritnig feling. I got up and walked towds the window. I loked out and saw a witch. she said come with me, So I went. she took me to a horable cave, she gave me blod and bones to eat. And she "said" I am a good witch. For ever and ever you shall be under my power. In the morning she siad here's your food and then she siad we have to go on a long gernee. She got out a bone randeer. I got on and she said geup so he galloped. I did not relese how long I had been ther. afchell she said we can break the spell of you being under my power. Only if you stay on this goat when it runs so I did and the spell brock. The End.

Bereavement

Two young girls write about the actual death of parents with simplicity and eloquence.

Dad *by Tiffany, aged 12*

I had a dad once like most of you. But there was something special about my dad . . . he loved football . . . he ended up playing for (his local team). I think that he always had a dream to play for them and it definitely came true.

My dad gave up football . . . because he got cancer. The cancer eventually went away and then I was born. . . . I am now 12. . . . Very quickly in February 1994, just two and a half weeks after my birthday, the cancer came back in different stages, eventually it was all over his body and he died.

Now it has been a year. It doesn't seem like a year to us. To this day we are still coming to terms with his death. My family, his friends will never forget him. He's a special person to us all.

After his death my two sisters and I went to a counsellor. Mine specialised in children.

Tiffany's view of counselling

I felt that I wanted to go to a counsiller because I thought that they could answer my questions, the mane one being 'Why?' I felt that I could not ask my mum because it would be too upsetting for her and too upsetting for me so I felt maybe someone I did not know would be able to help me come to turms with things.

When I met Anne (my counsillor) I felt warm and close to her. She was kind and understanding to me. I felt I could talk to her about my dad without feeling to upset. I really got to know her through the game we played and I thought that was a good start. [The game was called 'All About Me' and was developed for children by a Barnardo's counsellor, Peta Hemmings, see References.]

I started to relise that everything dies sometime and that my dad dieing was relisening him from the pain he was suffering through cancer. . . .

I wanted to tell people who have gone through the pain I had what Anne had told me . . . so I made a tape of some poems I had written about my dad. I even wrote a few letters to him. This meant I still keep in touch with him.

Anne really helped me and now I would like to see her as a speacil friend.

The first blossom from Tiffany
Dear Daddy
this rose tree
was bought for you.
This is the first
Blossom

I hope you like
this drawing it took
a long time

I will always
love you

P.S. I hope you are having
a good time with the
Angels

The experience of Tiffany's mother

'Can I go to a counsellor?' she said. It was a simple request but, like a stone in a pool, it sent out ripples of shock and struck me to the core, I felt inadequate.

I was given the name of a prospective counsellor and waited for her to call me to arrange an appointment. I tried to be calm and support my daughter's decision to talk to someone else, but I felt afraid. I was afraid that it wouldn't work out, but I was equally afraid that it would, and what would that say to me, to my daughter and to the world? That I was a failure and couldn't help my own daughter when she most needed me. My rational mind told me that I was over-reacting and that anything that would help Tiffany to deal with her father's death was beneficial, but strangely it didn't help.

I worried about taking her to someone else, a stranger, and leaving her for an hour and then picking her up feeling goodness knows how and me not knowing what this person had said. And if I wasn't able to help her now, how would I help her then, and would I mess up what the counsellor was trying to achieve by saying or doing the wrong thing? What would a counsellor say to her and would it be the sort of thing I would want her to say? Even though I knew that it was not for me to dictate what happened, I worried about the effect on Tiffany and the fact that I would be the one taking her home afterwards. What if the counsellor wasn't any good, what harm might she do?

When the call finally came, I felt sick and I wanted to call it off, but my daughter was so pleased I knew I couldn't do that, and I would have to get on with it and deal with my feelings, because this was something that was for her, and I wanted to make everything better for her and not let her down or ruin the experience just because I found it hard that she wanted to go to someone else.

My mother and I by Elizabeth, aged 13

My mother and I were never really close. We just have this mother–daughter bond that every parent has to their child. I thought she was very over-protective but now I see that it was just because she loved and cared for me.

On 10 December 1992 my dad took me and my brother into the dining room and told us about mum. I can remember his exact words. . . . 'Your mum has cancer and it can't be operated on. She's going to die.' I took a sip of a glass of orange squash on the table only to discover it was vodka and orange. Hot stuff. Through the tears (everybody's) dad told us about mum and exactly what would happen. He also told us about mum's choice. She had to choose whether or not to have chemotherapy which would prolong her life for another six months to a year. Dad wanted to help her make her choice. In the end she chose not to take it. Why prolong the agony? It was sort of like waiting for a time-bomb to go off. We could not stop it. We just had to wait. And wait. In that time you realise just how important your mother is.

On 7th January (Thursday) my mum died. She was 43. I had to try to cram everything I ever wanted to say to mum in my life into one month. It was impossible. Christmas will always be special to me now.

Elizabeth's goodbye

Mum's actual last moments were like something out of a fairy tale. Dad was sitting in a chair at the side of the bed and the nurse was standing beside Mum, [who] was asleep. I was lying on Dad's half of the bed beside Mum . . . listening to the regular sound of [her] hoarse breathing. And suddenly – nothing. Then it came. That last breath had been about a second late. . . . Dad looked back at me and crossed his fingers. He later told me that the anxiety and fear and worry in my face could not have been clearer if they were painted on my forehead in large red letters.

No, I don't think anxiety, fear and worry were the right words. This was some new emotion that I had never felt before. It's hard to describe. It was a mix of shock, disbelief, anger, love and in some ways relief. I tried to shout 'NO!' but nothing came. Then the breaths got slower and further apart and then – the next one didn't come. That was it. She had died.

Afterwards

After Mum had been taken to the chapel of rest we decided to . . . visit her one last time.

Dad went into Mum's room (well that's what I called it. Why not?) first to see what she looked like. Then he came back out, took my hand and together we walked back in. (My brother didn't want to go in.) As I went in the first thing I saw was Mum's face. 'Oh my God,' I said in a choked voice and buried my face in my Dad's chest and started bawling my eyes out. . . . Then I did something I will always remember. I walked away from Dad towards Mum . . . then kissed her gently on the forehead. When I turned round Dad was crying. 'That was the most beautiful thing I've ever seen . . . I couldn't even do that to my Dad when he died.'

The next half hour was really emotional. We kept kissing mum and stroking her cheeks, forehead and hands. . . .

When Dad called for me to come out because we were going, I just stayed by Mum's side. As [he] left a fresh wave of tears came over me. I looked at her in that blue and white gown, her pale yellowish face (yellow through the jaundice from the cancer). I just cried my heart out for two or three minutes. Then one last kiss, one last touch and I firmly turned my back and half walked, half ran out of the room.

Elizabeth's postscript

My mum died when I was 12. My brother was 11. We knew about her cancer for about a month before she died. It was strange knowing that soon she'd be gone while she was sitting there talking to me.

Some months later dad started applying to lonely hearts ads. At first I helped . . . looking through the ads with him and choosing ones I thought would be good. Through one of these he met Jane [and] . . . they started seeing each other as boyfriend and girlfriend. He told me he had never loved anyone like this before. This really hurt as he'd found someone that he loved more than my mum, his wife.

We met Jane one evening at a hotel bar. My brother Richard was really quiet and she had a go at him for this . . . and dad let her and even agreed with her. Richard went to sit in the car and I went too, part in protest, part in sympathy. After this Dad decided that we should go to counselling to try and get us over mum and to accept Jane.

I went with an open mind but in my heart of hearts I didn't think that I could get to like someone who had treated Richard that way – especially in front of me and dad.

The counselling with Anne helped me in that I could really let rip with my feelings without the risk of dad shouting at me or telling me to shut up. I also thought that if someone from outside our situation tried to explain how we were feeling, someone impartial, he might listen.

And he did listen – kind of. We had one evening where we told dad how we felt but with our counsellor present so he couldn't shout us down. This worked because for the first time we managed to discuss things like sensible adults. But on the way home my dad made his opinions about his relationship that he didn't want to give in front of our counsellor very clear. (But again, as it always had been, we couldn't say what we wanted for fear of him shouting and threats of what would happen when we got home.)

I think that dad wanted our counselling to help us get over mum and to like his girlfriend. But I think that evening (mentioned above) made him see that it wasn't all mine and my brother's fault, and that we did have some points to make. (Maybe dad was scared of us knowing he had made some mistakes and that's why he stopped us before we started saying how we felt.) I think he knew what his mistakes and problems were but he put them to the back of his mind as if to say 'If I don't acknowledge that you're there you'll go away.' Maybe.

My counselling helped me as an emotional outlet and it helped me realise that dad wasn't going to give up his love life for us (And why should he?) and if we made our feelings about his girlfriend known to him it was up to him what he did with that knowledge.

Anne's postscript

Five years after the death that so deeply disturbed this family, many of their difficulties have been resolved. Elizabeth, having done well in her GCSEs, is in her final sixth-form year and plans to go to university. She leads an active social life both in and out of school and has a part-time job. Richard, her brother, distinguished himself in his GCSEs and is now doing three A levels. The school's understanding and support, which began when their father told the staff of their mother's imminent death, has provided both of them with the continuity and stability so important to young people when home life proves difficult. Their father has become engaged to a new partner, but they do not intend to marry until the children have left home.

Counselling by Kerry, aged 14

To me counselling is when someone listens to your problems and gives as much advice as possible.

[The advice her counsellor, Anne, gave her helped Kerry to cope with dreams so scary they prevented her from going to sleep. Anne suggested she write down the dreams as soon as possible after they occurred. Putting them on paper seemed to get them out of Kerry's head, to distance and diminish their power. After reading them back to herself, Kerry saw that these dreams were her own creation, over which she had some control. By listening carefully to herself, she reached a deeper understanding not only of her dreams, but of the person she is. Gradually her nightmares and her fears subsided.]

Finally, here is Kerry's last word on the importance of listening: It is really important that someone listens to what a child or young person has to say because they need to be able to talk about who has died or what's on their mind and perhaps some guidance in the right direction. The difference between family and friends and a counsellor is, family and friends try to listen and sympathise and understand but are usually personally involved whereas a counsellor is usually a neutral person and has been trained to listen and help young people to cope with the bad times.

References

Carolin, S.S. (1997) Goldilocks goes to Nursery: The fairy tale in the early years classroom. Unpublished BA(Ed.) dissertation, University of London, Goldsmiths College

Chuilleanain, E.N. (1994) *The Brazen Serpent*. County Neath, Ireland: The Gallery Press.

Kelmer-Pringle, M. (1980) *The Needs of Children: A personal perspective*, London: Routledge.

Children's game

Barnados Publications, 'All About Me', tel.: 01268 520224 Ext. 267

2

PLEASURES, PITFALLS AND PERPLEXITIES

The content of counselling and supervision

Dorothy Eddi Piper

Introduction

One of the pleasures of working with young people is the sense of exploration not only of their 'story' but of what that story means to them. Similarly, one of the fascinations of supervising those who work therapeutically with young people, whether they describe themselves as counsellors, play therapists or child psychotherapists, is looking at their understanding of their work. This chapter discusses some of the pleasures, pitfalls and perplexities that have arisen in my own counselling work with young people aged 5–21, and in the work of supervisees using a range of theoretical orientations, who have been working in clinics, schools and colleges, social services settings, in private practice and in a variety of forms of youth counselling services.

The limited life experience of children

In listening to children, it is their perception of events that we need to understand, not our own construction of their meaning. We need to try to imagine the possible interpretations a small child with very limited life experience might make of an event or of what they hear and see around them. We should never forget that they will try to make sense of events by relating them to their existing knowledge, as James did.

James' mistaken guilt

James, aged 7, was not achieving his potential and often behaved angrily without apparent cause. His teachers were very concerned about him. He seemed to make good use of play therapy sessions and to make a good relationship with his counsellor. However, his behaviour remained troubled and he often turned his anger on himself. James' brother had special needs, having been brain damaged at birth, and so took much of their parents' attention. Although a case conference looked at this relationship, it did not seem to explain James' self-destructive behaviour and poor concentration. Then the counsellor overheard someone refer to James' brother as his twin and went back to look at the notes. She had missed the fact that James was a twin and no one else had considered it important, perhaps had not known, as the boys were in different schools.

It came to light that someone had explained to James what had caused his brother's disability, but they had not imagined what James might have interpreted from being the first born of twins when the second born had suffered brain damage because, as James one day explained to the counsellor, 'There wasn't enough air left for him to be born properly.'

Unspoken fears

From time to time counsellors suspect that children are harbouring fears or feelings that they are not able to express. Fears that, for us, can be dispelled by talking to friends or getting practical information, can become so frightening to a child that they cannot voice them and sometimes cannot even admit them to themselves. When this happens, the fears turn into a private nightmare that constantly demands energy to suppress its terrors.

One of the aims of counselling work is to enable children to experience themselves with a sense of power or control, a sense that they have some power in shaping their responses to their environment even if they cannot change the environment itself.

Creating the trusting relationship

Relationships in which people feel safe not only to explore their thoughts and emotions but also to risk changing, are trustful, encouraging, supportive, kind and firmly grounded, with clear boundaries and ethical ground rules (see p. 37). Young people will make full use of therapeutic opportunities when they feel safe to do so. However, their sense of safety and their readiness to deal with issues will depend on many things, some of which can be influenced by the counsellor, some of which cannot. People who work therapeutically with children are required to exercise their imagination, and counsellors beginning to work with children frequently need to be asked to imagine what it may be like for a particular child with their individual characteristics, history and present influences, to enter, leave and re-enter this counselling relationship, which is probably like no other the child experiences. There is no one right way to work with a client, no foolproof technique to follow. Our work needs to be appropriate to that particular child in their particular circumstances at the time.

As adults it is our duty to ensure that children are safe in our sessions; they, their carers and the community have a right to expect that of us. This means not just that we are trustworthy professionals in our techniques but that we have safe play equipment, child-safe furniture and that we think through the issues, for example, using paint that washes out to keep children safe from parental anger should any get onto their clothes.

Being congruent in the relationship

The child needs to perceive his relationship with the counsellor as trustworthy and the counselling environment as safe. For this to happen the counsellor must be personally integrated, grounded, genuinely consistent and stable. . . . children are very good at recognizing people who are not congruent and who are trying to play a role which is not consistent with the rest of their personalities.

(Geldard and Geldard 1997: 15)

We attempt to be congruent and genuinely ourselves and we need to be as open and honest with children as is consistent with our judgement of how such openness would improve the relationship or further the therapeutic activity. With most adult clients, we can discuss the effects on them of our interventions and disclosures. We need to be much more careful with children because they will interpret our actions and words in the light of their previous limited understanding and experience of adults. They may come to unhelpful conclusions, such as that they are themselves the cause of our behaviour or feelings.

When working with Patrick, a young man who had been very seriously abused, his counsellor was using a game that involved attributing emotions to squiggles that they each drew. It became clear that she was completing the squiggles very honestly and showing her underlying anger about his history, but because Patrick may well have thought that he was causing her angry feeling, she decided to be less transparent and deliberately to vary her responses.

Listening

To experience being heard and understood is a healing experience. It is the experience of being acknowledged and validated by another person that can enable people to validate themselves. Listening to young people in a therapeutic way helps them to achieve that validation and improve their self-esteem. To listen with understanding means making every effort to hear and comprehend what children mean by what they say and what they do; it means checking out that what we have heard is what we were meant to hear. If we reflect this meaning back to them, children have the chance

31

to hear for themselves what they have communicated, and such accepting listening can help them to grasp that the counsellor really does want to understand their perceptions and will accept these as valid.

Research findings support the positive benefits of being heard and understood. In a study by the Trust for the Study of Adolescence, young people who had attempted suicide stated that being listened to was the most important thing to prevent a further attempt (Coleman *et al.* 1995.) Talking and being listened to, and listening to music are cited by young people as being the most effective way of dealing with depression in another study of 1,500 young people (Friedli and Scherzer 1996).

Listening to non-verbal communication

Some of our most intense experiences are not transmitted in conversations. We may have strong feelings when watching a sunset or hearing a piece of music or through art or drama, and we can experience being understood by another person without exchanging any words. Play is one of the ways in which we can 'listen', as children communicate very effectively without words (see also Chapters 4, 6, 7, 9 and 11).

Why play?

Children can use play to check out their assumptions and perceptions: they can try out different consequences of different actions and see themselves in different roles. In play they can re-create events and exercise power over them. With the therapeutic attention of an adult, they may come to understand more about themselves and their world. The perplexity for the counsellor is that they themselves may never know what the child's play is about, for their role is to provide the safe, attentive space in which children can work things out for themselves. The adult does not need to know.

> We are looking for the child to create something in sand or play-room that makes sense to the child; if it makes sense to us too, that is a bonus. We listen to children with care and respect, hoping for insight on their thoughts; but we do not in fact need insight. It is enough that we should facilitate the work that the child needs to do, by giving him a language in which to do it. Barefoot play therapists should not aspire to high heels.
>
> (Newson 1992: 107)

Trusting children to do their own work

If we sometimes have to deal with not knowing what is happening in a session, we need to be persistent in our trust that a child will find a way to help themselves. Sometimes a young person will seem incapable of concentrating in class. The teacher will say that they either do stare out of the window or might as well be doing so. This distraction might be caused by thoughts of a coming pleasant event, such as a party, but it might be of an unwelcome event, in which case it is apprehension that takes up the concentration. This preoccupation can be conscious or unconscious. If a child accepts their life experience as 'normal', the only sign that there is something amiss may be this inability to concentrate. The child appears to be trying to puzzle something out but won't be able to say what they are puzzling about. We see a 'troubled' child, and therapeutic play may allow that child to symbolise the 'trouble' and to try to work out a sense of control or understanding or a coming to terms with it, in a way that frees them from the distraction of constantly having to deal with unsettling feelings. They may never know what the trouble was and may never verbalise it; alternatively, the understanding they come to through play may free them to talk.

Buried treasure

Sam was described as one such 'troubled' child. The counsellor had no idea of the meaning of what he was doing as he played with the sand tray and buried the little figures each week. Sometimes he removed a particular figure, sometimes he brought figures to the surface and buried them deeply again. The counsellor sat by him, silently concentrating on what he was doing and trying to feel what he was experiencing in this very intense play. In supervision, we puzzled about the meaning for this child who, at 6 years, was scapegoated by his family, ignored, undermined and blamed. A little exasperated, we eventually decided to stop puzzling about it and ask Sam what he was doing. Sam said that sailors were diving to a sunken ship to find buried treasure, but they couldn't find it. One of them, whom the counsellor took to represent Sam, wanted to stop the search.

Having begun to speak and been accepted, Sam talked more each week. He talked of his home and his feelings and welcomed the counsellor's attentive listening. After a few weeks, Sam announced that he would soon stop coming. He took all the figures and buried them, with 'himself' sitting above. He said with a satisfied smile that they were all searching but that he knew that 'Everyone has their own treasure inside themselves.'

Sam had the ability to make use of play therapy without any input from the counsellor except the provision of a safe relationship with concentrated attention. The counsellor had needed to sit without knowing until the time was right to ask the question.

The child's concerns might be different from ours

Creative therapy can help us to understand the real concerns of a child such as Dana and to realise that children may not have the same priorities as adults (see also Chapters 10, 11 and 12).

Dana's picture

Dana drew a picture of a large whale and a dolphin. The story she told about the picture was that the dolphin was injured by a harpoon fired by some men in a boat. The large whale overturned the boat and freed the dolphin. Then the whale and the dolphin together saved the men from drowning and took them to shore, but did not give them back the boat or the harpoon.

Dana's own story

Dana, aged 8, had been raped by a stranger while she was playing near her home. The counsellor experienced strong anger towards the rapist and fear for other children, as he had never been caught. Dana's reaction was complex. She was disturbed not only by her physical experience but also by the emotion she had picked up from her attacker, her knowledge of his confusion and unhappiness and his need to be rescued from his own disturbance. She expressed real concern for the perpetrator. Other concerns that she had were for her carers, who were being blamed by others for allowing her to play alone, which was something she had been used to doing quite safely. She wanted no one to be blamed for what had happened to her and she wanted to make the world happy.

Accepting the child's concerns

In the picture, the big whale was the counsellor and the dolphin was Dana. Because of the protective reaction of some adults, Dana found it hard to express her complex feelings and thoughts about her attacker. Adults sometimes cannot accept what children are experiencing, and tend to filter out words or actions that point to things that the adults find hard to handle. Those in Dana's life did not want her to feel any sympathy for her abuser; they ignored that part of her communication and so hindered her ability to be honest and open with them. In supervision, the counsellor had to struggle with her own reactions to the events to allow Dana a place for the full expression of all her thoughts and feelings. Using the painting and the story of it allowed Dana to symbolise what she was experiencing.

Beliefs and opinions

Certain explanations of strange sights in the sky are down-to-earth: they are weather balloons, tricks of the light or military aircraft; but some may be out-of-this-world: flying saucers, aliens or messages from a different planet. We choose to believe what seems to be within our understanding or we choose to remain in a state of not knowing. What is clear is that most people are happiest with an explanation that fits their existing knowledge. Similarly, children constantly strive to make sense of their worlds, and when something unknown occurs, they will invent an explanation that fits their experience at the time and with which they can feel familiar. However, these explanations do not necessarily square with the facts of a child's situation.

The child may be mistaken

The child who is sexually abused by a parent believes that they themselves must have been to blame. They have been brought up to trust that the parent is right, and because of their dependence on that parent for existence, it is too dangerous to contemplate any other explanation. The sequence of thinking might be: 'A bad thing has happened to me – it must be my fault – I must be bad – I deserve bad things.' Such a belief, and the child's consequent behaviour, provide a perplexity for the therapist. A child may not be able to accept that they are not to blame because that would mean thinking less of their parents. We can expect most adults to gain the confidence and self-esteem to move away from harmful people and activities, but few children can do this. The perplexity is that if, as counsellors, we cannot make changes in the actual environment of our client, what can or should we do to alter those beliefs that are harmful to the child's self-esteem?

Expressing our opinions

Should we express an opinion about our client's responsibility for events? We have to be very careful that we are looking at the issues from the young person's viewpoint before we venture to do anything other than help them to come to their own conclusions.

Mike: the lowest of the low

Mike, aged 13, who was tricked and sexually abused by a stranger and ashamed to tell anyone, described himself as 'the lowest of the low' when he was caught stealing from a corner shop. His behaviour reflected his opinion of himself. He was 'good for nothing' and put himself with company and in activities that reinforced that expectation. He was grappling not only with his perceptions of himself but also with the attitudes of peers and society which taught him that he would be unwise to tell anyone. His parents' reaction had re-inforced that view.

Elaine Dorfman, in her chapter on client-centered play therapy (Rogers 1951: 235), puts forward the view that therapists should never indicate their opinions or attitudes to the client but should only reflect back what they have heard through their attentive listening. I agree that, particularly in non-verbal work, it is important not to show judgements of the activity; however, when someone is operating on a belief that is clearly mistaken, then that belief may need to be corrected.

With Mike, listening was not enough. In supervision, having role-played Mike and tried to understand how he might be interpreting my behaviour, I decided that in this particular case I needed to express my opinion that he had not invited the abuse, express my outrage about the abuser and discuss with Mike my wish to warn the police to look out for the abuser whilst respecting Mike's wish to remain anonymous. Mike needed me to act as an adult and to do those things before he could believe that I meant what I said about him not being to blame. It was important that Mike altered his perception of himself as quickly as possible before his behaviour moved him from therapeutic help to the juvenile justice system. He was supported by talking not only in counselling sessions but also in a group of young people who accepted each other. The respect of his peers as they heard his story had an almost visible impact on his self-esteem.

Promoting self-healing

Much of our work in listening to young people is giving them a safe space in which to explore their perceptions of their experiences. In this way they can try out different perspectives and alternative strategies for coping and can develop their own intrinsic feelings of self-worth, thus giving themselves permission and time to heal.

Pete changed his perspective of himself without any need for the counsellor to give an opinion. He painted a picture of how he felt about himself at his first session: a huge tangle of string with a dark ball in the centre entitled 'Lost snail'.

His parents had decided to divorce after months of violent argument. Pete's reaction at their first attempt to separate had been so distressing to them that they had tried to stay together for a further six months, but he had remained disturbed and they had come for help as they attempted again to separate. The painting of how Pete felt at his final session was a beautiful silhouette against a night sky entitled 'A scarecrow dancing in the moonlight'. He hadn't changed his circumstances, but he had come a long way from the dark snail.

Pete had worked it out for himself

What Pete had tried to do was to take responsibility for his parents, both by blaming himself and by trying to put things right between them by being 'disturbed'. He had temporarily managed to bring them back together as parents to seek help for him. Over six months he had been able to reflect in his play and painting on the turmoil of his life and to gain a more positive perspective of himself. In sessions, Pete had taken complete control. The counsellor had not given any advice or any opinion but had provided the safe space for his own self-directed exploration through sand play and painting.

Contracts and boundaries

The ethics that counsellors and psychotherapists follow include guidelines about boundaries between counsellor and client and between the counsellor and others connected with the client. It is important that a child has these boundaries explained in language that they can understand, and their agreement to a contract is at least as important as the carer's agreement. Most children will have experienced adults misleading them with 'white lies', and a balance needs to be achieved that allows the counsellor to be open and honest with a child without confusing them or making the relationship so different from any other that it is worrying to them. I use a list of 'rules' or agreements that I share with children and their carers.

We agree that:

- I am not allowed to tell anyone what you do or say here but you are allowed to tell anyone you choose.
- If I thought you were in serious danger or might get into serious trouble, then I would have to talk with you about telling someone else about it.
- I will not talk about you to anyone else unless you are present or you tell me to do so, except that I have to talk about my work with my supervisor who helps me to do my work properly. She does not have to know who you are and I don't use your name when I talk with her.
- I do not have to do anything I don't want to do and you don't have to do anything you don't want to do.
- You do not have to come if you don't want to come.
- You are not allowed to hurt yourself or me.
- You will try to tell me if there is anything you don't like me doing or saying or anything you want me to do or say so that I can try to do my best.

I apply the essence of these agreements with all my clients, although the language I use to explain them is different according to the age of the child. However, parents and agencies are not always happy with these boundaries, and it is perhaps an indication of the way in which adults perceive children that they often expect me to break them, having thought that I did not really mean them. In situations where these agreements or their equivalents are not possible because of the nature of the counsellor's contract or particular circumstances, we have to tell children the truth and they will work within that knowledge.

Supervision

The British Association for Counselling states in the Code of Ethics and Practice for Supervision of Counsellors: 'The primary purpose of supervision is to ensure that the counsellor is addressing the needs of the client' (BAC 1996). Counselling and supervision are both 'helping' relationships and both to some extent aim to assist the client and the supervisee to be more effective in achieving their goals. A common dilemma in counselling children and supervising counsellors is who decides what the needs of the client are. The supervisory relationship is defined by Francesca Inskipp and Brigid Proctor as:

> a working alliance between a supervisor and a counsellor in which the counsellor can offer an account or recording of her work; reflect on it; receive feedback, and, where appropriate, guidance. The object of this alliance is to enable the counsellor to gain in ethical competence, confidence and creativity so as to give her best possible service to her client.
>
> (Inskipp and Proctor 1995: 5)

They also give the tasks of supervision under the headings:

- *normative* – involves professional and ethical considerations;
- *formative* – includes the educative task;
- *restorative* – refers to the counsellor's support and mental well-being.

The supervision triangle

Supervision can be viewed as a triangular relationship of client, counsellor and supervisor which includes the background influences on each member of that triangle. The client may have family, carers, peers, culture and a situation such as school in their background. The counsellor and the supervisor have a number of influences, some of which will be from the same source, such as a code of ethics that both agree to, and some of which will be different, such as their lines of accountability to employers. All three bring their personal history to the triangle.

In supervision sessions, we can sometimes notice a parallel process occurring in which the supervisee or the supervisor takes on the 'feel' of one of the others in the triangle and responds from that position.

The supervisory relationship

The supervisor's role is to form a working alliance in order to support counsellors to work to the best of their ability with clients. Counsellors need to be competent in their skills and to be confident in using them. To further this end, the supervisory relationship is most effective when it is experienced by both participants as one in which it is safe to risk exploration and change, and in this respect it parallels the counselling relationship. There are other similarities between the supervisory relationship and the counsellor/child relationship in that both have issues of power and control to address. The supervisor has responsibilities to the supervisee as a professional overseer and the counsellor of a child has the responsibilities of an adult to a child. The supervisor has to be sensitive to the possibility that the counsellor will consider them a superior rather than a colleague. We have already seen that, when we are in a relationship, as we are with a child, where the power we have is so much greater than that of the client, we need to work with great sensitivity, by constantly taking account of the possible ways in which this particular child may perceive and interpret our behaviour.

The formative and normative tasks of supervision

In supervision, too, decisions have to be made about when to give an opinion and when to patiently allow the supervisee to make their own decisions. The formative or educative task of the supervisor may mean giving information that the supervisee is not aware of or making suggestions for interventions. As in work with a client, the pitfall to avoid is to say: 'If I were you. . . .' We are not the other person and they have to do it their way if they are to be congruent in their work. Similarly, if we return to the counsellor's dilemma in working with Mike (see pp. 35–6), warning the police about the potential danger to other children had to be dealt with sensitively, both with Mike and his counsellor. However, it was part of the supervisor's normative task to look at this ethical issue.

The restorative task of supervision

To look into the eyes of a child remembering terror is one of the most uncomfortable feelings we can experience. To ask ourselves to go through that experience with many different children in the course of our work is very demanding. Yet we attempt as counsellors or therapists to be fully present in the interview so that we may be as helpful as possible to each child. It is essential that counsellors deal with the horror of the work in a way that takes good care of themselves and which frees them to work openly with all their clients (see also Chapter 3).

The child within

When we are working with young people, we will be accessing the child within ourselves at all its ages. Our own childhood traumas and developmental events will be involved in our perceptions of our clients' worlds and in our emotional reactions to them. It would be impossible to work through all our previous experience and 'sort ourselves out', but we do have a responsibility to be as aware as possible of the effects of our history on our interaction with children. If we expect therapists to be alongside children in their pain, we need to be very careful that therapists take care of themselves. I imagine a rack of seaside hats, each with a label, and perhaps the greatest pitfall is to put on the 'I'm a big adult, I can cope' hat. In their desire to put things right for a child, I see counsellors putting on these hats, most of which will take even the limited power they have from their clients, because they are adult- or counsellor-centred, rather than child-centred.

Some of the hats that I challenge supervisees about wearing are:

'Let *me* protect you.'
'*I* know best.'
'I'm angry with your carers.'
'Let *me* mother you.'
'What this child needs is X and *I* can give it.'
'*I* can't bear your pain.'
'Only *I* can have this special relationship with you.'
'*I* can't bear to say no to you.'
'I'll make "them" listen.'
'You should be feeling the way *I* think you should feel.'

Reluctance to deal with pain

We find the physical or emotional pain of children more difficult to deal with than that of adults. When that pain is inflicted deliberately or by lack of proper care, we are likely to be angry and sometimes enraged. If as counsellors we show our anger or even talk about it in sessions without very careful consideration, we may be increasing children's distress. But we do need to examine and discharge that anger. Often supervisees are reluctant to show their shock and distress or reluctant to use the time to look after their own needs in supervision sessions, when they think they ought to be looking at their detailed work with the client.

Sometimes, as a child paints a picture or recreates an event in play, the intensity of their pain in the non-verbal communication is very real, and a counsellor may be reluctant to revisit that pain in supervision. Nevertheless, we do need to understand stress, practise relaxation techniques and limit our case-load appropriately if we are to stay healthy for ourselves and for our clients.

Supervision can provide a restorative space for the discharge of emotion and the recharging of our compassionate energy.

Making counselling accessible

My concern as a supervisor is that counsellors and therapists should use their skills in the best way possible to provide a therapeutic opportunity for the client. Many of the young people who come our way have very serious problems that cannot be ignored and many are in a crisis that affects other people. If help is to be provided it must be provided in a way that both children and those concerned in their lives can accept. We are not in this work to practise a refined skill, like perfecting the playing of a musical instrument. We are in it to use that skill in the service of others, and we need to make sure that we do all we can to make it available and acceptable to them.

A young person such as Dave may enter the therapy room alone, but just outside the door there will be a host of influences, many of which will be very powerful in his life. Each person who had influence over Dave had a different investment in him, and the concerns of those people needed to be addressed sufficiently in order to allow Dave the freedom to use the counselling well. Because children are dependent on adults for so many aspects of their lives, we need to take into account the effects of that dependence both in counselling and on any practical problems which may affect their attendance at sessions.

Dave's other influences

In setting up sessions for Dave with his social worker, it seemed that everything had been considered. It was agreed with the social worker that Dave, aged 10 years, would be collected from school at the beginning of his last lesson of the day by a volunteer escort organised by the social worker. The Headteacher had agreed to this arrangement. After the session, his escort would return Dave to his foster mother who would keep his tea hot for him. The social worker's manager had already authorised the funding for Dave's sessions.

However, various difficulties arose which meant that the counsellor had to involve herself in administrative issues in order to help Dave make full use of his sessions. Session days were affected by the fact that Mum could keep tea hot only on certain days of the week, and Dave wanted to go to drama and cricket practice after school two nights of the week. Once sessions had started, so too did the difficulties: the teacher asked awkward questions because no one had explained to her where Dave was going; when Dave was sick, no one told the escort, who was upset by this; after a session in which Dave had been upset about an issue, he was rude to the escort who was then angry with him; the social work manager asked the counsellor for information about Dave's sessions in order to justify funding; the social worker asked for the counsellor's opinion about the foster mother's care; when Dave said he wanted to stay at school one day instead of attending, he was forced to attend because no one believed he had the choice.

Thus many different relationships and events can affect the counselling relationship, and a young person's ability to use the session well can depend on what they experience in the half hours on either side of the session.

The needs of carers

We are unrealistic if we expect all the people involved with a child to understand and accept counselling ways of working. Carers need to understand what the counsellor means by the ethical and boundary issues that are explained to them. Here is a pitfall that is difficult to deal with. Carers who want help for a child will often agree to the contract that the counsellor discusses with them without really understanding it, and later experience difficulty with an aspect such as confidentiality. One of the purposes of confidentiality is that of freeing a client to use sessions in any way they choose without fear of interpretation by others. However, it may seem to carers that it is just a way of professionals keeping them out of the picture. Counsellors spend many hours puzzling over boundary and confidentiality issues, and it is not surprising that others do not grasp their implications immediately.

Confidentiality, power and responsibility

A frequent issue in supervision is the balancing of the confidentiality agreed with the child client and the responsibility we have as adults to protect that child and any other children from harm. Each agency employing counsellors will have a policy on child protection issues. However, within that policy the supervisor and counsellor have sometimes very difficult decisions to make.

'Walking on eggshells'

Karen, a 10-year-old very depressed and withdrawn girl, had several times tested out the confidentiality of the sessions by finding out if the counsellor had discussed issues with her parents. She was showing signs of developing an eating disorder, and the willingness to communicate with her counsellor had taken time to develop. 'Walking on eggshells' was how the counsellor described the relationship. The child's suicidal feelings had been discussed several times in supervision, and after a session in which Karen had said that she would rather be dead than stay with her uncle while her mother went away on holiday, the counsellor was left feeling very anxious and frightened that she might harm herself.

Should the counsellor tell Karen's mother of her fears? Did the mother have a right to know that her daughter was expressing suicidal thoughts just as she was going away on holiday? What would the effect of breaking confidentiality be? Was the counsellor's fear about any of her own issues rather than to do with the client? In supervision, we looked at all angles and the counsellor decided that she had no option, for her own peace of mind, but to tell the mother of her anxiety. She did this by requesting an additional session and telling Karen what she had decided to do. She then spoke to the mother in Karen's presence. Whilst her mother's reaction was not sympathetic, a serious discussion followed and Karen eventually accepted her mother's departure and, in the event, seemed to be quite happy at her uncle's house. If Karen was trying to stop her mother going on holiday, she had done all she could. The counsellor was given an example of the mother's attitude to her daughter and had done all she could to keep Karen safe. The good counselling relationship continued, and after many sessions Karen recovered from her depression and began to deal with her situation more positively.

The counsellor's and supervisor's responses here were to a client who was a child. It is unlikely that had an adult been in comparable circumstances the counsellor would have acted in the same way.

Janie's story

A 13 year old, Janie was referred by her school to a counselling agency because she had few friends, was frequently absent from school, had very poor concentration in class and often seemed to be in a world of her own. Given a chance to talk to a teacher, she would do so non-stop, following them round the room describing details of what she had eaten for her tea or what had happened during her walk to school in the morning.

Janie's first task each morning was to get her brother ready for school, do the housework, make the beds and then get herself to school. Her father left for work very early in the morning and would return in time to cook the evening meal. Her mother was mentally ill and, on her return from school, Janie would often find the beds stripped, cupboards emptied out and furniture moved around to create a shrine in the living room in praise of a religious statue. In counselling sessions, which Janie was very committed to, she talked non-stop about anything and everything, about television, the weather, people she had noticed in the street. It took a lot of persistence ever to get her to talk about anything personal. Counselling her was frustrating and boring.

Unwilling counsellors

When Janie's counsellor was leaving, I could find no one willing to take her on, though Janie was very keen to continue sessions. In a supervision group, we pondered upon the value of sessions to her. Was she capable of making use of counselling? Were we misusing the resources of the centre which had a waiting list? When I contacted the Headteacher of Janie's school to say that we were thinking of ending the sessions the reaction was immediate. The Year Head phoned to say that there had been a marked change in Janie since counselling had begun, she no longer talked non-stop to staff, she had begun to do some project work and followed through on that interest. She still had few friends, but attendance had improved.

New thinking in the supervision group

In supervision, we drew a plan with Janie in the centre, and mapped out all the people and circumstances that had power in her life to see what power it might be possible for her to have in her own life (see Figure 1). We used dolls to represent what we knew of the people in Janie's life, to see how she might be feeling and thinking about her situation and what her hopes and fears might be in relation to each person. It became clear that Janie had no power to alter her mother's behaviour, and in the areas of control she did have when she tidied the house, her mother would destroy her efforts. Through her chatter about unimportant details, Janie escaped from her reality. What she understood about her mother and how she felt about her looked very important, yet she had never verbalised it. A new strategy was adopted of making suggestions to her about what she might be experiencing and seeing if this would help her to talk about more personal issues.

Using role play

We role played how the counsellor might approach Janie and identified some issues that might be tentatively put to her. It was decided that, once the new counsellor had established the relationship, she would say something like: 'I've been thinking about you this week and I wondered if you might be worried that you might get ill like your mother. And so I thought that I should tell you that that won't happen. Your mother has a very special illness and you can't catch it from her.' When she did so, Janie's

Who and what are the factors we know of in her life?
Use the dolls to map out how you see the factors in relation to Janie.
What might be Janie's perception of them? How close? How big? How safe?
How much power does she have with them?
What might her hopes and fears be of them?

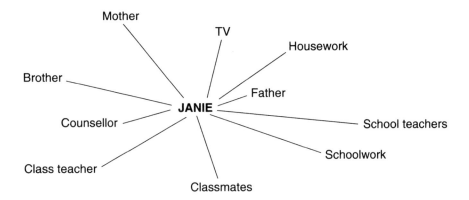

Janie's mother assumed huge proportions in the sculpt, with the counsellors using the biggest doll for her which overshadowed Janie. Father was seen to be close but small and dull; brother was seen as loving but a nuisance; the counsellor as bright and fairly close. Classmates were seen as attractive but rather frightening; class teacher as being supportive but other teachers as being impatient. TV was the only thing to distract from the problems. Schoolwork was seen as boring and housework anxiety provoking.

Figure 1. Supervision group exercise: sculpting

response was to weep for a few minutes and then to talk about something else. From time to time the counsellor would make another suggestion for Janie to consider, and gradually she began to make a limited attempt to discuss the issue, until eventually she began to take control of the session herself by introducing a personal topic.

When I saw Janie again for the first time in eighteen months I was amazed by the difference in her appearance. In the course of three years' counselling with several different counsellors, Janie had changed into a more self-confident and attractive young woman. Her face was no longer tightly screwed up, her turned-up nose was an attractive feature, and she now had friends.

Janie's powerlessness made us powerless

Janie's only power was to change the way she thought about herself. She could not change the erratic behaviour of her mother, and it had been unrealistic to expect that in counselling she could formulate words for her feelings and thoughts about her experiences. When she stopped her sessions, she was much more settled at school, had become an excellent swimmer and insisted that her brother come to the centre. We could very easily have given up on Janie, and described her as unsuitable for counselling. Had we made the connection between her powerlessness and our own feelings sooner, we would have saved several counsellors a deal of boredom and frustration.

Good enough sessions

Another pitfall that some counsellors fall into is that of judging the value of a session by its intensity. It was clear in Janie's case that this was not an accurate measure of value. Sometimes sessions are intense and sometimes they are not. Sometimes the counsellor's state of being dominates the mood of the session and sometimes not. Sometimes we get through as best we can and sometimes we are brilliant, but mostly we are good enough. One of the pleasures of working with young people is that they understand and accept that. On one occasion, having received some distressing personal news too late to stop a child from arriving, I decided to pull myself together and put on a brave face. He walked straight in, gave me a hug and said 'Eddi sad.'

It is the relationship that we establish more than any technique that we may use that allows the children to take what they need to heal their lives. Children are often at least as empathic as the counsellor, and maybe one of the most important elements in the relationship is that they pick up our loving intent. Perhaps Dibs, who began therapy speechless, sums up the essence of our work when he meets his ex-therapist and reflects on their sessions saying:

> 'I was frightened at first because I didn't know what you would do and I didn't know what I would do. But you just said "This is all yours Dibs. Have fun. Nobody is going to hurt you in here."'
> 'I said that?'
> 'Yes' Dibs said decisively. 'That is what you said to me. And I gradually came to believe you. And it was that way. You said for me to go fight my enemies until they cried out and said they were sorry they hurt me.'
> 'And did you do that?'
> 'Yes I found out my enemies and I fought them. But then I found out that I was not afraid anymore. I found out that I am

46

not unhappy when I feel love. Now I am big and strong and not afraid.'

(Axline 1964: 191)

References

Axline, V. (1964) *Dibs: In search of self.* New York: Penguin.

BAC (1996) *Code of Ethics and Practice for Supervision of Counsellors.* Rugby: British Association for Counselling.

Coleman, J., Lyon, J. and Piper, R. (1995) *Teenage Suicide and Self Harm.* Brighton: TSA Publishing Ltd.

Dorfman, E. (1951) Play therapy, in C.R. Rogers *Client Centered Therapy.* London: Constable.

Friedli, L. and Scherzer, A. (1996) *Positive Steps: Attitudes and awareness among 11–24 year olds.* London: Health Education Authority Publications.

Geldard, K. and Geldard, D. (1997) *Counselling Children.* London: Sage.

Inskipp, F. and Proctor, B. (1995) *Becoming a Supervisor.* Twickenham: Cascade.

Newson, E. (1992) The barefoot play therapist: adapting skills for time of need, in D. Lane and A. Miller, *Child and Adolescent Therapy.* Buckingham: Open University Press.

3

LEARNING TO LISTEN, LEARNING TO HEAR

A training approach

Penny Toller

Introduction

The new affluence of the 1960s and changing attitudes to work and leisure brought about a more child-centred family structure in Britain. These changes dealt a final blow to the idea that children should be seen and not heard. The development of counselling and mentoring in schools and that of helplines, such as ChildLine in 1986, indicates increasing acceptance that listening respectfully to children's feelings and experience is a source of healing, and that it can be offered by trained volunteers, as well as by more formally qualified professionals.

My own counselling and training work has taken place in three different settings: the first, a voluntary organisation that provides a telephone helpline for children and young people; the second, a state comprehensive school, and the third, an independent boys school with a prep school attached. Although these are organisations with significant differences in statutory responsibility and organisational style, my own approach and method of working have been broadly the same in each.

This chapter focuses on the experience of training volunteers to counsel children and young people on a telephone helpline and in schools.

Listening – the heart of the counselling approach

The approach to counselling offered in each setting is based on the understanding that it is through the experience of being listened to, accepted and truly heard by another person that we can begin to heal some of the pain and hurt of our human existence. No matter what theoretical model the counsellor uses, it is this area of contact that holds the potential for healing. It enables growth and change in clients but also in counsellors, if they are able to remain open to it.

Alice Miller has written that, even for those seeking help in their adult years, the capacity to heal damaging childhood experiences depends on this one condition: 'that there was *at least one person* in our childhood who affirmed our true feelings, and thus let us know that our true self could be seen by others and did exist' (quoted in Steinem 1992: 99). This listening approach suggests that such an experience of acceptance can form the basis of a model for training volunteer counsellors in the use of counselling skills, to enable children and young people to understand and cope with their distress more effectively. Training may take many forms, but its primary aim is to increase awareness of the complex forces that can aid or inhibit empathy between counsellor and client, and which open up or close down that therapeutic connection between them.

Although a kind heart is often regarded as a prerequisite for helping people, it is not sufficient in any way for negotiating the dangers and pitfalls of counselling work with children. Good training alerts trainees to the reality that the line between a counselling relationship that empowers a child and one that harms and is an abuse of power can be very difficult to recognise, and the road to hell may be paved with the best intentions.

Given a good enough level of counselling skills, training in awareness of the potential dynamics between child and counsellor is essential additional preparation. Self-awareness in a counsellor is as important as knowledge of counselling theory or counselling skills. Without it, the inner feelings and needs of the counsellor can drown out what is being said by a child. The content of this self-awareness dimension of training often arises out of the difficulties that are thrown up for a counsellor from session to session. I have found that these are usually not adequately addressed in counselling training devised mainly for volunteers working with adult clients.

Child-centredness

Though I counsel in a fairly intuitive way, by selecting skills and approaches that seem helpful in working with an individual client, my training is in psychodynamic counselling. It is more indicative to say that I counsel and train others from a child-centred approach. By 'child-centred', I mean working primarily at a child's pace, with and for the well-being of that child who is my client – not for the parents of the child, nor for the good of the client's whole family, nor for the good of the school, nor in the interests of society as a whole, but for that particular child. It may be that the counselling impacts positively on all or some of these other interests, but they are not the focus of the work.

A consequence of this child-centred approach is that I work mainly with children and young people who refer themselves. I recognise that many counsellors may not have this choice if they work in organisations in which children are referred by other adults, but it is still possible for counsellors to work in a child-centred way, however their clients are referred.

It is important to add that working in a child-centred way does not mean that the counsellor is willing or able always to follow the wishes of the child, which is a common misunderstanding of the term. The paradox here is that the counsellor is an adult with authority, knowledge and moral responsibilities, the most important of which is to protect the child from harm. Yet part of being child-centred is the attempt to empower children to find inner and outer resources to help themselves, rather than imposing adult solutions on them. It is a radical approach, raising several fundamental questions about power and responsibility in the relationships between children and adults, which add further complexity to a counselling relationship.

Power and responsibility

Part of the therapeutic holding that a counsellor can offer comes from the confidence of knowing this terrain of power and responsibility well enough to hold the power where it is appropriate and to let it go to the child at all other times. A counsellor's confidence or insecurity in this area will often be sensed unconsciously by a child and its impact on the counselling process is immediate, as the relationship becomes less safe for both: one being concerned about what may or may not be disclosed, the other less certain it is safe to trust.

In counselling adults, client-centredness is a central tenet of the relationship, a mark of good practice. It is not always so in counselling young people, since parents and teachers often regard themselves as having a legal and moral right to set the agenda for any counselling work and may look to see improvement in the child's behaviour that meets their own needs first. That a child is an individual, with feelings and wishes that may be different from those of other members of the family or from peers, is an attitude that cannot be taken for granted amongst those adults who have power over children.

Headteachers, too, though most would say that their work is ultimately for the well-being of the individual child, have to juggle this principle with other pressures from the child's family, the interests of other pupils and their parents, teachers, the governors and the local reputation of the school. In a fee-paying school, parents pay directly for their child's education in a competitive education market, which can make the relationships between Head and parents particularly problematic when difficulties with children arise.

Young people know, at some level, that adults inhabit a complex world of responsibilities and loyalties. Frequently, the first question to a counsellor is about confidentiality. Put another way, it is implicitly about checking out who the counsellor is working for – 'How far are you for me or are you really working on behalf of the authorities to breach my defences and find a way of making me what "they" want me to be? When the chips are down, whose side will you be on?' Even on the helpline, which advertises itself as a confidential service for young people, many callers check this out or ask for reassurance about call recording or tracing.

Setting safe-enough boundaries for client and counsellor is essential preparation for all counselling work. Children and young people in particular need to feel safe enough to begin to talk before adults can listen effectively.

Making a safe space: setting the boundaries for listening

It is fundamental to a client's sense of safety that counsellors are able to take responsibility for their own boundaries. They must be clear not only about their own professional ethics but also about their areas of accountability. Counsellors employed within the state education system, for example, are bound by statutory responsibilities as employees to report to the Headteacher disclosures of physical or sexual abuse made by students.

Regular on-going supervision is essential for anyone counselling children, partly for support with these difficult issues of power and pain and partly to aid the process of personal development, which is one of the (often unexpected) gifts of this challenging work. It is also important for a counsellor working within an organisation with its own legal and institutional code of practice to have thought through how this might affect work with clients.

If Joanna is being bullied, the strategies she considers with her counsellor need to take into account the school's approach to bullying, how far it is taken seriously and what procedures are in place for dealing effectively with complaints. If Joanna's distress is likely to be met with the attitude that bullying is a normal part of growing up that she should be able to cope with, it is important that this can be acknowledged and not simply explained away as another of the fears and fantasies that may also be part of Joanna's feelings about the school. In my experience, it can sometimes be difficult for adults to acknowledge that an organisation that ostensibly cares for children may have developed a culture that, in some areas, is insensitive or even abusive.

Working with others who work with children

Institutional policies and procedures provide the framework in a school within which everyone must operate. But there is a much more flexible area within working relationships, for example between a counsellor and a teacher, that can be developed by individuals to become an important resource for supporting a young person with difficulties. The area of goodwill, good working relations, co-operation, an understanding of how other people work and their view of the situation are all about *how* things are done within the rules. A counsellor's own sense of safety and support can depend on how such relationships are developed. How this might be done is a training issue, since it requires not just interpersonal skills but also some understanding of how organisations work.

Unless they have been clients themselves, teachers may have some expectations of counselling that are unrealistic. Unless these expectations are adjusted, they set the counsellor up to be seen to fail. For example, the remark that 'John says he went to see the counsellor last week but he doesn't seem to be any better' contains the underlying assumption that counselling can offer a quick solution to long-standing problems.

A counsellor might also want to be pro-active in giving other people a clearer understanding of what it means in practice to work in a child-centred way, especially as this can easily be misinterpreted as taking sides against parents and teachers. Reducing the mystique of counselling facilitates a more co-operative way of working with colleagues. It may be a fundamental part of an experienced counsellor's preparation for work with clients to consider how to contribute to the in-house training of colleagues, with whom co-operation and goodwill are important. A shared, basic understanding of how the counsellor and the teacher operate differently in the school, and some mutual appreciation of the pressures and dilemmas of both, might be a starting point.

Hostility, misunderstanding and a lack of respect for counselling do not provide the kind of environment in which the vulnerable will want to seek help. Maximising support for the work of counselling from within the organisation can also act as a useful container for the anxieties of the counsellor, who might otherwise expend large amounts of energy defending personal boundaries to ensure a safe working place.

Confidentiality

In the first meeting with the client when the issue of confidentiality is addressed, it is the counsellor's responsibility to have a clear policy already formulated and to be able to answer any questions raised by the young person clearly and honestly. The client may want to know what the circumstances are in which the counsellor would involve someone else.

Training exercises: boundaries and confidentiality

The issues of boundaries and confidentiality can be explored helpfully in training sessions. The following exercises might provide the basis for one or several sessions in which trainees are asked to:

1   Devise a form of words to explain to a client how they work and what their confidentiality policy is. Explore how these might be similar/ different for a 7 year old, 11 year old, 14 year old or 16 year old.

2   Consider different scenarios presented to the group which they discuss before deciding if/when they would break confidentiality and how they would talk to the client about this decision. A useful example might be to consider two or three different clients who have at some time expressed suicidal feelings.
    Issues of confidentiality for the client, risk, counsellors' anxieties and responsibilities and outside referral can be discussed.

3   Explore in discussion when and how they might consider referral of clients who are abusing drugs/alcohol or presenting difficulties around food and eating, and how factors such as age, class, ethnic group, gender, sexuality and disability might influence these considerations.

4   Characterise their own ethics in the practice of their counselling. What is the fit between the counselling work and the work of other groups in the organisation, e.g. teachers? Where are the areas of potential misunderstanding and/or conflict between the counsellor and other groups of workers? What can be done to minimise these?

5   Devise policy and principles for contact with parents/carers of clients.

6   Explore personal attitudes to child protection agencies such as social services and suggest how these might influence work with clients, especially referrals to these agencies.

7   Explore institutional accountability: to whom in the organisation is the counsellor responsible? What are the counsellor's areas of autonomy? What, if any, are the statutory responsibilities of the organisation and how might they affect counselling work with young people?

Inside the safe space: the counselling relationship

Children and young people bring their past experience of adults into every counselling session. Particularly in the early sessions, it may be difficult for them to imagine a relationship in which they will not be punished or judged, controlled or manipulated, one in which it is safe for them to explore their feelings without having their privacy violated and where their individuality and personal wishes will be respected. Acquiring the skills, knowledge and attitudes to offer such a relationship to any client forms the basis of many counselling training courses. But counselling children is different in some aspects that need particular focus in training. These centre around the difficulties of listening to children's pain.

Trainee counsellors need help to learn about several aspects of hearing about children's suffering:

- It is a painful and stressful experience in itself, with a quality different from the experience of counselling adults, perhaps because it is so easy to identify with the vulnerability of children.
- Part of this difference is that it evokes powerful feelings and memories from the counsellor's own childhood, which may inhibit the ability to respond appropriately to what the child is saying.
- Listening to the reality of some children's lives can horrify and challenge the adult's own sense of the basic goodness of life and precipitate a kind of spiritual or existential crisis in the counsellor, especially where abuse of children is involved.

Listening to a child's pain may evoke any or all of these feelings in the counsellor:

- sadness and pain
- anger on behalf of the child
- anger with the child for causing pain to the counsellor
- despair for the world
- helplessness
- the desire to do something, to act, to rescue
- denial
- sympathy
- identification
- empathy
- blame
- shock
- embarrassment.

One important aim in training people to listen actively to children is to enable them to recognise and name these feelings when they arise. Part of this aim is also to encourage acceptance that there is nothing 'wrong' with what they feel. It is difficult for some trainees to admit, for example, that they can feel angry with a distressed child; but the importance of self-awareness can hardly be stressed too much. To attempt to listen actively without being able to recognise your own feelings is to disable the counselling process before it can begin.

What is crucial is that trainees develop an awareness of their own individual pattern of response to hearing the pain and distress of children. They can be helped to do this in different ways.

Exploring the counsellor's response to hearing children's pain

Using video material

In a training session on loss for volunteer telephone counsellors, the trainers first show a short BBC video (BBC 1993) of an interview with a 10-year-old boy about the sudden death of his father. His mother confirms on camera that her grief was so overwhelming at the time that the needs of the boy were overlooked, with serious consequences for him in the years after. It is painful viewing.

After viewing the video, trainees are given a structure to identify their learning. The first exercise is to identify the feelings raised in the group by what they have seen and heard and then to consider each trainee's response. Wanting to leave the room, weeping, blaming the mother, intellectual discussion about the nature of loss, anger towards the trainers, focusing on practical solutions to the family difficulties, being distracted (the video contains footage of the family dog, which was much discussed), together with feelings of loss and grief around their own bereavements are some usual responses shared in the group.

What trainees are usually able to get in touch with is that counselling children is intrinsically difficult work. Each individual finds a way of defending against painful feelings. I have noticed among trainees a tendency sometimes to expect themselves to be heroic in their work with children, in the sense that they are self-critical about any reaction that is not 'strong'; as if the vulnerability of the child disqualifies the counsellor from any vulnerable feelings of their own.

This is one area where the integration of some theoretical understanding is crucial. Showing in training how projective identification works as part of empathy introduces the idea that some of the feelings a counsellor has in the session may be the client's unexpressed feelings, which the child unconsciously projects and which the counsellor then unconsciously picks up. These processes form another mode of communication besides words. This helps to explain why, unless there is openness to feelings, there can be no empathy or authentic connection with a child. The importance of recognising feelings raised in a counsellor and accepting that they 'go with the territory' transform them from a distraction into being an important part of the counselling interaction that can be used to gain a better understanding of each child.

What matters most is the development of an attitude of cautious respect and tentativeness towards the feelings that come up in counselling, a tolerance towards perhaps not knowing in any final way whose feelings they are, and yet good enough skill and confidence to use them constructively to bring greater empathy and insight into the relationship.

The main difficulties for counsellors are in distinguishing between:

- their own immediate responses and feelings
- the child's feelings both expressed and projected
- the conscious and unconscious feelings evoked from the counsellor's childhood past.

Exploring the feelings raised in the relationship between the child and the counsellor is a never-ending process in counselling work.

Self-awareness – the counsellor's childhood

There is something about listening to children that can evoke very powerful memories, experiences and feelings from the counsellor's own childhood. In my experience, this can take counsellors by surprise, especially if they have previously been working only with adult clients. The depth of their response may be painful enough to compound the difficulties of effective listening already considered, but it is an area that can be directly addressed in training in the following ways:

- using a trainee's own early life material for role play practice
- exploring early memories in group discussion
- working through some of the inner child exercises pioneered by John Bradshaw (1990) either in groups or privately at home
- keeping a journal of work with regular entries to record memories, reflections, dreams, reactions and feelings triggered by what has come up through the work. This is a useful way for counsellors to stay in touch with their own process and development, and can provide rich material for discussion in supervision.

Motivation

There is one particular question that is essential for counsellors to ask themselves when deciding to work with children, namely: 'Why do I choose to work with children and young people rather than with adults?' Some of the most common answers volunteers give when asked are:

- 'I had a terrible childhood. I've survived and want to give children the kind of help I never got.'
- 'I've had a privileged life. I want to give something back.'
- 'I just love children.'
- 'I want to help someone.'

These are some of the conscious motives that lie behind the generosity of people who give their time and energy as volunteers. The difficulty is that these motives tend to make the trainee's initial response to a child one of identification or sympathy rather than empathy. Seeing their own childhood pain reflected in the client and/or feeling sorry for the client are elements of empathy, but if they dominate, can inhibit a truly empathic stance.

Identification – 'I think I understand because the same sort of thing happened to me' – and sympathy – 'I'm sorry that you are unhappy' – are responses based on the counsellor's feelings and experience. They can make a contribution to empathy – 'I'm open to what you say about how you feel' – but are not sufficient in themselves. Empathy allows the client's feelings and experiences to be the focus. Carl Rogers wrote about the meaning of empathy:

> It involves . . . being sensitive, moment by moment, to the changing felt meanings which flow in this other person, to the fear or rage or tenderness or whatever he or she is experiencing. It means temporarily living in his/her life, moving about in it delicately without making judgements; it means sensing meanings of which he/she is scarcely aware, but not trying to uncover feelings of which the person is totally unaware, since this would be too threatening. It includes communicating your sensings of the person's world . . . frequently checking with the person as to the accuracy of your sensings and being guided by the responses you receive. You are a confident companion to the person in his or her inner world . . . you lay aside yourself; this can only be done by persons who are secure enough in themselves. . . . Being empathic is a complex, demanding and strong – yet also subtle and gentle – way of being.
>
> (Rogers 1980: 142)

Exploring the difference between empathy, identification and sympathy is a key training exercise, especially important in developing self-awareness in counsellors.

Empathy and the counsellor's frame of reference

Over-identification with a client makes listening with empathy very difficult. It is tempting to assume, for example, that because Joanna is being bullied at school, a counsellor who also was bullied as a young person will understand better. Yet the counsellor's experience, which is evoked by what the child is saying, can actually act as a distraction from looking at how Joanna experiences being bullied and what meaning it has in her individual life.

Being empathic is about allowing clients to talk from *their* frame of reference about *their* meanings and concerns, not the counsellor's. The more work trainees are able to do to identify their own frame of reference – where they, as counsellors, are 'coming from', in terms of personal history, filtered through generations, gender, ethnicity, race, sexuality, disability – the less these factors will intrude into the client's space and time. Empathy is also about respect for difference, training to recognise the sort of assumptions we make as individuals under the banner of 'common sense', which in fact do not adequately honour difference – both social and personal – in other people's lives.

I recall one group training session in which a trainee described speaking to a boy who was upset because he felt his mother did not love him. Upset herself by his distress and wanting to comfort and reassure, the counsellor's initial unexamined response had been to say 'Oh, I'm sure your mother loves you.' However sympathetic and well-meaning, this was not an empathic counselling response. It led to a revealing discussion around the counsellor's assumptions about mothers and her need for the child's situation to be better than it had been presented, or, in other words, about the counsellor's social and emotional frame of reference closing down the client's opportunity to be heard.

The temptation to rush to action

From the training point of view, perhaps the most difficult response to a child's distress is the impulse of counsellors to deal with their own feelings of helplessness by trying to 'rescue' the client, either emotionally or through practical intervention of some kind. In other words, this is when counsellors try to solve children's problems on their behalf rather than helping and empowering children to help themselves.

The impulse to act is a tricky area, as practical intervention may sometimes be essential in terms of child protection. The aim of training is to enable counsellors to be more aware of their own responses to what the client is saying and better able to assess what is appropriate. Western culture tends to reward action/doing more than being/staying with, and this can increase anxiety in the counsellor about being blamed for 'not doing enough', when actually what is needed therapeutically is to stay with the feelings. Regular supervision provides important support in helping counsellors both to think through and to take account of the feelings involved in assessing the risks to children.

The counsellor's feelings of helplessness in the face of the distress of Paul, a boy who has recently experienced the break-up of his parents' marriage and who wants them to get back together, may include Paul's feelings projected onto the counsellor. This double burden of feelings may distract the counsellor into discussing what can be done to bring about a reconciliation or into offering empty assurances that Paul will soon get used to his new life. The impulse to solve Paul's problem for him is an attempt to cope with the counsellor's own helpless feelings by trying to be more powerful and effective than in reality a counsellor is able to be.

Such inappropriate reassurance by the counsellor does not allow Paul the space or time simply to experience his feelings of loss and helplessness, which is essential if he is then to find *his own way* of coping with what has happened. The reality is that it is not ultimately in Paul's power to reconcile his parents; his helplessness is real as well as felt. The counsellor must be able to stay with that feeling as well as explore the areas over which Paul has some control and choice.

When counsellors take control inappropriately, they may compound children's feelings of powerlessness and wound their trust in adults even further. There are, however, other situations in which it is the counsellor's job to challenge feelings of helplessness and help mobilise practical support for children. A child who is being bullied in school may need intervention by adults. Part of the counsellor's skill is to be able to make an assessment of each different situation and work with the client on agreeing a strategy. Clients may themselves expect instant answers to their problems, and there can be enormous pressure on the counsellor to offer a solution. Another response that trainees soon recognise is the desire to push the child towards another adult, a family member perhaps, in the hope that they can effect a solution.

A child-centred response is to work at the individual's pace, asking how a child would like things to change, identifying together differences that can be made and being able to accept what cannot at present be changed. Using adult knowledge and experience to help children help themselves is empowering. Offering solutions is a way for counsellors to feel better about what they have heard. This response, which puts the counsellor's feelings before the needs of the child, is unhelpful and potentially damaging to that child.

Parents/carers and the counsellor

The relationship between the counsellor and a child's parents/carers is another area that can be explored in training in preparation for actual contact. This relationship may be more problematic when working from a child-centred stance, as the counsellor may need the co-operation of parents at some stage, but this has to be gained without compromising the central relationship with the client.

Unlike most adults, children have little control over their practical circumstances. Where adults can decide to change their living arrangements or leave a relationship, children do not have these options for acting on their feelings. It can be frustrating and painful for the counsellor to have to accept that Sarah, a child frightened and upset by the violent rows between her parents, has no alternative but to stay in the situation that is hurting her and to adapt to it.

In my experience, young people often ask their counsellor to act as facilitator or negotiator on their behalf in any situation in which they feel it is important to express their feelings or point of view, for example with parents, teachers and social workers.

When Lee is angry and rude to his mother, he says it is because her relationship with her new boyfriend betrays the memory of his dead father. Lee's mother, on the other hand, regards this relationship as the first sign of hope of recovery after the shattering loss of her husband. She feels let down by her son's hostility and determined he will not be allowed to spoil her chance of happiness. If Lee requests it, part of the counsellor's role can be to facilitate better understanding between them, but this is a delicate process, depending largely on the extent of the mother's willingness to take part in the process. It is a non-starter if she expects the counsellor to see their problem only in terms of enforcing discipline in the home.

Taking a child-centred stance is to work towards enabling young people to speak for themselves by exploring with them what they want to say, in what ways it is difficult to say it and how these difficulties might be overcome. Being present while Lee and his mother try to find a better understanding, offers Lee support in communicating directly with his mother, rather than acting his feelings out in destructive ways. The counsellor may have strong feelings about how Lee's mother deals with his behaviour, for example, it may trigger identification with her as a parent struggling with a 'difficult' child and/or identification with Lee as 'misunderstood'. It may even raise envious feelings to see in action sensitive parenting that the counsellor may have wanted but never experienced in childhood.

It is worth examining with trainees their attitudes to parenting so that they can be more aware of their stance on different styles of parenting, including their attitudes to their own parents and how they feel they were treated by them during their childhood. Again, this is essential work to develop awareness of the counsellor's personal issues so that they can be more easily distinguished from the child's in the course of their work together.

Conclusion

Learning to listen to children in a counselling way is not an academic process but a practical invitation to cultivate that openness of heart that allows both learning and unlearning. What we learn is the capacity to reflect on our personal history, how we became the person we are, the attitudes, culture, difficulties and pain of that becoming, so that we do not confuse our experiences and feelings with those of the children who confide in us.

Active listening includes learned skills and abilities, but they are not the point of arrival. That is a constantly developing process of working at our relationships with children to keep them free from our own life material while we listen. It is complex work and we often need to set aside our superiority of knowing as an adult, to allow ourselves respect and humility in the face of a child's difference, so that we can actually listen to what they wish and need us to hear.

References

BBC (1993) Family Matters programme.

Bradshaw, J. (1990) *Homecoming: Reclaiming and championing your inner child*. London: Piatkus.

Rogers, C.R. (1980) *A Way of Being*. Boston: Houghton Mifflin.

Steinem, G. (1992) *Revolution from Within*. London: Bloomsbury.

Suggested reading

Axline, V.M. (1990) *Dibs: In Search of Self*. Harmondsworth: Penguin.

Miller, A. (1990) *The Drama of Being a Child*. London: Virago.

Part II

MULTICULTURES, MULTIFAITHS

Ear

You

Eyes

Undivided attention

Heart

Chinese character 'to listen'

Art Therapy: The person-centred way
(Liesl Silverstone 1997: 24)

4

COMMUNICATING
WITH A BLACK CHILD

Overcoming obstacles of difference

Lennox K. Thomas

Introduction

My earliest experiences of listening to children came about as a result of my work as a children's officer. Listening in such a context seemed natural and unself-conscious. Allowing time and space as a keyworker for a child to talk about their day at school or their plans for weekends or visits home to family was part of a routine encouraged by senior staff. Being available in this way to a child would inevitably lead to an unfolding of the child's history of difficulties. The publication 'Communication with children' (Winnicott 1964) was the first influence on my learning and ability to listen and make sense of what children were saying to me. This article was most encouraging. Mrs Winnicott believed that listening would be therapeutic and would help children to establish a sense of their own identity and worth in relation to other people. I was alerted to understanding the significance of play and the role of the favourite teddy bear, cuddly toy or doll.

After a training in social work, working in children's theatre and a child observation training, I began work as a probation officer. My caseload was mostly made up of divorce court welfare work and preparing reports on parents and children appearing before the juvenile courts.

Making a connection

Many years went by before I was able to make a connection between how social and attitudinal factors affect the lives of ethnic minority children and, moreover, the effect that ethnic difference might have on their psychological development in a society where they were relative outsiders. It was from the experience of working with children, adolescents and adults from minority ethnic backgrounds that I developed an interest in black child development.

Little has been written about the therapeutic process when working with children of African and Asian heritage. To consider specific issues in this context might be new to many people. People who talk to children or who listen to children's information in a quasi-legal or therapeutic setting may not have considered the particular issues of power, culture and race as being possible obstacles to their task. The priority given to children's welfare in the 1989 Children Act has made some impact, but the intricate issues of providing a context and developing a relationship with black children have not been much discussed in professional literature.

Such children need to be thought of specifically, individually and culturally, since the situation and experiences of children in general may not help workers to understand those complex relationships that are present in working with children of African or Asian descent. It is my view that children in these cultural groups experience different developmental pathways to the 'standard orthodox child' often mentioned in text books or child development schemas. Thinking along general lines about children obscures the particular issues of development for black children, children with disabilities, those from deprived backgrounds and others from ethnic minorities. Some case histories have appeared (Boston and Szur 1983; Smith 1987; Hopson and Hopson 1992). However, the impact of contextual difference of skin colour and the effects of racism on later psychological development has yet to be researched. From my experience, child development theories have never featured the experience of black children in a white society, nor in a multicultural society. Thus a whole range of diversity and difference is often missed, and therapeutic work with these children can sometimes bear poor results. Interesting work has been done by Sinason (1992) and Bichaud (1996) on self-esteem and self-concept with abused children and young people with learning difficulties, and we have much to learn from this pioneering work. What is of key importance is the issue of self-esteem and self-love of those from groups who experience discrimination.

Identification by proxy

Thomas (1995) puts forward the notion of 'identification by proxy'. This takes into account the social context in which black children are raised in a society that does not privilege them or sometimes discriminates against them, leaving the children to use their own antennae to figure out who will be kind and fair to them and who will not. This experience affects the degree to which a black child is able to disclose information about themselves honestly, or to make an identification with the white worker, based on the proxy or pretend self that is put forward to engage with the worker for self-protective reasons. Unless the worker is able to understand the barriers that exist to communication and has the capacity to surmount them, the child will not be helped.

Gurmail

Gurmail, an 8-year-old boy of Indian heritage, came to the teacher's attention after he had described his weekend at circle time in the classroom. He said that the family had gone to church and Sunday school. The teacher, knowing that the family were practising Sikhs, found this information incongruous. Thinking that he might have said this in case the other children would not understand the word for his own place of worship, the teacher spoke to him afterwards. She asked him if he really went to church, or if he did not want to be too different from the others in the class. Nervously, he agreed that this was the case. A caricature of this position is the African or Asian descended child using the stock answer 'fish and chips', when asked by school friends and others what they had for tea the previous day. This might be the answer that is given even if it might not have been the case. Seeming so apparently English, such a response is easier, and would not attract curiosity or ridicule. A sensitive teacher would be able to help this child to express their cultural difference openly with pride and confidence. In Gurmail's case, his teacher recognised that he was trying to obscure his difference by what he had said. She was later able to talk in the class about different forms of worship. In doing so, she was able to include his way of worshipping as well as others. An important step was taken by the teacher to include Gurmail and others who were not churchgoers. This positive example helped to restore his sense of pride in his difference.

Such a situation places the onus on the professional not only to be keenly attuned to the child's psychological needs, but also to help them to work through the protective barrier in order that real communication can be made. An understanding of why the child's defence needed to be erected in the first instance has to take place. If a child assumes a false or proxy self, it is unlikely that their utterances or communication will be authentic, or that the worker would make effective communication with them. The adult would be unable to listen to or hear the child's real concerns or psychological needs. Asian and African children have a protracted struggle in their bid to gain a positive sense of themselves. The consequence of not achieving this might be detrimental during the various stages of their lives. Whilst the most exaggerated examples of self-hatred in black children have been noted by Maxime (1993), Ahmed *et al.* (1986) and Wilson (1978), these writings have not yet had the full impact that they deserve on therapeutic work with black children in the United Kingdom. Indeed, there has been a significant lack of response from psychotherapists, although child care social workers have grappled with these issues for some years at a policy level. The approach to therapeutic listening to these children appears to have lagged behind, possibly because of the paralysing effect of political correctness and the way in which workers have understood this.

Living in a dual world

One wonders whether or not proxy identity and self-hatred in black children will become part of the diagnostic categories for professionals who have to listen to children. Many black children and young people who have difficulties in adulthood have not had the opportunity to be listened to and understood by professionals that they met during their earlier lives. Those working with black children need to have a clear understanding of the role and function of the families in which they live in order to make better communication and really understand what the children say. The notion of the black family as one that is built to equip their offspring with the skills of survival in a racist or prejudiced society certainly has to be taken into account. Moreover, children's allegiance to home and family might present a conflict for them in taking into their confidence someone whom they do not know, and might have learned not to trust. Conflict may arise between what the child learns from home and family about the unsafe or racist outside world, and white professionals' wish for them to be open and honest. Communication between them will be affected, and preparation has to take place. Home as a safe place, a retreat or as a haven from the outside world, is not just a social construction for young children, but also a psychological construction that might serve the function of keeping out white authority and, sometimes with it, the white racism that devalues and diminishes them. It could be argued that the child of African or Asian descent inhabits a dual world in a society where racism and discrimination are rife. In *Home is Where We Start From*, Winnicott describes such a dual world in terms of the true and false self and talks about the ways in which the individual has the capacity for splitting:

> In health, this splitting of the self is an achievement of personal growth; in illness the split is a matter of a schism in the mind that can go to any depth; at its deepest it is labelled schizophrenia.
> (Winnicott 1986: 66)

Internal splits are ultimately not helpful to black children. The experience of talking to a white therapist and appearing to be engaged, yet being hesitant to talk about being racially abused by another white person some hours earlier, puts the child in a difficult position.

In *Playing and Reality*, Winnicott points out the importance of context and the environment for psychoanalytic practice. Whilst he speaks generally here, it is of particular importance for those children who are different, that workers do not ignore their context and environment. Failing to recognise the particular situation of the child renders therapeutic intervention a blunt instrument at best and at worst useless. What happens to the child outside the sessions cannot be ignored, particularly if the person of the worker might in some way pose a threat to the child: 'I draw attention to the fact that . . . the behaviour of the environment is part of the individual's own personal development and must therefore be included.' (Winnicott 1971: 62–63)

Black children are not held and supported by the environment in a racist society like ours, because many of their developmental needs are ignored or not even thought about. For example, a white student, having observed a black 2 year old in a nursery for a period of a year, decided that a couple of black dolls might make a suitable gift to the nursery. Although one quarter of the children were of African, Asian or mixed descent, there were no black dolls or other representative materials in the nursery. Holding, contemplating, relating and loving the image of oneself is one of the ways in which children learn to love themselves and other significant people in their lives. She thought that if all play were with white dolls, to which only the white children could easily relate, the black children would learn to privilege whiteness, regarding themselves ultimately as invisible. Consequently, they would learn to pay homage to whiteness through the sacrifice of their own self-hood. Children learn through play, and in studies in the USA (Clark 1963), black children indicate a preference for white friends more often than for other children like themselves. They considered the black dolls, which they resembled, to be ugly or not nice. Similar studies in the UK (Davey and Norburn 1980) found that children of primary school age had an awareness of ethnic difference and black dolls were not considered as favourably as white dolls. Perhaps by having greater access to images of themselves, black children might achieve a greater degree of self-love.

The case of Susie

Susie was fostered by a white family after her mother's separation from her father and the subsequent distress and neglect of herself and her daughter. Susie's Caribbean parents kept in touch with her, her father by cards and letters and her mother by occasional visits and telephone calls. Susie had been with the foster family for two years, since she was 6 years old, when she was sexually abused by a 13-year-old white boy, who lived a few doors away from her foster parents' home. During the course of the abuse, he called her 'black shit'. At bath time she asked her foster mother 'Am I black shit?' Shocked, her foster mother reassured Susie, who went on to describe the incident. She seemed more upset about the name calling than about other aspects of the abuse of being touched and being made to touch the boy's private parts. The incident set off for Susie a series of questions about her identity and acceptability within the foster family. She was not happy with being 'black shit' and proceeded to work at unravelling this in many forms. Through her questions she clearly sought assurance that she was acceptable and lovable and probably that she was not really black at all. She was not entirely sure about who she was, but she wanted to be white, the same as her foster parents and their older daughters. It seemed that she could not accept anything other than this. Whilst the split in Susie's concept of herself was becoming apparent only as a result of this abusive experience, she was being held and contained by caring and skilful foster parents. For others, without support, this confusion can develop into a hatred of themselves, distancing them further from an acceptance of their ethnic or racial identity.

The experience of living in a society where the formation of a positive black identity is against many odds, poses fundamental problems for black children. Many black children and adults alike are in various stages of a process of re-claiming a sense of their worth and identity. Even when family relationships are nourishing, the reality of the external world frequently gnaws away at the child's sense of themselves. Familial love and acceptance can sometimes serve as the only fortress against an encroaching and damaging external world, and the home has to perform the function of continually and subliminally topping up self-esteem and self-love in the African and Asian child, often against the tide of their own experience outside the home. These outside experiences, which frequently seem bent on diminishing esteem, often render the black child invisible, since so little recognition is given to their existence. Wilson (1978) describes what he terms schizoid play, which appears to be the process of approaching whiteness *en route* to the development of a proxy identity. Wilson excludes the experience of girls by using 'his' or 'him'. I would like 'his' to read 'their', because the use of the inclusive pronoun enables the quotation to be helpful.

> Commensurate black heroes and figures are absent. In this child's mind the attributes of his white imaginal heroes and figures may become attributes of whites in general and not the attributes of the black 'heroes' and 'figures' which are absent from his imagination. The black child's imaginal and imitative play may surreptitiously lay the foundation for his own growing feelings of inferiority, his own self-hatred and rejection of his people. It may lead to his frustrated attempts to identify himself as white or to deny his blackness.
>
> (Wilson 1978: 106)

How can we really listen to what is communicated by the whole authentic child?

Why do many white workers so often miss identifying and diagnosing identity confusion or related disorders in Asian and African descended children? Could it be that the framework for conceptualising these behaviours is beyond the personal and practical experience of these workers? Or that the very process within the child, of developing a transference, love or identification blinds the worker to what is really going on? Until these issues are worked with and understood, the black child will not be listened to and their presenting psychological distress will not be dealt with, because it is not fully understood. Although it is not an easy task, the worker needs to understand the context of the child's situation, which might differ greatly from their own experience in a number of ways.

Rashid

Rashid, 14 years old, was referred for therapy because of what his social worker considered to be his self-destructive behaviour. He was accommodated by the local authority when his mother was no longer able to control him. He was disappearing from home, returning at all hours, and occasionally sleeping out, while giving no explanation for this. He had appeared before the youth court for shoplifting a year earlier, and whilst his stealing appeared to cease, his behaviour worsened. He was rude at home and his mother felt it was a poor example for the four younger children.

Rashid was the second of six children born to his parents. He had a brother of 18, two sisters aged 12 and 10, and two brothers aged 8 and 7. His father, who was much older than his mother, died when Rashid was 9 years old after a long illness. His older brother, Ahmed, became very supportive at home and was changed after the death of their father. Ahmed is reported to have been in trouble with the police and involved with gangs when their father was alive.

Discussing his past seemed to upset Rashid, who would say from time to time, 'Well, what can you (meaning himself) do about it? No point getting upset.' I had the impression from those words that they had been repeatedly said to him, and now, in turn, he said them to other people. He had fond memories of his father, who although frail and ill, was very involved with his children. Rashid remembered the stories about Bangladesh, and his father's adventures as a merchant seaman. He seemed, on the one hand, very able to talk and value our sessions, but he was also guarded about his feelings. Asking him why he stayed out late so often from the children's home silenced him, or provoked a tough guy response. He said that he spent most of his time with his mates and that he was old enough to look after himself.

Rashid found it easy to engage with me. I think that his street lifestyle and his choice of African-American rap music probably made it easy for him to make a connection with me as a black man. The tough nonchalance of this image seemed attractive to Rashid, who wore clothes and trainers as the hallmark of this style. He boasted that he had a lot of money and knew how to get it. This half-revealing, half-concealing comment seemed to be inviting a question that I knew would create some tension. It would give Rashid the opportunity to be evasive and to derive the great satisfaction of holding on to what he knows. The therapeutic contract did not require me to jeopardise our relationship in order to fill in the gaps in Rashid's life for the social workers involved. Holding on to my curiosity and my assumptions was crucial if I was to establish a good relationship with him.

Rashid was very sad after his father's death. He said that his older brother became close to their mother, and helped her a great deal, especially with the younger ones. His brother had made a promise to the extended family to keep out of trouble, and he seemed to have kept this promise. Thus Ahmed became a responsible Muslim son, leaving little space for Rashid to do anything else but to fill the role of the difficult one.

Rashid hated his older brother and felt criticised by him. Ahmed had been a rebel when he was younger and therefore no different to himself. Rashid said that if Ahmed had not upset his parents so much, his father would still have been alive. He was critical of his mother for allowing his brother to boss them all around. He felt justified in his staying out late and doing as he wanted. Whilst he felt that he was not treated well by his family and had resolved, in his own words, 'not to get upset about it', he set about paying them back by making them worry by his frequent absences until he was accommodated by the local authority.

I discovered the extent to which Rashid was prepared to put himself at risk in his bid to show them or teach them a lesson. He took my concern some weeks earlier about putting himself at risk literally and asked casually one day how people 'got AIDS'. After a very general reply to what I thought was the curiosity of an early adolescent, I discovered that Rashid was on the fringe of a group of boys who performed sexual favours for local men who had a particular liking for Asian or Afro-Caribbean boys. Rashid thought that he was very clever to be in the position of always having money in his pocket, and of knowing how to get it. I was surprised by the way in which he was able to talk about this issue. With hindsight, he needed to have been in therapy for six months to check me out, and feel some degree of safety in the therapy in order to say this.

Rashid wanted to be treated with respect and to be allowed the space to talk about what he wanted, at a time when he wanted. Adult clients are often able to negotiate with their workers the timing of sensitive material, but children do not always have the skill or power to do this. I tried hard to work at Rashid's own pace and suspected that he had something important

to tell me. I also realised that Rashid enjoyed the power of knowing something that I did not know. In order to be really available, I had to be
patient and listen. Because Rashid had prepared me so well in order to
recount his story, I had not displayed shock at what he had to tell me. To
some extent, he might not have considered me as someone who could understand his story.

Engaging with difference

It is sometimes said that it is not possible for us to work therapeutically
beyond what is our own experience, but the capacity for visualisation, spec-
ulation and empathy seems not to be taken into account here. Since most
African descended and Asian children have therapeutic contact with white
professionals, it does not augur well for their receiving appropriate and
sensitive help, if this statement were true. It is possible to learn, and to
hold on to, the working assumption that we will not know everything.
Most professionals have the rudimentary skills of making contact, observing,
putting the child at ease and being able to use play to facilitate the
therapeutic relationship. The experience of working with cultural difference
is part of the dynamic where not only the client might be different
but where we, also, as workers are different in the therapeutic space. Experience of such differences in an encounter can have quite a profound effect
on us. I have never forgotten the powerful emotional impact on me during
my early career when working with a client who recounted her childhood
experiences in a Nazi concentration camp some twenty-four years earlier.
We can learn to accommodate our different feelings and thinking in order
to make sense of such an experience, so that our racial and cultural difference, or our lack of understanding of a child's life, is not an obstacle in
therapy.

While working with a black child, we need to have an understanding of
what our own unconscious storehouse might contain in relation to black-
ness, race and difference. We have to ask ourselves: What have I learned
about black people over the years and what might get in the way of me
making meaningful contact? We have to ask ourselves: What is it like to
be a child of African or Asian heritage growing up on this council estate
or in this leafy suburban area? How might this child understand or deal
with the experiences of fear or threat to his or her personal safety? What
might it mean to this child to be sitting in this room with me, and how
will this child relate to an experience with me, who hitherto might have
been a figure of threat in the outside world? What processes does this child
have to go through in order to make me a safer and helpful person able to
listen to them? As well as the stored-up unhappiness or distress for which
the therapeutic help is sought (probably school exclusion, low scholastic
achievement, physical or sexual abuse or bullying), how can the two of us

create a safe place where these issues, as well as the issues of our difference, can be explored and really understood?

Another issue might be, how can I as a professional take account of the child's future social and psychological well-being if I am clueless about their personal context and history? What can my assessment be about? Might it be based on a false premise? Might it be based on my ignorance about what this child's life is really about? In order to really hear the child, how can I attune to the very many differences between us and how can I use those points of sameness between us in our contact? It is often the case that professionals are unable to hear the pain or distress because of the distance that has sometimes been erected both by the child and sometimes themselves, through the haze of cultural difference.

Learning to work interculturally

Working in a psychotherapy centre that puts the needs of black and ethnic minority children and adults first, certainly focuses attention on how the land lies from their perspective. It can be both a confusing and challenging task to think about the so often neglected needs of these children and young people. Non-ethnic-minority professionals need to consider the issues of fear and safety for children with whom they are working and to discover ways of putting them at ease. It is very important to think of one's own background, one's own childhood and how it felt to be in the presence of an adult who might represent power and fear; to recall the first meeting with the school nurse or the dentist, of whom we were told that we should not be frightened. Having heard previous information from our peers about these adults, such assurances seemed hollow. As children, we went to such a meeting with great caution and held ourselves together in the hope that we would survive. It is also important for the worker to consider what the superiority of their own whiteness might have meant to them as children, and whether or not in adulthood they are able to give this up as a prop to their own self-esteem and personality in order to really meet a black child on neutral ground. Being a child raised in a culture or ethnicity that fought and won wars, controlled an empire, provided an international language and generally ruled the waves, confers a certain security and pride. This would not be the experience of the black child in the United Kingdom. For them the historical markers and structures that demonstrate their greatness as a people and as individuals do not exist in the school system, nor are they reflected in society at large.

Supervisory support

The challenge of therapeutic work with children and young people from backgrounds that might differ from our own can take place only within the supportive context of a supervisory relationship. Supervisors need to be experienced in doing this work, and should not be defensive about engaging with difference. The worker also needs to be courageous enough to stick with the painful material, even when the feelings evoked might be a sense of guilt for being white, or how other white people might have oppressed or are oppressing this child, in a direct way or indirectly, by placing obstacles in the way of their development of selfhood and pride. Feeling a sense of racist guilt might indeed be evident in the work, but it is not helpful to the child. Personal exploration of these issues is a process that the worker needs to engage with in supervision or consultation, sometimes outside the agency. This sense of uselessness and guilt can de-stabilise and de-skill helpful workers unless it is discussed in a supervisory relationship or in the worker's own counselling or non-managerial consultation.

Self-awareness

Working across cultures can present both workers and clients with challenges to their own identity, values or world views. Working with children can sometimes put us in touch with times in our own lives when we might have been vulnerable to the will and power of others.

Black and white workers alike might become engaged in the unlearning of certain things about themselves accrued from childhood as a result of the distortion of the worth ascribed to black and white people. This can sometimes be the unlearning of negative attributes, personally or racially based (Thomas 1992) that might have served as an obstacle to positive and realistic development. Others might have to work through gender or social class issues that might have oppressed them, or deal with a false sense of confidence because of the positive attributes conferred on their group. If positive selection is done at the expense of other social groups, we are left in an unrealistic position. On discovering this, we have to learn our own true worth, not that which is given to us because of the colour of our skin, our gender, sexuality, able-bodiedness or social class.

We have lived through a time in our society when groups of people were relegated to social positions because of their gender, social class or skin colour. These ideas have been challenged by social and political pressure groups who wanted to redefine their position in the social structures. These changes have inevitably given rise to a gradual re-ordering of the way in which we are valued as people. Psychological or personal changes seem to lag behind social and political changes. This time-delay can sometimes be evident when we make a statement in an unguarded moment and immediately realise how prejudiced we still are. The residue of prejudice that might give way to an act of discrimination needs to be engaged with. Being the source of shame in many workers, this aspect of their own developmental needs can often be ignored in order to preserve their self-esteem and protect their psyche from the further rigours of change. Personal change and personal development, if successful as a preparation for listening and engaging with children, will enable us to have greater access to ourselves. In becoming more aware of how we impact on children and how they impact on us, we can be better skilled to hear their stories.

Listening to children and bearing witness to their pain as well as endeavouring to provide them with therapeutic help requires us to know about the process of working through personal difficulties.

A welcoming atmosphere

Working with a child either briefly or long term requires regularity and a comfortable room with toys or play materials that are appropriate to the children's age. Adolescents too might sometimes wish to discover the contents of the play box and the dolls' house, and for some this can be a cautious and self-conscious beginning in their discovery of their own playfulness. Black and white dolls in the play box are sometimes alone, or in sets of families: Asian, African Caribbean or white European. The small pipe cleaner dolls appear to be a favourite of under 10 year olds. One little 8-year-old boy was able to recreate his mixed parentage family with these dolls. Plasticine, plastic building blocks and other toys can be used, a room containing a sink is helpful for children who might like to use paint, or felt tip pens and paper. Children can talk about their drawings and make their own interpretation of what they see. Often the workers' interpretations can be intrusive and stem the flow of the child's discussion. Interpretation, if made at all, should be done with great care and in a form of words that the child understands. Often it is the workers' excitement at their discoveries that leads them to interpret using complex ideas that may be inaccessible to children. Waiting can be very rewarding when the child eventually arrives at their own insights and shares them with the worker. Hand puppets are useful because the child will give them their own voice and characteristics which will speak for them in snippets of dramatic play. Story telling, toy cars and animals can also be used in this way.

Ensure a welcoming atmosphere in the room and other areas of the agency. Do the pictures or posters on the wall reflect the children who use it? Are Asian, African and other children pictured and do children with disabilities also appear?

On beginning to talk to a child, I have found it helpful to introduce myself and sometimes say a little about how some children use the time in the room. This depends very much on the child's age and knowledge. Some children ask if I will tell other people about what they say. Surprisingly or not, very young children might pose this question about the boundaries of confidentiality. This question has to be answered honestly, and the child will need to be told that some things they say might have to be told to someone else. It is important to tell a child that you will talk to them first so that the best way can be found to let someone else know. Sometimes, the child might be able to select the most helpful person to tell from among a choice available.

Conclusion

There are as many obstacles to professional workers listening effectively to black children in distress as there are obstacles to the development of a positive balanced identity in a black child. Of these, racism, internal colonisation and being a minority in a large majority society all play their part. One of the most significant obstacles is the invisibility of these issues to professionals charged with providing treatment and help to black children. Therapists can become sensitive to these issues and can be able to work therapeutically with black children. I believe, however, that many will steer clear of this work because of the many challenges that doing this might pose to their own learning, and unlearning. I have described some of the issues involved in listening to and helping African and Asian children therapeutically. Doing this in the context of what they have to face in the social and psychological situations of their day-to-day lives is somewhat unusual. Many workers engage with these children as if they were white, thereby missing the stories of the children's struggle with obtaining a positive sense of their racial identity.

There are difficulties for both children and workers in their bid to overcome problems of communication and receptiveness. In terms of our future, health and social service workers need to further develop their methods of working therapeutically with black children. Missing this opportunity will increase the frightening problem of the increasing numbers of children and adolescents who move into adulthood with severe psychological and psychiatric problems. The concerns expressed about the disproportionate numbers of black adults with mental health problems need to be addressed much earlier with those children we can already identify as users of children's services.

> They felt hated and they felt despised. These feelings were exacerbated by the sense that the views embodied in the harassment were widely held. It is extremely difficult to maintain a sense of self worth against such relentless persecution as the children here described.
>
> (ChildLine 1996: 24)

ChildLine studied calls made to them about racism by children. This report, from the best-known British agency for listening to children, presents sad and compelling evidence of the need for skilled work with ethnic minority children. Workers might be reluctant to engage in this work because the preparation to do this could pose a threat to their personal identity. It is my belief that we need to engage with the challenge of this threat, not only to realise our own identity in our multicultural society, but also to meet the needs of its children.

References

Ahmed, S., Cheetham, J. and Small, J. (1986) *Social Work with Black Children and Families*. London: Batsford.

Bichaud, S. *et al.* (1996) Measuring change in mentally retarded clients in long-term psychoanalytic psychotherapy: The draw a person test. *NADD Newsletter* 13 (5) September, 6–11.

Boston, M. and Szur, R. (1983) *Psychotherapy with Severely Deprived Children*. London: Routledge & Kegan Paul.

ChildLine (1996) *Children and Racism*. ChildLine, Royal Mail Building, Studd St, London.

Clark, K.B. (1963) *Prejudice and Your Child.* Boston: Beacon Press.

Davey, A.G. and Norburn, V.M. (1980) Ethnic awareness and difference among primary schoolchildren. *New Community* 8 (1), 51–60.

Hopson, D. and Hopson, D. (1992) *Different and Wonderful: Raising Black children in a race conscious society*. New York: Simon & Schuster.

Maxime, J. (1993) The Importance of Racial Identity For The Psychological Wellbeing Of Black Children. Vol. 15, No 4, page 173–179, Association of Child Psychiatry & Psychology.

Sinason, V. (1992) *Mental Handicap and the Human Condition*. London: Free Association Books.

Smith, E. (1987) Shared work with children in care and their families. *Journal Of Social Work Practice*. 2 (4) May, 13–28.

Thomas, L.K. (1992) Racism and psychotherapy: Working with racism in the consulting room: An analytic view, in J. Kareem and R. Littlewood (eds) *Intercultural Therapy: Themes, interpretations and practice*. Oxford: Blackwell Scientific

Thomas, L.K. (1995) Psychotherapy in the context of race and culture: An inter-cultural therapeutic approach, in S. Fernando (ed.) *Mental Health in a Multi-ethnic Society*. London: Routledge.

Wilson, A. (1978) *The Developmental Psychology Of The Black Child*. New York: Africana Research Publications.

Winnicott, C. (1964) Communicating with children. *Child Care Quarterly Review* 18 (3).

Winnicott, D.W. (1971) *Playing and Reality*. London: Penguin.

Winnicott, D.W. (1986) *Home is Where We Start From*. London: Penguin.

5

CHILDREN, SPIRITUALITY AND RELIGION

Margaret Crompton

Introduction

Children's spiritual experience

Tina, a nominal Christian, was 10 when she discussed the fundamental questions of life with an adult who knew how to listen to children:

Tina: And I thought, how do little ladybirds know where they are . . . ?

Adult: When you think about that, does it make you feel different?

Tina: Well, sometimes it feels like I just popped out of my body and blow somewhere else. I don't know why it just feels like that and sometimes I think 'how did we get here?' and just stop in one place for a moment and think 'why am I here?, how did I become here?' and stuff like that. . . . All over, just like a tingle starting from your head down to your feet.

[In a later discussion]:   Well, there was a time I told you that I stop and think 'How did I get here and that?' . . . Well, that's when I just switch on to God. . . . That's when I start . . . thinking about Him.

(Nye 1996: 2/10-1)

Joanna, also 10, described her innermost feelings and experiences. For her:

. . . spiritual refreshment was found in an imaginary garden, where it was always sunny and peaceful, in contrast to the gloominess of home life and endless chatter of her noisy sisters. . . . Without the

79

encouragement or knowledge of her secular family she had developed her own spasmodic prayer life.

(Nye 1996: 2/16 7)

In her garden, Joanna would think about God and find fulfilment for her 'soul-felt needs in a way that formal prayer (she would repeat just one she'd heard at Brownies) could not'. Joanna was nominally Christian but 'intrigued and somewhat comforted by her understanding of Hindu beliefs about reincarnation and a cycle of life' (ibid.).

Only in her garden could this girl nurture the spiritual aspects of her life and soon, as she entered adolescence, the door to that garden might close. Rebecca Nye, who interviewed both Joanna and Tina during research into children's spiritual experiences, comments that:

> Joanna and other children of her age seemed to feel that there was something 'silly' in all this, and would soon need to find new ways of withdrawing to secret places; otherwise this source of spirituality would be closed altogether.

(Nye 1996: 2/17)

Children and young people of any age and background share with Tina and Joanna experiences that may be described as spiritual and which may, or may not, be associated with religious faith.

The purpose and content of this chapter

This chapter reviews some ideas about spirituality, religion and children in the context of practice within social work and other settings. It is hoped that readers will be stimulated to study these topics further, seeking 'a common currency of shared understanding' with both children and colleagues (OFSTED 1994: 8). Since this area has, to date, received little attention in training and literature, the emphasis here is on ideas illustrated by brief references to the experiences of a number of children.

Working with and on behalf of children and young people, in whatever setting and however focused, means being concerned with the well-being of the whole person. This holistic approach recognises as fundamental the integration of all aspects of life. The interweaving of physical, cognitive and emotional experience is widely accepted. Loss and bereavement, for example, may lead to ill health, impaired concentration and depressed spirits that reinforce, and are stimulated by, one another. However, while the word *spirits* may easily be used in such a context, *spirituality* is not universally regarded as integral to life.

Definitions of spirituality have been developed within such disciplines as education, medicine and social work. The existence of spirituality is assumed in the UN Convention on the Rights of the Child (1989) (ratified by the UK in 1991), which requires governments to 'recognize the right of every child to a standard of living adequate for the child's physical, mental, *spiritual*, moral and social development' (Article 27). The Education Reform Act (1988) instructs schools to provide curricula that promote '*spiritual*, moral, cultural, mental and physical development' (emphasis added). (Since the concept of *spiritual development* can present problems, readers may prefer the idea of *spiritual well-being*, as in Article 17 of the UN Convention.)

In contrast to the Education Reform Act (1988), the Children Act (1989) requires attention to *religious* well-being but no reference is made to spiritual nurture. For many people, spirituality and religion are inseparable, and religious beliefs and observances form the foundation of life. However, if our attention is directed only towards religion, the spiritual experiences and needs of children who have no formal religious belief or affiliation may be overlooked or even discounted.

The religious backgrounds of people may range from deep devotion to declared, even antagonistic, non-belief, which means that talking about spiritual matters may be comforting or may sometimes cause embarrassment. Nevertheless, whatever the beliefs and attitudes of adults, children have both rights to, and needs for, attention to spiritual and religious aspects of their lives. It is also worth reminding ourselves that experiences associated with spirituality and/or religion are not necessarily conducive to well-being and may even have connotations of distress, neglect and abuse, with implications for all those who care for children.

Spirituality

Defining spirituality

Many people reject the whole idea of spirituality because of associations with religious beliefs that they find unacceptable. However, spirituality is not necessarily connected with religion. For example, the British Humanist Association Briefing, *The Human Spirit* proposes that:

> the 'spiritual' dimension comes from our deepest humanity. It finds expression in aspirations, moral sensibility, creativity, love and friendship, response to natural and human beauty, scientific and artistic endeavour, appreciation and wonder at the natural world, intellectual achievement and physical activity, surmounting suffering and persecution, selfless love, the quest for meaning and for values by which to live. . . .
>
> Humanists see these qualities as the highest part of the human personality but yet as part of it, having evolved naturally.
>
> (BHA Leaflet)

In discussing spirituality in relation to the care of the whole child, John Bradford, a chaplain missioner with The Children's Society, proposes a three-fold concept embracing human, devotional and practical spirituality fitting closely together and complementing the whole. This concept has 'multi-cultural and multifaith applicability'. Bradford (1995) suggests that human spirituality consists of *being loved, feeling secure, responding in wonder, being affirmed and sharing together* – all essential experiences for the well-being of every child (indeed, every person) yet not necessarily associated with religion. Readers may find it interesting to compare this definition with their own ideas about life and spirituality.

Spiritual development

The key word in the present discussion is *experience*. Whilst some articles in the UN Convention and various definitions refer to *spiritual development*, that concept presents problems. Readers who wish to pursue ideas about development are referred to James Fowler's (1981) taxonomy of faith development; this proposes six stages (of which the last can be attained only by such exceptional people as Martin Luther King and Mother Theresa).

Difficulties in devising models of spiritual development include the implication that people move from a less valued to a more valued state, suggested by the terms *underdeveloped, developing* and *highly developed*. Such models also imply an agreed definition of maturity (Nye 1996: 2/13). Readers are advised carefully to consider implications of definitions, legislation and statements of rights based on developmental models and concepts. For example, is a child's spiritual experience recognised as rich and mature, irrespective of chronological age? It is important also to ask whether ideas about spirituality are based on concepts of progression (from 'immaturity' to 'maturity'), regression (from 'perfection', having come from God, to imperfection, as the individual grows away from God), or cycles of reincarnation.

Spiritual experience

Whilst ideas about development are stimulating, readers may find studies of children's experience more accessible and useful. Rebecca Nye and David Hay (Nottingham University) studied spirituality through contact with randomly selected groups of school children, finding 'Even in the most resolutely secular boy (. . . usually a boy), evidences of spiritual sensitivity.' They sought not to discover 'the presence of spirituality, but to understand how it becomes suppressed or repressed during the process of growing up', considering that 'children's spiritual awareness is artificially blotted out by secularised society' (Hay 1995: 1271).

Children who were interviewed often described experiences, ideas and responses that could be identified with those of adults. These were clustered into four *core qualities of spiritual experience*, defined as *sensing a changed quality in 1) awareness; 2) value; 3) mystery; 4) meaningfulness or insight* (detailed introductions may be found in Nye 1996: 2–8). These core qualities link with Bradford's (1995) category of 'Human spirituality'.

Children express experience that can be described as *spiritual* in many ways and at any age. Edward, who was studied from birth, was described at 2 as 'oozing spirituality' with 'all the capacities and predispositions of an individual who has an awareness of the spiritual dimension of . . . life'. Spirituality was expressed through a capacity for silence and reflection, concentration and delight in play, happiness in his own company and 'the capacity to become totally absorbed in what he attends to – a picture, some music, a puzzle'. Physical, cognitive and spiritual aspects were integrated and he displayed 'a highly developed capacity for delight', rejoicing in 'each new possibility, whether it is the unexpected brightness of colour, any representation of the sun, moon and stars or the rhythm of music which instinctively makes him dance'. He could experience 'ecstasy, totally absorbed in and drawn towards realities outside himself' (McClure 1996 : 9).

The vocabulary used to describe Edward is, surely, applicable to every child, whether it is associated with a concept of spirituality or not. The quality of his experience is, equally, that which we desire for all children. When a child displays no delight, no sense of wonder, no integration and interest in meaning and value, we feel that abundance of life and quality of care are desperately deficient, however comfortable the physical environment and elegant the education. If attention to spiritual well-being is lacking, physical, cognitive and emotional life cannot thrive and the whole child is deprived.

Coles (1992) conversed with children in many countries, associated with several religions, including Christian, Hopi, Jewish and Muslim, as well as those children 'less interested in religion as such than in the kind of spiritual rumination many of us have had, regardless of our agnostic or even atheistic inclinations'. He wanted to 'learn from young people that exquisitely private sense of things that nurtures their spirituality', which one boy described as ' "My thoughts . . . , when they suddenly come to me, about God and the world and what it's all about" ' (Coles 1992: 36, 37). Coles' writing reflects the *core quality of sensing meaningfulness* described by Nye (1996: 2/8).

A residential social worker found that all children known to her throughout fourteen years of work were 'deeply concerned with moral and religious questions: "What sort of person am I? How am I to live my life?" '. She became 'convinced that the search for meaning and direction is of critical concern for children . . . [particularly] when their image of themselves is cloudy or flawed', and she emphasises that although such questions may not be answered, they need to be addressed (Cairns 1990 : 27). Whilst we constantly ask or meet such questions, children cannot always formulate their anxieties into clear sentences and hearing the question entails listening behind the words.

Whether or not readers feel comfortable with vocabulary associated with spirituality, such definitions, models and studies identify extensive implications for practice in all settings, taking into account recent legislation and the UN Convention requirement that children's right to a standard of living adequate for *spiritual* development/well-being should be recognised (1989).

Religion

Respect for children's religious backgrounds

For many children and their families, spirituality is inseparable from religious faith. Attention to and understanding of children's religious backgrounds, beliefs and observances is an essential means of demonstrating respect for, and interest in, every aspect of their lives. Introductory information can be obtained through reading (see References), but the most important and effective source is children themselves, their families and local religious congregations, remembering that every religion comprises numerous denominations with different protocols of belief and observance.

The UN *Convention* (Article 14) requires governments to 'respect the right of the child to freedom of thought, conscience and religion', a provision with important implications for all concerned with children's care and well-being. Article 20 states that religious background should be taken into account when children are accommodated apart from their families, reflected in the *Children Act* (1989). While children live with their families of origin, fulfilment of everyday religious obligations can be taken for granted by them and perhaps even regarded as boring and unimportant. However, interference with ordinary routines of life caused by bereavement, parental divorce, or accommodation away from home, may threaten children's sense of security and identity.

Attending to religious observances when children are away from home

There are many ways in which we can attend to children's needs and demonstrate respect for religious beliefs and observances. For example, when children are placed in foster/residential/medical accommodation, a statue, sacred book, rosary, picture, crucifix or prayer shawl might be included in the luggage, at least as a familiar object from home and maybe with deeper significance. Such objects should be treated with respect and touched only with permission from the child and/or parents.

Attention should always be paid to religious observances regarding dress, cleanliness, care of the hair and body and diet (including forbidden foods, preparation and fasting). Distress and offence may be caused by ignorance or indifference. A Muslim baby, for example, was given pork by a nurse who considered that, since the ingredients were mashed together, no one would know that the child had eaten haram (forbidden) food. It was easy to ignore the request of the parents for attention to their religious protocol, for the baby did not know and could not report on, or object to, the meat.

Older children may feel unable to speak. For example, Roxana (9), also Muslim, ate meat while in care despite religious and parental prohibition, because she did not wish to appear different, which 'suited staff greatly'. Eventually, however, she was able to express 'anxiety and feelings of guilt, she worried about betraying her mother and wondered about punishment from God' (Ahmed *et al.* 1986: 59). Although the child was silent, surely her non-verbal behaviour shouted clues to those whose task it was to care for her.

Festival times may be especially difficult for children who are separated from, or experiencing difficulties with, their families of origin; they may feel increasingly disorientated and isolated from their parents as the religious/spiritual texture of everyday life is torn and discarded. A Jewish boy placed with gentile foster parents was described as 'indifferent' when asked if he would like to celebrate Pesach (Passover) (Department of Health 1992: 134). It may be that his family was non-observant, but, equally, the social worker may not have understood the significance of this festival, which is essentially celebrated within the family. Indifference is a common response to questions about sensitive matters; it is important always to listen behind the blank face, the flat tone, the expressionless words.

A sense of identity with family and religious congregation is initiated at, and sometimes before, birth, in such ceremonies as baptism (Christian), chhati (Sikh) and jatakarman (Hindu). Throughout life, change of status (for example, initiation into adulthood) is marked by a ceremony identifying the *rite of passage*, and those of us who work with children need to discover their individual beliefs and traditions to ensure that appropriate celebrations are available to them. Even if people profess no active faith, beliefs taught in childhood have a powerful influence throughout life.

Looking after Children *questionnaires*

Respect for religious beliefs and observances is inherent in basic good practice in all settings. *Looking after Children* questionnaires (Department of Health 1995), designed to improve communication with children in local authority care, acknowledge the importance of religious background and observance through such questions as: 'Do the carer(s) share the same religion as the child's birth family? If not, what efforts are being made to help the child follow the religion of his/her family of origin?' Older children are asked 'Do you belong to a particular religion?' and offered a range of responses from: 'No, I am not interested' to 'Yes' in which case they are asked: 'If so, do you have enough opportunities to attend religious services?'

Questionnaires can form only the basis for thoughtful discussion between children and adults. It would be easy for those who are not interested in, or are hostile to, religion in general, or a particular religion, to dismiss these questions as difficult or of little relevance. For example, when a girl announced that she had become a Christian, a social worker told a colleague (also a Christian) 'I'm glad you were there – I wouldn't have known how to respond.' Yet both professional practice and everyday life require individuals to respond to many matters of which they have no direct experience, or about which they have personally strong feelings (Crompton 1998: 152).

Learning about religion

Opportunities to fulfil religious obligations can be of deep importance. Nourjahan Kharbach (for Barnardo's), for example, found that of the children surveyed on an estate in Oldham, a high proportion expressed interest in learning about their religion, reading the Quran and performing salat (worship) (1996: 18). For some children, however, religious obligation, including education, may involve distress. Julia Ipgrave learnt from Muslim children in Leicester and Strasbourg about 'strict methods . . . used to maintain control [in mosque classes], including beatings, throwing objects at pupils, and getting them to stand for given periods of time in strange and uncomfortable positions', but 'most children interviewed seemed in favour of such methods of discipline as an aid to learning and a way of combatting sin' (1995: 5). We need to listen carefully to children's descriptions of, and attitudes towards, the requirements of their religions.

Worship

All outward religious observances are expressions of the core of religion which is worship, the integration of the whole person – spirit, mind, body and emotion – expressing reverence for, and in communion with, a deity, whether in private or within a congregation.

A powerful account of the meaning of religious worship was recorded at Helen House hospice by Mother Frances Dominica in conversation with Garvan Byrne (11), who had been severely ill throughout his life and died soon after the filming. The nun asked:

'Garvan, is making your communion important to you?'
'Yes, and it was a very joyful experience, my first Holy Communion, and meeting Christ in Holy Communion I found was

86

a great joy and very, sort of, mysterious, very peaceful. It was the only time I could seem to talk to Him about my deepest problems, and have a really good talk to Him about them, and what I felt and ask Him for his help. He always answered me back, and my way of praying is just praying with an open heart to Him so that I get the open answer back. Yes, it was a very important time and my very first time was extremely the happiest day of my life, I think, that very first day I took it and His coming to me was very special.'

(Byrne 1985 [video])

Thoroughly listening to children, in whatever setting and for whatever reason, implies attending, with respect and interest, to religious background, obligations and beliefs.

Some implications for practice

Experiences associated with spirituality and religion can contribute to the well-being of the whole person. However, effects of distress, neglect and abuse must also be considered. Nye identified both delight and despair in children's experiences (1996: 2/8). Whatever the setting, we may encounter indications of inhibited spiritual and/or religious well-being, and thus of the well-being of the whole child.

Anxiety and fear

It is often difficult for children to express or explain anxieties and fears, which may be stimulated by misunderstanding and lack of information. For example, children may fear death and future destiny (which may involve divine punishment), especially if harbouring some 'guilty' secret. Children may believe that they are sinful because they have committed an actual offence or failed to attain standards set by religious teaching. They may fear inescapable divine intervention; a child who had been taught that God is omnipresent hid under the sheets and asked: '"If God is everywhere, can he see me here?"' (Crompton 1990: 54). Fallacies about religions can stimulate inappropriate reactions: Muslim children expressed fears of 'demons' in Christian churches and cemeteries, having been told 'that churches were full of ghosts' (Ipgrave 1995: 67).

Children may manifest difficulties in behaviour and communication relating to such experiences, past or immediate, which they often cannot put into words. Non-verbal clues, for example listlessness, may reflect a child's state of mind and be described in everyday expressions such as 'she's in low spirits', 'he's dispirited' or 'show some spirit!'.

Adults easily miss signs of distress, even desperation. A young woman recalled her childhood from 8 to 11 as '"pretty agonising . . . subject to severe panic attacks which *nobody seemed to notice. I couldn't expect them to at that age of course"*. She thought she had '"reached a religious crisis at *a ridiculously early age* [and was] *quite unable to cope with it"*' (Robinson 1977: 159) [emphasis added]. The implications of her sad comments give us much to think about. Indifference to her agonies as a child rendered this young woman confused, self-deprecating, unsure of her right to notice and nurture, perhaps lacking trust in other people. Her religious crisis does not seem to have resolved into positive faith and a joyful view of life.

The spiritual environment

Spiritual well-being is impaired by neglect. Hay notes the damage to children's spiritual awareness by 'secularised society' (1995: 1271), and everyone knows an 'Edward' whose delight in life has turned to indifference, even despair, whose spirituality no longer even trickles. A beautiful environment is not essential for spiritual fulfilment, but it is hard for children to experience wonder and mystery in brutal and brutalising circumstances.

Yet children can respond to, and make their own, opportunities. 'Mark' found meaning and precious memory in a rubbish tip where he had played with siblings and friends before his removal from home. When he later visited the site with his social worker, he was devastated to discover that the tip had vanished beneath acres of tarmac. His whole body and tone of voice demonstrated his despair and bewilderment as he asked the profound and unanswerable question, 'Why do things have to change?'. The tip had provided an arena for delight and discovery when, as a little boy, Mark had been secure and happy. During his absence from his lost home, it had held the best of his memories, but now it became the focus for his painful recognition of transitoriness. While the social worker provided a peaceful environment, Mark drew the beloved tip, filling the picture with remembered objects and recreating, in memory and on paper, the essence, the spirit, of his place. Discovering and mourning the loss of the physical tip was a significant event in Mark's spiritual journey. For the social worker, being with him, attending to his sad demeanour, listening to his grief and enabling Mark to engage with and express his feelings, was an important contribution to his spiritual well-being. This was a kind of listening for which adults in all settings too often consider that they have no time (Crompton 1995: 347).

Spiritual abuse

Children who are abused, in whatever form, are consequently abused spiritually. The capacity for trust and self-esteem, for giving and receiving love and expecting security and affirmation, community and sharing, is assaulted; delight and wonder are all too probably replaced by despair, anger and guilt. An analysis of effects of sexual abuse on disabled children, for example, includes self-blame, anger, hatred, lack of confidence, bitterness, fear, powerlessness, guilt, rejection, isolation and depression (Kennedy 1995a: 146–7).

When children associated with a religion suffer abuse, trust in a deity who should have offered protection is challenged, especially if both abuser and deity are male. Children may respond: '"Where *was* God when I was abused?"; "I knew that I had committed a terrible sin of some kind, and that I was evil; I was going to Hell."' Survivors may be expected to '*heal quickly* because people have prayed for them, and want to see the power of prayer' and may be blamed for 'failing' to be healed because '"You must be blocking God's healing by some sin. . . ."' (Kennedy 1995b: 12, 13). Terrible distortion may be caused by the use of the word 'love' by abusing adults.

Whilst adults who have no concept of spirit or soul cannot be accused of deliberately assaulting the child's spirit, abuse may be perpetrated by a minister or other adult in connection with activities concerned with a religious organisation. Since these adults profess belief in a spiritual dimension, they must, by implication, be abusing the spirit. Ritual (aka satanic) abuse has been defined as 'the involvement of children in physical or sexual abuse associated with repeated activities ("ritual") which purport to relate the abuse to contexts of a religious, magical or supernatural kind' (McFadyen *et al.* 1993; Hobbs and Wynne 1994: 216). In a television series on child abuse one commentator suggests that official reluctance to believe in such practices gives abusers 'the message that the more crazy things you do with children, the more the children will not be believed and you will be safe'. Valerie Sinason (1994), a consultant child psychotherapist, has compiled a substantial, practice-based introduction to this complex and controversial subject.

Offenders

Particularly strong feelings are aroused by children who commit serious crimes and who may be described as *evil*. Jane Newsome (independent representative, Voice for the Child in Care) notes that:

> Young people . . . in care or secure accommodation . . . feel that it doesn't matter what they do because they are not worth much and anyway no one bothers about them. The media often compound this feeling and even suggest that [these young people] are less than human.

In consequence, they have no motivation 'to behave as human beings, with all the dignity, responsibility and thought that requires'. Some children 'feel that they are in some way controlled by evil. That what they have done is the result of this evil and that therefore there is nothing they can do to stop themselves.' Others speak of people who held 'demonic power' over them (cited in Crompton 1996: 4/46–7, 44). Concepts of evil and demonic power have spiritual/religious connotations with which we need to engage if we are really to listen to children.

Death, bereavement and loss

Spiritual and religious aspects of death, bereavement and loss are of relevance in all settings. Hospices, for example, are concerned not only with dying children but also with their bereaved parents and siblings. Suicide and termination of pregnancy may or may not involve consideration of the nature and meaning of life, responsibility for other people and possible punishment after death. Children may be told euphemistic stories about death and/or afterlife that can cause deep anxiety and injure trust. Yet the ability to grieve is part of loving, and sadness is the partner to joy.

The effects of bereavement may be expressed in many ways and noted at home, school and place of worship. Alfred Torrie (husband of Margaret, the founder of Cruse Bereavement Care) notes the difficulty in communication for young children who cannot say what they feel: 'Silent or preoccupied with material things, adults often say "he isn't grieving! He doesn't seem to care".' Relations may be puzzled 'when an able child falls dramatically in school performance, or behaves wildly or retreats into a strange silence' (Torrie 1978: 5). Older children, like adults, find difficulty in expressing feelings about loss, especially if we seem indifferent or encourage them to 'cheer up'.

Conclusion

I would encourage readers to be aware of spirituality and religious devotion in all children, irrespective of background, intellectual ability or level of communication skills.

This chapter began with the words of a young girl seeking meaning and learning the wonder of life. It concludes with the words of Nigel Hunt, who was not deterred by Down's Syndrome from living abundantly and writing his autobiography. Two years before his death, he achieved the ambition of becoming an altar server in his parish church. His book is full of wonder, joy, awareness and love, and shows great spirit:

> As soon as we got on the coach started to roar up the long curved road and when we got to the edge, Foo! What a long way down. I started to sing at the top of my voice and as I sang I saw people making a snowman and having a snowball fight. It really was something: and, do you know, it snowed the minute we were up there.
>
> (Hunt 1982: 56)

Ideas about spirituality and religion in the context of children and those who care for and about them have been reviewed briefly. Engaging with aspects of spirituality and/or religion can raise anxieties and cause distress, and although it has not been usual to include consideration of these topics in literature and training connected with counselling, education, medicine and social work, it is hoped that opportunities for consultation and training will become more readily available.

Really listening to children involves giving attention to the well-being of the whole child – body, emotions, mind and spirit.

References

Ahmed, S., Cheetham, J. and Small, J. (eds.) (1986) *Social Work with Black Children and their Families*. London: Batsford.

Bradford, J. (1995) *Caring for the Whole Child: A holistic approach to spirituality*. London: The Children's Society.

British Humanist Association *The Human Spirit: The Humanist perspective on spiritual development in education: BHA Briefing*. London: British Humanist Association.

Cairns, K. (1990) Climate for learning. *Social Work Today* 21 (38): 26–7.

Coles, R. (1992) *The Spiritual Life of Children*. London: HarperCollins

Crompton, M. (1990) *Attending to Children: Direct work in social and health care*. Dunton Green: Edward Arnold.

—— (1992) *Children and Counselling*. London: Edward Arnold.

—— (1995) Individual work with children, in K. Wilson and A. James (eds) *The Child Protection Handbook*. London: Baillière Tindall, 334–53.

—— (ed.) (1996) *Children, Spirituality and Religion: A training pack*. London: CCETSW.

—— (1998) *Children, Spirituality, Religion and Social Work*. Andover: Ashgate.

Department of Education of Science (1988) *Education Reform Act*. London: HMSO.

Department of Health (1989) *Children Act*. London: HMSO.

—— (1992) *The Report of the Inquiry into the Removal of Children from Orkney in February 1991: part 2*. London: HMSO.

—— (1995) *Looking after Children: Questionnaires*. London: HMSO.

Fowler, J. (1981) *Stages of Faith: The psychology of human development and the quest for meaning*. New York: Harper & Row.

Hay, D. (1995) Children and God. *The Tablet: educational supplement*, 7.10.95, 1270–1.

Hobbs, C. and Wynne, J. (1994) Treating Satanist abuse survivors: The Leeds experience, in V. Sinason (ed.) *Treating Survivors of Satanist Abuse*. London: Routledge, 214–17.

Hunt, N. (1982) *The World of Nigel Hunt: The diary of a Mongoloid youth*. Norwich: Asset Recycling Ltd.

Ipgrave, J. (1995) *God and Guna: The religious education of Muslim children*. Leicester: unpublished study.

Kennedy, M. (1995a) Perceptions of abused disabled children, in K. Wilson and A. James (eds) *The Child Protection Handbook*. London: Baillière Tindall, 127–52.

—— (1995b) *Submission to the National Commission of Inquiry into the Prevention of Child Abuse*. London: Christian Survivors of Sexual Abuse (CSSA).

Kharbach, N (1996) *Working Together in Westwood: The single regeneration budget bid for Oldham*. Liverpool: Barnardo's.

McClure, M. (1996) How children's faith develops. *The Spirituality of Children: The way supplement*, 5–13.

McFadyen, A., Hanks, H. and James, C. (1993) Ritual abuse: a definition. *Child Abuse Review* 2: 35–41.

Nye, R. (1996) Spiritual development, in M. Crompton (ed.) *Children, Spirituality and Religion: A training pack*. London: Central Council for Education and Training in Social Work 2: 6–19.

OFSTED (1994) *Spiritual, Moral, Social and Cultural Education*. London: Office of Standards in Education.

Robinson, E. (1977) *The Original Vision*. Oxford: The Religious Research Unit.

United Nations (1989) *The Convention on the Rights of the Child*: UNICEF (1995) *Information pack*. 55 Lincoln's Inn Fields, London: United Nations Children's Fund.

Sinason, V. (ed.) (1994) *Treating Survivors of Satanist Abuse*. London: Routledge.

Torrie, A. (1978) *When Children Grieve*. Richmond: Cruse.

Video/television

Byrne, G. (1985) *Encounter: Garvan Byrne talks to Mother Frances Dominica*. Birmingham: Independent Television.

Kelly, L. (1997) *The Death of Childhood*, Channel 4.

Recommended reading

Allan, J. (1988) *Inscapes of the Child's World: Jungian counselling in schools and clinics*. Dallas: Spring Publications.

Armstrong, H. (1991) *Taking Care: A church response to children, adults, and abuse*. London: National Children's Bureau.

Bird, G. (1996) East meets West: secular individualism in Western social work values and practice, and its interface with the 'collective' in Asian faith perspectives, unpublished thesis, University of Leicester, School of Social Work.

Henley, A. *Asians in Britain* series: includes (1982) *Caring for Muslims and their Families: Religious aspects of care* (1983) *Hindus/Sikhs*. Cambridge: Health Education Council/National Extension College.

Hill, L. (ed.) (1994) *Caring for Dying Children and their Families*. London: Chapman & Hall.

Holm, J. with Bowker, J. (eds) *Themes in Religious Studies* series: includes (1994) *Rites of Passage, Worship*. London: Pinter.

Rausch, D.A. and Voss, C.H. (1994) *World Religions: A simple guide*. London: SCM Press.

Rose, D. (1992) *Home, School and Faith*. London: David Fulton.

Walshe, J.G. and Warrier, S. (1993) *Dates and Meanings of Religious and other Festivals*. Slough: Foulsham.

For a fuller discussion of the ideas introduced in this chapter see M. Crompton (1998) *Children, Spirituality, Religion and Social Work*, Andover: Ashgate.

Training material

The Central Council for Education and Training in Social Work (CCETSW) training pack *Children, Spirituality and Religion* (Crompton 1996), whilst primarily intended for practitioners and carers in social work agencies and establishments, contains materials that are relevant to a wider range of settings. The pack includes original papers on Buddhism, Christianity, Hinduism, Islam, Judaism, Rastafarianism, Sikhism and Spiritual Development, together with ideas that can be used within formal training programmes or by small groups or individuals. It also contains suggestions about communication and Social Work Practice units which focus on such topics as abuse/neglect, bereavement, learning disability and offending.

Part III

AT WORK
WITH CHILDREN

If children live with criticism, they learn to condemn.

If children live with hostility, they learn to fight.

If children live with fear, they learn to be apprehensive.

If children live with tolerance, they learn to be patient.

If children live with encouragement, they learn to be confident.

If children live with praise, they learn to be appreciative.

If children live with acceptance, they learn to love.

If children live with approval, they learn to respect.

If children live with recognition, they learn it is good to have a
goal.

If children live with honesty, they learn what truth is.

If children live with fairness, they learn justice.

If children live with security, they learn to have faith in themselves
and others.

Anon.

6

CHILDREN AS TEACHERS

Listening to children in education

Colleen McLaughlin, Mary Carnell and Lynne Blount

Inside each child there is a story that needs to be told – a story
that no-one else has yet had time to listen to.

(Winnicott 1984: 21)

Introduction

In this chapter, three teachers write from three different positions in the
education system. One is an in-service educator in counselling and guidance and a researcher, one is a teacher in a primary school and one is the
team leader of a primary behaviour support service; each sees their role as
primarily concerned with listening to children. First the context of education as a work setting will be explored and then case studies of work with
children will be described. The issues for those listening to children in
education are integrated within these case study examples.

Voices in education

This chapter is concerned with listening to the child's voice. In education
at the moment there are many voices and it seems at times that they are
all shouting very loudly. When the authors began teaching, there were
fewer voices and, at risk of romanticising the past, the prime voices were
the child's and the teacher's. However, in the last decade in particular,
many more voices have joined the chorus and some are being heard more
publicly than they were. The voices now belong to politicians, parents, the
media, economists, moralists and educationalists, in addition to the child
and the teacher. All of them have very clear views on the role of the school
and the teacher and they are often in conflict. The languages they speak
are different. Some talk the language of money, some of management, of
standards, of accountability and some of the rights of children. This can be
a confusing cacophony and schools are now the locus of much debate about

which values and whose values are important and where efforts should be placed. Such debate and confusion can sometimes make it hard for teachers to listen and means that a clarity of focus is needed. It means that this is a very particular setting in which to work with children.

The school as a work setting

There are certain aspects of school life that need to be considered when thinking about how we listen to children in education and the things that can block or facilitate such listening. School is a place that children have to attend by law and they come in large numbers, so that the group setting and managing the group preoccupies teachers and others a great deal. This means that there are issues of control that can militate against listening openly to children. The non-judgemental approaches derived largely from counselling have to be juggled with concerns about order and fairness. Teachers are asked to be judges of behaviour, learning and standards and to assess these with grades and marks, all of which makes teaching very public. Teachers are time limited in a way that no other profession is. There is no 'free' time in teaching: there is no leeway. Life is governed by set slots, curriculum syllabuses and often by bells, so flexibility has to be very cleverly managed. Children are almost always in groups, and seeing a child alone in privacy is the most uncommon activity to occur in a school. The role of teacher is also multifaceted. There are concerns for the child's learning, welfare and development, as well as the expectations of others who hold schools and teachers accountable. Teachers must balance being in *loco parentis*, educator, public servant, keeper of the peace and welfare worker. Role tension comes from moving fast from one aspect to another. So at one point a teacher may be 'disciplining' a child, at another marking their work and at another listening to them. These are similar to the roles of parents, but many teachers find it hard to accept that they are all able to be combined and this can militate against listening to children. They can develop a false polarisation between the different aspects of the role of teacher. Equally, teachers place a different emphasis on the various aspects of their role. Some are primarily subject-centred, some child-centred, and some behaviour-centred.

A teacher is the one adult, apart from members of their family, with whom children have regular and prolonged contact. Consequently, the teacher may be a significant person with the power to be a respectful adult able to provide a type of listening that children may not experience elsewhere in their lives. So there is often tension underneath the role of listener as well as great power.

Listening and recent developments in education

Just as there are different voices in education at the moment so there have been very different developments, some of which have strengthened the importance of the case for listening to children and others that have not. There has long been an interest in promoting counselling and counselling skills in education. Almost all the recent thinkers in the humanistic counselling field have written at length about education, and many of their ideas currently underpin initiatives in the field of classroom management and work with individuals (Glasser 1969; Hamblin 1974; Rogers 1983). The interest was limited at first and tended to stress the role of counsellor in education, drawing on the American model of specialist counsellors in schools. The shift has been away from the idea of an individual specialist counsellor to teachers working at different levels. In this view, all teachers learn some of the skills and concepts of counselling that would enable them to listen and respond to individuals and groups, whilst others would have more specialised training and be able to work in more depth. This has meant an increase in training for counselling and listening. This training has largely been in-service rather than initial, and ranges from introductory-level courses to more in-depth work. The work is largely based on humanistic approaches, although teachers' approaches are very eclectic due to the complex and practical bias of the work. In the case studies that follow there are elements of cognitive behavioural and person-centred approaches, and play or art therapy are also used.

Recent examples of how listening to children has been developed in schools can be seen in initiatives that have arisen from the issues around bullying and in the development of personal and social education, as well as school improvement. Historically, bullying was seen by many as a necessary part of school life, as was the physical punishment of children. Just as thinking and practice develop in pedagogical approaches, so they are also changing in schools. Generally, the notion that children feel and suffer as adults do has been taken seriously, leading to the introduction of activities and programmes that deal with bereavement, transition and other major emotional events in children's lives.

There has been a big development in helping children to listen to each other as well as in helping adults to listen seriously to children. Two examples are 'circle time' and peer counselling. Circle time is a structured form of listening. Children sit in a circle and share the time to talk about feelings and events that are top of their concerns. This work has become common in primary schools and is being extended into some secondary schools. It is also being developed for work with staff groups (Mosley 1996). Some schools have responded to bullying in many ways, first and foremost by taking seriously what children say. A few secondary schools have established peer counselling schemes of children who listen to children, in which an experienced, trained adult educates the students in basic listening attitudes and skills. These students then act as listeners and facilitators for the other students in the playground. They can always refer and consult with the adults and care is taken for them not to bear inappropriate or unnecessary responsibility (Cowie and Sharp 1996). These peer counsellors also receive supervision and support from an experienced adult. The concept of supervision or time to reflect on your practice is one that is only just entering teaching. Great strides have been taken in terms of the best practice, and children have become the greatest teachers of where our efforts should be placed and how we should work.

The school improvement movement is now enhancing this trend of listening to the pupil's voice. There is encouragement and practice about including students in the planning and decision making of the school, as well as in giving feedback to the teachers. This aims to develop commitment and a sense of belonging to the school community as well as being based on the principle that children should be seen *and* heard.

However, there are other trends that contradict these developments. The education system has undergone radical reform in the last decade. The reforms have increased the openness to scrutiny and accountability of schools, as well as prescribing the curriculum. In addition, the idea of competition between schools has been implemented. This has had different effects. One has been that teachers have become concerned to meet the heavy new demands placed upon them. Some feel that teachers have shifted to becoming curriculum- or syllabus-focused rather than child-centred. Others dispute this. Whilst these changes are debatable, some trends are measurable. There has been a huge increase in the exclusion of students of all ages from schools, and the biggest increase has been in the numbers being excluded from primary schools (Parsons and Howlett 1996). The analysis of this issue is complex. Some argue that young people have become more problematic, others that problematic behaviours are less acceptable and that teachers under pressure are less willing to listen and deal with the issues. There has been a change in the public nature of the debate, with the language of the market place being used a great deal. This has included much deliberation about standards, which can result in a concept of standardisation in which those who do not fit the norm become less acceptable in schools. The many voices that are clamouring to be heard may mean that the child's voice is less likely to be heard. However, what is clear is that children still want to be listened to and value it enormously and many teachers still want to listen primarily to the child's voice.

Young people's views on listening

Recently we conducted interviews with a group of students who had been part of a scheme that offered them a personal tutor to listen to them regularly (McLaughlin 1997). These interviews, and the quotations from them that follow, confirm previous work that showed that students value the particular contribution of teachers as listeners (McLaughlin *et al.* 1995). These students were very clear about what sort of listening they wanted and its effects in their lives. They talked about the difficulties they took with them into school and particularly the difficulty of 'bottling things up'. One student said this about when she bottled things up: 'It's just like I have to be bad and that and I have to take it out on the teachers sometimes and I do and I get detentions.' All of them talked about the importance of being listened to. 'I talk to her and she understands.' 'It's just she listens and she is a good teacher. . . . She just understands how I feel. . . . I can tell her anything. . . . She always knows how I feel.' They wanted the opportunity to talk. 'Just that it is a really good idea, I think, for children like, well me, that need the help to talk to someone. Not every child can actually bottle it up, because they could do something serious, like kill themself or something.' 'We talk about whatever's worrying me, we talk about everything. It's good to have someone to speak to if you've got problems and if you need help with homework and things, it's handy. Sometimes people need someone to speak to.' 'It's helped me with my homework and it's helped me to understand things and I feel a lot better having someone to speak to.'

They were all clear that confidentiality was important. 'I don't want everyone knowing.' 'There's someone there you can talk to and it's all confidential. . . . It's very important, because, I mean, you don't want people talking about things what are nothing to do with them, to other people. Especially as it's not their business.' They felt the importance of individual attention – 'Because they [teachers] don't have to deal with a whole class of people it's only dealing with one person, so you get their whole attention, don't you, and you get them to yourself.'

When asked what this listening and individual attention did for them, they had much to say. One talked of getting it out of her system: 'Being able to talk to her about it has helped me to change. Getting it out of my system. "Cos usually I keep it all bottled up inside and I don't say nothing but when I am with Miss I can tell her everything that happened and then it's out in the open.' Another talked about increased feelings of loyalty, "Cos I think I've got to prove to her that I can be good and prove it to her and my Mum.' There was a link between being checked on and being cared for. 'That's the good thing about it, because you know she's always checking up on me. That tells me that she's actually trying to help me, so I should pay her back in some way.' In the sessions with the personal tutors, the students were engaged in a range of activities as well as being listened to. There was goal setting, the discussion of strategies for dealing with difficult situations and emotions, particularly anger. They also worked on issues around self-esteem. One student described how this transferred outside the sessions. 'I wrote up a list of things that were good about me. Yes, it was helpful. Yes because whenever you feel like that, you can sort of say it in your head.' Another said, 'We write tasks for the next week, I don't lose my temper easily and I do what I want for a change and stuff like that. We write them down and I put it in my pencil case and I can just look at it and then I'll know.'

All of them were sure that without this form of supportive listening and active work they would not cope with the difficulties of the school situation. 'I'd have been really, really bad. I could have been suspended and that I reckon.' 'I don't think I'd be as happy in school. I don't think I'd actually probably come some days if I didn't have a personal tutor because I'd be so fed up and if I didn't complete homework I wouldn't probably come.' 'I would have been kicked out of school straight away.' These students were being listened to by teachers who had received some basic listening skills training and were asking for more as the scheme progressed. They had met regularly as a group to receive some group supervision. The students valued the individual and particular attention given by this form of active listening.

We offer two case studies from teachers who work in schools; one is based in a primary school and has an uncommon and particular role, the other is part of a county's behaviour support team.

Case study 1: Listening to children and parents in an infant school

The school, the children and the teachers

Children's chatter is everywhere in our infants' school. The 4 to 6 year olds are generally brimming over with energy and enthusiasm and eager to share their world with us, their teachers. Ask any class teacher in our school how much time they are able to assign each day to listening to each child in their care, and the answer would be 'nowhere near enough'. New demands imposed on teachers have meant listening time per child is at a minimum, and for some children this means that their access to the only 'listening' adult is therefore blocked.

In our school we have many children whose days do not start peacefully and for whom sleep does not come easily. These children arrive at school tired, often late, without breakfast and with a catalogue of domestic disasters to pass on to members of staff before any learning process can possibly begin. Distressed children may fail to learn, and in some cases their behaviour may become unmanageable within school. Class teachers are unable to respond to the needs of these children as classroom lessons begin. As home/school link teacher, I have the privilege of being timetabled to meet the needs of the families and children who may need a listening ear as school starts.

My background training is as an infant teacher with additional qualifications in counselling and child protection. The flexibility of my role as home/school link teacher leads me (with parental permission) to be a listener for some children whose home life is so tangled and chaotic that a helping ear such as mine is invaluable. I have strong links with most external agencies to our school and the adjoining junior school, health centres, social services, family therapy centre, church, school health services and the nearby nursery school. I do not know of one professional who is not frustrated by the pressures of insufficient budgets, leading to an over demanding work pace which at the end of the day means little time for listening, whether it be to adult or child. Our technological world of computers, video systems and television has meant that the 1990s child has less and less access to qualitative listening at home or school and therefore benefits from time with an adult such as me.

Teachers are responsible on a fairly long-term basis for children's welfare and should therefore be able to note changes in a child's individual behaviour more quickly than some adults. In our school, class teachers pay special attention to change in a child and will generally pass on their concern first to the parents, then to the Headteacher and then possibly me.

Listening to children is emotionally demanding: I have had to learn to tolerate feelings of rejection, guilt and anger in order that some children may be free to communicate their feelings. It is easy for children to sense when adults cannot handle their own feelings. A finger tap or aggressive questioning will contribute to a child's feelings of vulnerability and neediness, and thus silence them. It is vital that children do not witness the adult listener's inability to cope with their own re-awakened memories of childhood. It is easy to make children mistrust their own reflections and take away their voice. My responsibility is to do the reverse, to take each child seriously and to indicate in whatever way is necessary that I want to listen and try to understand. I hope that by communicating their feelings they will one day be able to trust in others, learn to think and feel for themselves and positively discover the art of living.

My training in counselling skills has helped me to reflect on the most appropriate method of helping the more troubled children in school. I am fortunate in sharing the use of a tiny, warm room, spacious enough for lots of toys and books, all helpful when fostering conversation in a young child. The toys are plentiful in baskets full of puppets, dolls, hospital workers, vehicles, furniture, trees, flowers, animals and 'cuddlies' – all bought at minimal cost from local jumble sales. In addition I have a shelf full of play-dough, bright paper, pens, envelopes, postcards, musical instruments, disconnected phones and much more. I generally find play is a prime mover in encouraging children to talk in a relaxed way. Infant school children are limited in their ability to verbalise thoughts and feelings adequately, and often the trigger of play figures is a useful mode of communication to even the most 'blocked' child. Play generally establishes rapport, and prompts something, somewhere within that child to work from (see Chapter 11).

In an individual session (of about thirty to forty minutes) I leave the child free to structure the play sessions. Some children as young as 4 have had such little experience of play that every basket of toys can be emptied all over the floor! They lead, I follow, observing the items chosen from the wealth of material within the room. Some children will need encouragement to play, will be very distressed by outside sounds and will check for approval. It may be that this child is punished at home, in which case time is essential in building up trust. What follows are some brief outlines of case studies to illustrate the level I work at in school.

The children

Jade

Jade, aged 5, was referred by her class teacher and parent to see me. She had enormous difficulty playing with friends in the playground without conflict, and in her first session played out this scene in sand and said: 'My teachers tell me never to hit out, and to tell them if I'm hit. My mum says I must bash the children that annoy me and not tell the school.'

Jade had needed help to understand her loyalty to her mum's instructions and to adapt to an alien code of behaviour in school. She only saw me twice before establishing a non-aggressive way to play in the playground. Mum understood our code of behaviour and simultaneously supported Jade in her actions.

Tom

Tom, aged 6, whose family was breaking down while his mother was receiving psychological help, came and talked openly in his first session. He placed all his family in the sand tray. His play centred on violence and death and included Tom gently killing his mother and then burying her tenderly, putting flowers on the grave and staying by her side. This boy had witnessed his mother trying to take her own life, followed by the suffering and misery that she had encountered as she wrestled with her illness. It seemed Tom wanted a neater package for Mum and wanted to support her through the turmoil. For many 6-year-old children, death does not appear permanent, so at the end of a session he would say 'Mummy is better now.' Much of my work centred on empowering Tom to cope with his life's circumstances. The issues were so powerful that he was referred with his family for therapy.

Nick

Nick is 5 years old. His class teacher and mother had asked me to see him, as they believed he had become a silent, sad little boy following the death of his father a month previously. He had been told that his father had died in a road accident. He had in fact died from a drug overdose and had been ill for some time as he battled with his addiction. Nick had been very involved with nursing him at home, but was unaware that he might die. His mother gave me the above information and agreed for Nick to be seen only if I promised not to tell him how his father had really died. I agreed in the hope that, through talking, Nick might arrive at the truth himself. I was prepared to face his mother once we had reached that point. Nick had become aggressive in the playground, resented adults, rarely smiled and kept telling his class teacher that he wanted to be home with his mother; he wanted to be at home until he could be convinced and reassured that his mother wouldn't die too.

My aim was to help Nick develop appropriate ways of dealing with his loss and build on his memories of his father to explore his grief. By the third of our six sessions, Nick had begun to express his feelings openly and easily by drawing pictures. He drew one for Dad, and asked to show it to him outside. We walked to the middle of the playground and he held it horizontally to the sky and talked through the drawing with his dad. He wanted me to be there and introduced me to his father. By the fourth session, drawing had become a tool in communication, Nick had made a book for his father and left time at the end of the session to show his dad in the playground.

Nick had developed his own method of communicating powerful feelings of love, loss, anger and confusion through his drawings and pictures. His mum found it easier to help him this way and likened it to story telling, 'but a real story'. Nick became less dependent on chatting to Dad as time went on, and openly told his friends that his dad lived in heaven and would never be with us again. 'I remember loads I did with Dad and I've done pictures and photos, so I don't forget.'

Nick needed someone to help him accept his father's death, and by the end of six sessions he had begun to contribute in class and become less aggressive and angry (see Chapter 10).

Listening and play

Some children need many sessions before they begin to trust me and so allow themselves the freedom to explore the turmoil within. When a child gains control of the sessions and is enjoying directing the play or conversation, my job begins. Being a good listener is crucial to the detective work needed to unravel the trouble; listening well can be tiring and I use all my senses to pick up small cues that will be relevant to reflect back to the child.

In my experience, success depends on the children accepting me as a reliable and consistent figure in their world. For those children who have experienced rejection and child abuse as part of life, it is important to show repeatedly my understanding, empathy and concern. For most children, play is the starting point. Once it has begun, children often open up feelings that for them are too painful or difficult to verbalise in conversation. The sand tray is a favourite and many children choose to place their chosen figures in scenes relating to home or school life.

By listening to children as they play, I try to reflect back the feelings expressed in their play and enable them to acknowledge and recognise those feelings, thereby helping them to begin the healing process. My skills and experience are still developing, and I am aware of this, so I will always discuss with supporting agencies any concerns that may emerge. I find to my distress that waiting lists for family appointments are so long that families have often broken down and further trauma has been experienced by the child before adequate help is available. For some, the adults in their lives whom they have grown to love have let them down, resent their presence and treat them with such coldness and sometimes abuse, that problems develop for the child that could have been avoided if somebody had time to listen to the needs of the family.

Listening to parents

My role as home/school link teacher in an infants' school enables me to listen to parents too. If schools do not listen to parents, it is unlikely that teachers will be effective listeners to children. By being a 'listening' school, I believe that we will help families to share some of their feelings and lead the way for this practice to be used in the home. It is important that a listening adult is easily accessible to children to help them manage anger and hurt.

I scratch the surface of the mounting problems in the children's lives; my job appears to be unique in our authority, and yet, in my opinion, necessary. Neighbouring schools are just as much in need of such help, and yet their cries, so far, are unanswered.

Case study 2: Working from the outside

The role of a behaviour support teacher

The role of a behaviour support teacher is to support pupils with emotional and/or behavioural difficulties in mainstream and some special schools across all age ranges. The Local Education Authority provides a statutory service for pupils with a Statement of Special Educational Needs, and schools are able to subscribe to the service for support with pupils at stage three of the assessment procedure in accordance with the Code of Practice for Pupils with Special Educational Needs (DFE 1994). Most pupils referred present with a complexity of needs as well as emotional and/or behavioural difficulties. My work involves listening to teachers, parents and pupils and then advising schools on the negotiation, implementation, monitoring and evaluation of a programme of support, which may involve referral to another agency for specialist support.

> The effectiveness of any assessment and intervention will be influenced by the involvement and interest of the child concerned. Schools should, therefore, make every effort to identify the ascertainable views of the child or young person. Positive pupil involvement is unlikely to happen spontaneously.
>
> (DFE 1994: 14)

All interventions are agreed only after I have listened to the young person's own perception of their difficulties, as it is not unusual for staff to be unaware of the views, feelings and/or the circumstances that exacerbate the young person's inappropriate behaviour. Many young people exhibiting behavioural and/or emotional difficulties in a school environment have few opportunities to describe and discuss their difficulties because staff have little or no contact time. Any time away from the classroom is spent in preparation, marking or record keeping. Some teachers may be reluctant to use contact time actively because of a strongly held belief that a child's behavioural difficulties in school are caused mainly by family dysfunction over which teachers have no control.

Even if the value of listening is recognised, some teachers find it difficult to alter their pedagogical role, which has traditionally involved the giving of both admonishment and advice. Therefore they judge young people by commenting on their behaviour and erect further barriers between them.

As behaviour support teachers, we are in a unique position to support schools in the provision of quality interventions that facilitate long-term changes in a young person's behaviour. We have the time to listen and also have a firmly held belief that schools can have a powerful and beneficial effect on a child, despite family difficulties. We also have direct experience of the resourcefulness of children, who are able to recognise the potential of any opportunities they are provided to change and develop. Most of all, we have relinquished our traditional teacher role for that of the learner, and allow children to teach us about their perception of the problem and the environment that they experience, as well as the context in which their behaviour occurs.

We are able to listen in a way that does not attempt to advise, teach or discipline. Many children actively test for safety before taking the risk of telling their stories. They may swear, choose to be insulting or behave in a destructive way, and then await the expected teacher or parent reactions. During this testing time, we need to be able to demonstrate by our actions that we are interested, willing to learn and able to accept these children and their behaviour without criticism of any kind.

Vulnerability and listening

Perhaps the most valuable gift we bring to work with children is our capacity to remain vulnerable, whilst accepting our discipline and role.

(Winnicott 1984: 23)

The journey into the self-perceived world of an insecure child with a behavioural difficulty is always an emotional experience for the listener. Feelings generated by the helplessness of a vulnerable child can invade our emotions and prevent active listening. On such occasions, the borders between empathy, sympathy and collusion need to remain clear if a child is to be empowered. The listener cannot afford to be overwhelmed by disclosures, as this can hinder the professionally helpful response that has to be made (see Chapters 2 and 3).

There is an expectation when counselling adults that they will be empowered by the counselling process to take control of their lives, make choices and learn more effective coping strategies: 'The end of the counselling process is characterised by action' (Mearns and Thorne 1988: 141).

The needs of a vulnerable and often helpless child, however, require the listener to be able to undertake 'differentiated' listening. While absorbing the contents of the story being told, we need to be able to recognise the learning needs of the child and their possible relationship to the events in the story. We are also expected to pick up from the story those skills that a child will need to learn to enable them to become empowered and avoid learned helplessness. Consideration also needs to be given to what can be changed in the young person's immediate environment to prevent the same events occurring again.

Listening and responding to the 'here and now'

The background

Jon was 9 years old and attended a rural primary school. He had been a pupil there for approximately eighteen months, having attended two schools in other counties, from which he had been excluded. Jon was referred to

Behaviour Support by his Headteacher, who stated that the school was unable to deal with his 'aggressive' behaviour at playtimes any longer, and if support was not immediate he was likely to be excluded. Whilst contact had been made with Jon's mother, she had refused to come into school. The school had interpreted this refusal as a failure to care.

Observations of Jon in the playground and classroom revealed that he was unable to play appropriately with his peers, and on occasions his attempts to communicate by approaching from behind and grabbing anything he needed to borrow provoked 'aggressive' responses from his peers and further exclusion from the group. Jon's Headteacher regarded him as a serious 'aggressor' whom she felt was 'disturbed' and would be better placed in a residential school.

The interview

I began the interview with Jon by explaining about my job. I finished by saying that a little bird had told me that sometimes he wasn't very happy and that maybe, if he wanted to, we could make a plan together that could help him change the situation. His face looked very thoughtful for a minute and he said, 'What sort of bird was it?' I explained what the phrase meant and asked him to tell me something about himself. At this point Jon became very agitated. He stood up and began pacing up and down the staff room floor, waving his arms and raising the level of his voice: 'I always get the blame, I do. They call me names so I hit them I do. I know I shouldn't retaliate but they deserve it for calling me names, they do. I'm an easy wind up I am. Like when I was in Mr Harris's class they said I tore a picture but I didn't and then I got told off and he shouted at me he did and I didn't do it. I hit the boy who did it and they said I couldn't go to that school anymore they did. I always have to play on my own I do. They won't let me play they won't. I can't stop hitting I can't. They deserve it they do. I always get the blame and my mum knows it's not always my fault, she does, but she won't come up to school anymore. She just sits and cries for me so I don't tell her what they say to me anymore now I don't. So I would like a plan because I don't like school and I don't think anybody likes me. One day I'll bring my dad's gun in I will and shoot everyone I will. There must be something very wrong with me. Do you think there is something very wrong with me? There must be because two schools have said they don't want me, they have. They made me stay at home, they did. The children say I talk funny. I don't talk funny do I?'

At this point I reassured Jon and asked him which particular children called him names. He named two boys in his class, but added, 'they are the worst they are, but everyone does it even the infants they do. I can't work in my class I can't. I keep thinking how sad I am I do and they are making me not concentrate they are and then they laugh when I get told off they do. I would like a plan, yes, I would. My mum said someone might come, she did. I do want a plan I do. Can we make it now can we?' The explosive way in which Jon revealed his story and his perception of events came as a shock both to myself and later to his Headteacher, whose own perception of his difficulties had been quite different.

It is not until right at the end that Jon mentions his feelings and the recognition that the way he feels is affecting his ability to work in school. He's not lazy, just sad. It is not unusual for young people to have a clarity of understanding about cause and effect that adults can find more difficult to understand and relate. The story provided a vital insight, not only into Jon's behaviour but also into his other special needs, which, if left without being targeted for improvement, would continue to ensure that relationships with his peers would always be difficult. All the adults involved in Jon's education learned a great deal from his story. It was a catalyst for several different layers of intervention by the behaviour support team and changed the way in which the school responded to pupils with behavioural difficulties.

Jon was able to negotiate a reward programme that targeted his communication skills as well as his concentration; this was implemented by his class teacher and monitored by a teacher assistant. Group intervention provided Jon with the opportunity to take part in the resolution of the bullying he had been subjected to, and his class teacher began to set up activities to promote friendship and appropriate play skills which benefited other children as well as Jon. The Headteacher and staff, who were distressed that they had not taken more appropriate action sooner, began to set up systems to prevent bullying.

Jon's story demonstrates the importance of listening to young people but also how important and crucial it is for adults to believe, learn from and act on what they are told without judgement, admonishment or advice. Underestimating or trivialising the value of what a young person has to say because of their age, or in the belief that they have nothing to teach us, will prevent us from gaining a valuable insight into the environments we create for them. We may have the impression that our education systems and procedures benefit every child, when in reality they fail to serve or protect an increasing number. However disturbing a young person's behaviour may be, an opportunity to share their perception of their difficulty is the starting place from which they can begin to take control, own their behaviour and recognise that they can change. Without adults who have the time and skills to listen, some young people will become trapped in a system that perpetuates feelings of powerlessness which in turn encourage inappropriate behaviour.

Within a few weeks, Jon's behaviour began to change positively and he made friends with another pupil. After a negative experience of the education system, Jon's mother came into school for the first time to receive the first of several 'Good News' certificates.

Children's voices in education

These case studies are from two educators whose primary role is to listen to and be advocates for distressed children in schools. There are other developments, already mentioned, to listen to children as part of the daily life of schools: 'There is now increasing recognition and acceptance that children's views and perspectives need to be heard both as an ethical imperative and also as a matter of practical utility and efficacy' (Davie and Galloway 1996: 3). These moves are slow and not to be found in all schools, but they are part of a trend that is to be welcomed.

The case studies have shown that schools are complex settings, with many voices clamouring to be heard. Teachers strive to balance the demands. Some are conservative and find it difficult to take the child's voice seriously. Those of us who work in the listening field find it both demanding and rewarding. We find that children are our best teachers and that teachers need also to be learners.

References

Cowie, H. and Sharp, S. (1996) *Peer Counselling in Schools: A time to listen*. London: David Fulton.

Davie, R. and Galloway, D. (1996) *Listening to Children in Education*. London: David Fulton.

Department for Education (1994) *Code of Practice on the Identification and Assessment of Special Educational Needs*. London: HMSO.

Glasser, W. (1969) *Schools Without Failure*. New York: Harper & Row.

Hamblin, D.H., (1974) *The Teacher and Counselling*. Oxford: Basil Blackwell.

McLaughlin, C. (1997) Unpublished interviews with students in one school.

McLaughlin, C., Clark, P. and Chisholm, M. (1995) *Counselling and Guidance in Schools: Developing policy and practice*. London: David Fulton.

Mearns, D. and Thorne, B. (1988) *Person-Centred Counselling in Action*. London: Sage.

Mosley, J. (1996) *Quality Circle Time in the Primary Classroom*. Wisbech, Cambridge: LDA.

Parsons, C. and Howlett, K. (1996) Permanent exclusion from school: A case where society is failing its children. *Support for Learning* 11 (3): 109–12.

Rogers, C. (1983) *Freedom to Learn in the Eighties*. Ohio: Charles Merrill.

Winnicott, C. (1984) *Face to Face with Children: In touch with children*. London: British Agencies for Adoption and Fostering.

Resource packs

Blount, L. and Szpakowski, J. (1998) *Promoting Positive Behaviour: The Essex approach. Resource packs for primary and secondary schools*. Chelmsford: Essex County Council Learning Services. £99 each.

7

CHILD PROTECTION

Facing up to fear

Barbara Smedley

Introduction

My name is Barbara Smedley. I have worked in child care all my working life. I believe passionately in the uniqueness of each individual, the striving of each human being for self-actualisation. In particular, I believe in the rights of children, their need for love and security, and to be understood. Many of us, as adults, have lost touch with the child within ourselves, and this has resulted in our becoming immune to the pains we once experienced. We therefore fail to see the hurts that all children experience and, in particular, the terrible pain that neglected and abused children feel.

I have worked as a child care officer, social worker, trainer, student supervisor and middle manager in a number of child protection settings and have managed and practised within a therapeutic team at a residential family and community centre for abusing families. I have designed and line managed high-quality family and community centres, respite facilities, youth projects and child sexual abuse treatment centres. As an independent social worker, I have worked as a guardian *ad litem*, expert witness in adoption and child protection proceedings, and have helped Romanian authorities to transform an orphanage into a range of community and family resources. For the past few years I have practised non-directive play therapy with children who have emotional and behavioural difficulties.

In essence, I have worked with many hundreds of children over the years, abused and hurt in a system that was very often not able to meet their needs. I have contributed to the 'Orange Book' (DoH 1988), have an M.Sc. in Social Services Management and a Diploma in Non-directive Play Therapy. Yet I am afraid to write this chapter.

I carry fears, like other human beings. These fears prevent me from expressing myself in the way I really want to. My fear of exposing my inadequacies was based on shame and humiliation experienced in, amongst others, the school setting. No one has an idyllic childhood. No one escapes childhood fears. We have all experienced shame and humiliation. But we have repressed those fears, those bad feelings, and it is not until something triggers them that we have the opportunity to confront them and to move forward in our lives – both personal and professional. In order to help neglected and abused children, we need to face and understand our own fears before we can begin to really understand theirs. Child protection dominated by fear and anxiety becomes risk insurance.

Child protection or risk insurance?

Undeniably there are organisational reasons why child protection social workers are prevented from really understanding the abused children with whom they work. For instance, they operate within organisations that are caught up in a cycle of anxiety. 'Anxiety runs like a vein throughout the child protection process [and this results in] blunted emotional responsiveness, reduced sensitivity, inadequate reflection, and dangerous decision-making' (Morrison 1997: 196).

There is also compelling evidence (Parton *et al.,* 1997) that social workers are undertaking not child protection work but risk insurance. They operate in a hostile environment, constantly under media pressure, and suffer verbal and physical abuse from male and female users of services. Some, like myself, have received death threats, others have been stalked and/or have had their cars and homes vandalised.

The consequences of the work can result in emotional, psychological and physical stress for social workers, all of which militate against attending to children in need of their help, who require them to be emotionally competent.

There is overwhelming evidence that we do not listen to children. For instance, it seems that weekly there is widespread coverage of abuse in children's homes throughout the United Kingdom. Parton *et al.* (1997), in their research into how child protection work is accomplished, found that children's voices were virtually absent from social services files: 'It seems children as subjects with their own views and interests are very marginal to child protection policy and practice' (1997: 226). They also noted that children's voices were absent from the report *Child Protection: Messages from research*:

> Whilst it is reported that children's hobbies, activities, family and social relationships were explored in interview with the children themselves, nothing of this content is mentioned as relevant. Indeed the distinction between what the children said and what their parents said is not clear from the document. Whilst their voice was sought, even in this limited way, it was clearly not relevant to record in relation to the messages from research. The child's voice

is missing in the overview document in the same way it was missing from our files.

(Dartington Social Research Unit 1995: 227)

(But see Chapter 13.)

Government reports and inquiries highlight the need to communicate with children, for example the Utting Review (1997). There are other reports such as, for example, *The Challenge of Partnership in Child Protection: Practice Guide* (DoH 1995) and books including Owen and Pritchard (1993), Butler and Roberts (1997) and Kemshall and Pritchard (1995) which explain how to interview children. Yet rarely do these publications address the very real difficulties in working with children whose behavioural and emotional problems prevent them from communicating, for instance those who are silent or those who have no control over their anger. Few writers address the problems of fear that arise in the worker. Exceptions to this are Bray (1991) and Bray and Pugh (1997), who give examples of sensitive work on listening to sexually abused children through the medium of play, highlighting some of the barriers to communicating with them. They also acknowledge that 'The emotionally charged content of child protection and therapy goes to the very heart of the worker's sense of self' (Bray and Pugh 1997: 144).

Hearing, understanding and self-awareness

The Utting Review, whose author heard directly from children, said 'Looking after them would be easier and much more effective if we really heard and understood what they have to tell us' (Utting 1997: 7). My fear is that local authorities, in accepting the recommendations of the review, are unlikely to address the root problems inherent in *listening* to children, and will instead institute mechanistic procedures to ensure that children are heard. Children will be failed by us yet again, because society will continue to deny that children who are involved in the child protection process experience a range of feelings, including the deeply pervasive shame and humiliation that accompany neglecting or abusive experiences, plus fear, guilt, great sadness and anger. Their basic human need for love and security has been cruelly shaken, they have been betrayed, usually by adults and often by members of their family. A frequent consequence of such betrayal is that children's cognitive, emotional and spiritual development is affected and often impaired. Depending on their own unique history, children may display a range of behavioural and emotional difficulties that are symbols of their underlying hurt. We will not reach children unless we can convey to them our openness to understanding their deep hurt, and we cannot do this if we deny our own pain.

In order to be alongside children in this way, social workers need great sensitivity and self-awareness. They must be aware of their own feelings, not in order to re-work them at the expense of the children they are trying to help, but to have a deep respect for them; because in understanding and valuing our own feelings, we begin to unlock the door to a trusting relationship being established with a child. As we will see later, children know when adults are authentic, they know if we understand about childhood pain. We must never underestimate the importance of our communications with children.

Introducing Adam, Lisa and Daniel

In order to demonstrate the crucial role the child protection social worker has in communicating with children, I quote the perceptions of three children between the ages of 12 and 14 who were involved in the child protection process in different parts of the country. All three struggle daily to survive the consequences of their abuse.

Adam, Lisa and Daniel, as they wish to be called, had the courage to face up to terrible childhood hurts and have now undergone therapy. They were enthusiastic about contributing to this chapter, thus sharing their insights about how social workers could communicate with children.

Adam

'I thought the first social worker was an evil bitch because she had no feelings: she just wanted me to tell what happened. She sat with a form asking me whether I wanted to press charges – she asked questions instead of asking me about my questions. . . . If they push you too much you try not to answer questions, you get upset. They should back off a bit. . . . They introduce themselves but just assume you are who they came to see! You know you have to answer the questions but you're scared to death because you may have to go away – to "foster". They shouldn't ask questions until the kid feels more comfortable. You shouldn't rush kids because it's like you don't have any feelings. It's really hard and it's like the social worker doesn't always believe you. They're collecting evidence. How can you prove it happened? They want you to have tests – who wants to have tests? They say, "Why won't you have tests?"

'It's because you know it's gonna hurt, bring back really bad memories. They don't understand. You want to say, "You have it done to you, see how you feel." I felt useless, just like being walked over. You already feel bad! It hurt – they don't even know you! You have to think about what happened. You didn't rush me in counselling, but with a social worker you can't take your time. You don't want the hurting feelings to come so quick because then you feel depressed and do something stupid. You want to be treated as a human being, not dirt – there just to answer questions – you need to be treated with respect, like they expect to be treated. They wonder why kids slit their wrists, go into hospital, and ask, "Why?"

115

'I did it because I was hurting. The questions did the hurting because they bring back everything you've tried to forget. It needs to be easier, not so fast. They want you to bring it all up straight away. Everything that happened. It's like they don't really want to know. They ask you questions then go away. . . . You feel worse 'cos it was hard and then they go. . . . When they don't listen you feel upset, because you answered their questions so you ask yourself, "Why did I answer if they don't do anything about it?" They did not see I was hurting – it was like they thought I was a bad person.'

(Adam had lived with his mother whom he loved, his violent father, and his siblings. He had been sexually abused since he was very young by an older brother. Although left at home after he disclosed the abuse, he took matters into his own hands and asked to be accommodated by the local authority. He is now the subject of a care order.)

Lisa

Lisa, too, had feelings about the way in which the investigative interview took place: 'I've been lied to – by the child protection worker. I trusted her and she lied – she said she was a social worker and she wasn't, she was from child protection. I didn't think they would lie to me. Never again. I felt let down. Betrayed. I told her what happened. Everything flared up – my whole diary was read. It wasn't allowed to be private, and even if I said, "I don't want you to see it," they had a camera on me and on my diary. I wish I'd never written in my diary. I should have known what they were going to do. They should have told me. It was awful.'

(Lisa had cared for her mother and profoundly disabled sister until her mother died from an overdose of drugs and alcohol when Lisa was 9 years old. Since this time she and her sister have lived in a foster home. Too ashamed to tell anybody about indecent assaults that had taken place at a local leisure centre, she tried to make sense of the experience by writing in her diary, which was subsequently read by her foster mother.)

Adam and Lisa are able to articulate the feelings they experienced during the investigative process. Their comments are not given as instruments of blame against social workers. Indeed, I and others, when reading these accounts, will recall occasions when our own practice has failed children; occasions when we did not 'tune in' to their feelings. The examples are to highlight how easy it is to fail children at a crucial stage in their lives, the time when they desperately need someone safely and sensitively to help them.

These children remind us of the crucial role social workers play in their lives. In re-telling the story of abusive incidents, they re-experience the pain, humiliation, betrayal and abandonment associated not only with the abuse, but with other aspects of their lives. As Adam said, 'Social workers can make you feel your life's not worth living. They can make you feel like a piece of dirt or make you feel really good. You expect a social worker to be nice, to treat you with respect. But what happens? They pressurise you, they don't give you time to relax into telling what happened. It's just like you're the next job.'

Daniel

Daniel's experience of the child protection social worker was positive: 'She was nice. I knew she understood because when she didn't she asked me again, another way, and I explained. I could tell she cared. If I'm talking to someone and they don't look serious, I know not to trust. If they weren't really interested they would not be answering my questions properly. You know when they don't care. It's a waste of time. I wouldn't talk to anyone who didn't understand kids. The first woman who was gonna counsel me, I knew, "No!" When I saw you I knew it was OK. Well, I had to test so really it took three or four times because I need to go step by step. I can trust you and I can tell you something that won't get around. I even trusted you to see my mum and sister because she wouldn't stop calling me those names. I knew you wouldn't take their side because you knew the real problem.'

Daniel's account indicates that the social worker conveyed her respect for him as a human being, and in a safe setting he was able to ask questions that were troubling him, for example confidentiality. He felt he had been listened to. (Daniel had been violently sexually assaulted by an older boy at a time when his father was in the final stages of a terminal illness, so he did not disclose the abuse until several years later when he heard of an assault on another child. His school work suffered as he tried to cope with his shame and humiliation, plus guilt and fear that people would find out.)

Messages for social workers

In reading the transcripts of my interviews with the children, I found the same message for social workers not only in respect of the investigative process, but in all stages of child protection work. They wanted social workers to really understand them, their pain, their needs, and that they needed time. The need to be heard and understood was of paramount importance.

Lisa said: 'You should say in the book that adults should really listen to children. Any child who has a problem needs to be listened to. Social workers should try to understand what children are really trying to say, explain any questions the children have, and if they feel left out they should be made to feel important, wanted and loved.'

(In therapy, Lisa did not discuss her abuse; her overriding need was to work on her guilt at her mother's death, about which she had not talked to anybody. She worked on this symbolically, through the use of the play room.)

The following quotations highlight the joy when children feel they are understood:

> *Adam:* 'The one (social worker) I've got now just goes for it. She pays attention to what I want. She listens. I say what I want and she helps me straight away. Yeah – I've got big shields around me now.'

> *Lisa:* (referring to the placement conference that took place after her sixteenth and final play therapy session) 'I didn't think I was getting through. I went over the same thing three times and I didn't think I was getting my actual meaning across. It wasn't until I read the review notes that I realised I had got it across. I thought they would all think I was stupid and I realised – HEY – they understand!! That made me feel so good – so happy – I couldn't believe it! I knew you understood but I didn't think the others would.'

Another example is from my interview with Daniel when he was using the metaphor of a loan company to explain the difficulty of trusting another person. Note my less than adequate response – instead of tuning in to him I was trying to analyse the material in my head!

Daniel:	Trusting is harder than you think. I'll explain.
Barbara:	OK.
Daniel:	If I run a loan company and I give you £3,000 it has to be paid weekly. You say you can only pay monthly. You're trusted to pay monthly and you can only pay £50.
Barbara:	Yes. . . . (waiting for the next bit)
Daniel:	Do you understand?
Barbara:	Well . . . er . . . you're trusting you'll get it all back?
Daniel:	Ha! You don't understand do you! (Gleefully) I'll explain another way. If you have a catalogue and someone bought and they moved house, the catalogue is gone. If I order and paid first payment and went away, that's not trusting.
Barbara:	It is difficult for me to understand.
Daniel:	Oh, Barbara! Look, if I lend £100 off you, you want it back next week, and I can't pay you, that's not trusting, is it?
Barbara:	Ah! Trusting really is a two way thing.
Daniel:	See, trusting is harder than you think!

The following heartfelt excerpt is from Adam: 'Social workers need to know their own feelings and remember they are adults and can cope better with their feelings, and the pain for them is not so bad. When you're young you're bound to hurt more. Social workers think "So what – it's just a kid with hurting feelings." They don't remember when they were kids and they hurt just the same. Maybe they were doing what I was doing – only perhaps I was ten times worse! They could then say, "Yeah, I remember my pain. I understand his." They'll realise the kids are going through a lot more pain than they went through. The feelings – hurt, sad, useless, stupid. Thinking I'm not worth anything. If they don't have feelings for me, why should I have feelings for other people? Then you feel like dirt.'

Adam then exposed very early childhood pain and linked it to the cycle of abuse (without realising it) to explain to social workers why it was important to understand feelings: 'At home I got confused about feelings because things weren't right. You're brought up to think giving feelings out is OK, then someone ruins that and treats you as if feelings are no good, so you grow up thinking that. Then you bring up your own kid to think feelings are no good, so they get into a lot of trouble 'cos the kids won't know anything different. You'll end up like people won't want to know you. Who wants you if you can't care for somebody else? Or if you can't love somebody? Who's gonna like you? Everybody in the world needs to be loved and to have someone care for them.'

In these excerpts from the transcript it is possible to sense the very poor self-image of the children and how easy it is to increase their suffering. The social worker cannot remove the hurt, but equally must not compound it. Therefore sensitive handling of the child's pain, which runs with self-awareness, knowledge and understanding, is crucial. As Adam says, 'If they don't have feelings for me, why should I have feelings for other people . . .? Everybody in the world needs to be loved and to have someone care for them.' Note also Lisa's comment that every child needs to feel important, wanted and loved.

Non-directive play therapy

Another issue that needs to be considered here, is that these children entered play therapy for between sixteen and twenty-four sessions of one hour. Non-directive play therapy enabled each of them to become articulate, to get in touch with their feelings, and to become assertive, challenging and self-confident (see the exchange between Daniel and me). Also at one point during my interview with Adam, he said, as I was asking him to explain something particularly difficult for me to understand, 'Barbara, you're doin' my head in!'

I refer the reader who is prepared to learn more about this approach to the work of West (1992), Wilson et al. (1992) and Ryan and Wilson (1996), who explain the theoretical framework of child-centred, or non-directive, play therapy, and fully demonstrate the approach through case examples throughout.

In brief, the model uses stages of cognitive (following Piaget) and emotional (following Erikson) development within a framework of attachment theory. A grasp of these is essential in order to understand the stage at which children are functioning, as it is improbable that neglected, physically, sexually and/or emotionally abused children will function at their chronological age. Depending on a child's unique attachment history, developmental stage, and age when the abuse occurs, thinking and feelings are likely to be distorted and confused, as the child does not have the means to unscramble the confusion. It is crucial for communication to be established whereby such a child feels safe and totally accepted.

Non-directive play therapy uses symbolic play as the means of communication. The therapist provides a secure environment for children in the play room where there are adequate toys and equipment to provide a range of media for them to express themselves symbolically. Therapists need to be genuine (to be themselves), to have unconditional positive regard for a child (akin to love but without the connotations usually attached to the word), and to have accurate empathy (the ability to show they really care). They must provide consistency, for instance in terms of time, venue, reliability, limits and boundaries in the play room. Careful planning and preparation is required, as is time to reflect and record after each session (see also Chapter 11).

I believe that social workers can use some of the tools used in play therapy, provided that they believe in each child's unique capacity to resolve their own problems. It is important for workers to believe in themselves as talented and unique human beings, to understand and accept the hurt child in themselves, to be aware of gaps in their knowledge and understanding, and to be committed to filling those gaps through reading, supervision, training, consultancy and, yes, personal therapy. They need to take pride in their profession and their work, to take responsibility for themselves, for the work they do, and to make decisions about whether working with children is for them. It is painful as well as joyful! They require self-awareness, a deep regard for each child they work with, the ability to reflect accurately the emotions that the child is feeling, the capacity to enjoy play, and, very importantly, excellent supervision.

The way I work

I work with children of both sexes, of different nationalities, from 5 to 16 years of age. All have behavioural and emotional difficulties. They may or may not have been abused or neglected. I see them as children first, and accept whatever issues they want to work on. In this way they direct the pace and they can symbolically express those issues that are the most pressing for them at any particular time. Every child will use those toys or equipment that suit them best. Most at some time will use the sand tray, regardless of age, and many love dressing up. I never persuade a child to use anything in particular. I always, when introducing children or teenagers to the play room, explain that they can play with anything they wish, the time is theirs – 'special time'.

I sometimes see children in their own or their carers' homes and always carry a variety of small toys with me, including finger puppets, doll's house dolls, babies' bottles, guns, swords, stick-on farmyards, villages, houses, zoos, playdough, revolting noisy goo, crayons and paper. This approach met with approval from one teenager who commented that it was 'real cool'. He said, 'Social workers don't bring crayons, puppets, or things like that. It would be helpful if they did because those things can help you relax, gives you time if you don't want to answer. You can pretend to be interested in something like a book, hide your face in it when you're embarrassed. If social workers carried stuff round with them in their cars for when they see children and teenagers it can help them when they're fidgety. Kids could use anything they want as long as it helps them talk. If they're helping, you don't feel stupid.'

Robert

Robert was 8, chronically neglected and physically abused when he was referred for play therapy. I met him in his placement and naturally he was very uneasy, would not make eye contact, and was very fearful. We communicated through finger puppets. He chose a robin for himself and an owl for me. He kept the robin. When Robert arrived for his first play therapy session, he sat like a cornered and frightened animal in the rear of the social worker's car, screaming obscenities and refusing to get out. I said gently that it must be really scary to think he had to come into this strange building, but it was OK not to. No one would make him do what he didn't want to do. I said I was sorry he was so frightened. I also said that if he would like to come another time, that would be fine, but I understood if he did not want to. Right now, perhaps he would feel better if his social worker took him back to. . . . I visited Robert at his placement the following week and he avoided me. I left the owl finger puppet with a note saying that owl would like to spend some time with robin, if that was OK. Robert came to play therapy the following week, having overcome his fear. No mention was made of the puppets. As often happens with chronically neglected children who are in a safe place, he very quickly blossomed in self-confidence. At the tenth and final session he wanted to be videoed, to take photographs of himself, me and his foster mother when she came to collect him, and was joyful in his play.

David

Physically abused children have to contend with great fear, and many cope with the fearfulness and anxiety of an imminent physical attack by inviting their own physical abuse. David, a 10-year-old boy, had, since early childhood, been abused and scapegoated by his father, with whom he identified, and he is now the subject of a care order. David bullied, intimidated, and constantly goaded other adults and children into physically abusing him, as though the only attention/affection he knew was of a violent kind. He had attempted to drown another child.

David could be both charming and aggressive, and did not present as fearful, indeed he was totally without limits and boundaries. In his first session, which he eagerly attended, he wanted to drown everything in water and to run screaming throughout the building. I acknowledged that he wanted to pour water everywhere and maybe he was very afraid or very angry about being in the play room, but I would not allow anything to happen that might hurt him or me. He calmed down, accepted the rules of safety and never again infringed them. David is in continuing need of help, as he has yet to unscramble the terrible hurts and injustices that have been poured on him by his parents, and he needs a placement that will provide safety and security. His anger and aggression are directed towards other human beings, yet his gentleness, sensitivity and warmth were also displayed for my benefit in play therapy. I hope his future will not be as bleak as I fear it may be.

A postscript from Adam

Adam experienced another kind of fear. He was feeling so pained, hopeless and afraid, that during one of our sessions he stood up, wanting to throw himself through the window to the conservatory glass roof beneath. I felt his fear and reflected this. I stayed seated, and quietly talked to him about how I wanted him to be safe. This is what he said about interviewing someone who is suicidal: 'If a kid is so unhappy he wants to, say, slit his wrists, you listen to him, try to do what he says, do your best. If you can't do it, explain why. Sit down, relax, wait till he calms down, make sure he's safe. Accept the kid's fears. Put yourself in that position, you feel so unhappy you're going to slit your wrists. What would it take to stop you? Social workers should remember the kid is scared, nervous.'

Adam had another fear – he told me during a session that his beloved nephew, just months old, was in danger of being sexually abused. We discussed what action he might take. He confronted his fear, and arranged to talk in my presence to the child protection worker. 'I love him. I was worried he would be hurt, so what do you do? You have to cross your family, piss your sister off, to make sure that someone you care for, who's just been born, is safe. I think myself, it's better for him to be safe than go through what I've been through. I don't want him to be brought up the way I was. It's not exactly a nice thing to wish on anybody. I never would wish it on anybody.'

Adam put his heart and soul into helping me to write this chapter. He understood its purpose completely and his words speak volumes. The profundity of his inner wisdom is inescapable. At school, Adam feels like a 'no hoper' – he has what are euphemistically called 'learning difficulties' – and he has been permanently excluded from school. At a soul level, he knows how deeply I care about him and that who he is is absolutely fine with me.

Summary

If troubled children are to experience a sense of their own value and worth, social workers need to convey to them that they understand their fears and terrors, and that they accept them as they are. This involves:

- conveying a real respect for each child
- allowing time to build a trusting relationship
- understanding how to communicate non-verbally as well as with words
- making the environment within their control safe.

It also requires social workers to act in a trustworthy way, not coercing or directing children, nor making promises they cannot keep.

Perhaps most difficult of all, people who wish to work successfully with children need a commitment to developing an understanding of their own fears and childhood pain and of how that pain limits them both personally and professionally. If they cannot face that pain within themselves, they are prevented from being able to provide a context in which a child can be truly listened to. If overwhelmed by inner fear, the worker cannot listen and does not hear, and so communication does not happen. The result is an interaction that is arid and mechanistic. The child reveals nothing, the worker discovers nothing. True child protection must be an interactive process.

In conclusion, I want to share an anonymous poem with those children and adults who feel that they are worthless and are fearful of their perceived inadequacy.

> Our deepest fear is not that we are inadequate
> Our deepest fear is that we are powerful beyond measure;
> It is our light not our darkness that most frightens us.
> We ask ourselves, "Who am I to be brilliant, gorgeous,
>   talented and fabulous?"
> Actually, who are we *not* to be?

Notes

[Author] I must pay tribute to my dear friend Madge Bray from whom I have learned, and will go on learning, so much about truly listening to children. Her sensitivity, courage and friendship have inspired me to develop my own unique capacity to listen and 'be', not only with children but with myself.

[Editors] We wish to thank Barbara Smedley for writing this chapter when our original author, Madge Bray, was unable to do so.

References

Bray, M. (1991) *Poppies on the Rubbish Heap: Sexual abuse – the child's voice.* Edinburgh: Canongate Press. Second edition (1997), London: Jessica Kingsley.

Bray, M. and Pugh, R. (1997) Listening to children: Appreciating the abused child's reality, in J. Bates, R. Pugh and N. Thompson (eds) *Protecting Children: Challenges and change.* Aldershot: Arena.

Butler, I. and Roberts, G. (1997) *Social Work with Children and Families: Getting into practice.* London: Jessica Kingsley.

Dartington Social Research Unit (1995) *Child Protection: Messages from research.* London: HMSO.

Department of Health (1988) *Protecting Children: A guide for social workers undertaking a comprehensive assessment.* London: HMSO.

Department of Health (1995) *The Challenge of Partnership in Child Protection: Practice guide.* London: HMSO.

Kemshall, H. and Pritchard, J. (1995) *Good Practice in Risk Assessment and Risk Management.* London: Jessica Kingsley.

Morrison, T. (1997) Emotionally competent child protection organizations: Fallacy, fiction or necessity?, in J. Bates, R. Pugh and N. Thompson (eds) *Protecting Children: Challenges and change.* Aldershot: Arena.

Owen, H. and Pritchard, J. (eds) (1993) *Good Practice in Child Protection: A manual for professionals.* London: Jessica Kingsley.

Parton, N., Thorpe, D. and Wattam, C. (1997) *Child Protection: Risk and the moral order.* Basingstoke: Macmillan.

Ryan, V. and Wilson, K. (1996) *Case Studies in Non-directive Play Therapy.* London: Baillière Tindall.

Utting, Sir William (1997) *People Like Us: The report of the review of the safeguards for children living away from home.* London: HMSO.

West, J. (1992) *Child Centred Play Therapy.* London: Edward Arnold.

Wilson, K., Kendrick, P. and Ryan, V. (1992) *Play Therapy: A non-directive approach for children and adolescents.* London: Baillière Tindall.

Recommended reading

Bates, J., Pugh, R. and Thompson, N. (eds) (1997) *Protecting Children: Challenges and change.* Aldershot: Arena.

Butler Schloss, E. (1988) *Report of the Inquiry into Child Abuse in Cleveland 1987.* London: HMSO.

Department of Health, Department of Education and Science, Welsh Office (1991) *Working Together Under the Children Act 1989.* London: HMSO.

Department of Health (1992) *Memorandum of Good Practice.* London: HMSO.

Miller, A. (1987) *The Drama of Being a Child and the Search for the True Self.* London: Virago.

Miller, A. (1991) *Banished Knowledge: Facing childhood injuries.* London: Virago.

Miller, A. (1995 reprint) *Thou Shalt Not Be Aware: Society's betrayal of the child.* London: Pluto Press.

Training

The University of York offers training in non-directive play therapy. For further information, please contact Kate Wilson at the Department of Social Policy and Social Work, University of York, York YO1 5DD (telephone 01904 433 490; fax 01904 433 475). I recommend readers interested in this highly effective method of working with children to contact Kate Wilson or Virginia Ryan at York University; both have researched and written extensively on non-directive play therapy, and I cannot recommend their Diploma course too highly.

8

'WILL IT HURT?'

Children and medical settings

Penny Cook

Introduction

Children of all ages may encounter medical settings of various kinds, and the people who work in them, for differing reasons and at any stage in their development. Many of these occasions are for what adults would call routine visits, such as immunisations, dental check-ups, and school medical examinations. From a child's view, however, such visits may be new experiences and possibly quite traumatic, unless the child has been prepared for what will happen.

Unfortunately, many children find themselves in the doctor's surgery or hospital because they are sick or have had some sort of accident, and in these cases there will not have been enough time to prepare them or to allow questions and fears to be discussed. Adults close to children often try to protect them from pain and fear, perhaps because of their own difficulty in dealing with a situation. It is almost invariably more helpful if children are given the opportunity to ask questions, to be heard, to be given honest information and to share feelings with the family and relevant health professionals.

This chapter considers some of the situations in which children are in medical settings and explores the issues for these young people. It is only by understanding the child's point of view that adults are really able to help, so I hope that this chapter will be read with the focus on the needs of children.

Medical settings where children may be involved

1 Children who are relatively healthy come into contact with those who work medically in a variety of circumstances. They need regular dental checks, recommended vaccinations, checks by a health visitor and, later, by a school nurse or doctor, which may involve hearing or sight tests

and perhaps lead to visits to an optician. Also children may need to be examined by a General Practitioner when they are unwell.

2   Some children may visit the outpatient clinic of a hospital for speech therapy, occupational therapy or physiotherapy. Such a visit may be required for the diagnosis and treatment of some specific acute or chronic medical condition and may involve investigations such as blood tests, X-rays, or scans.

3   Children may receive emergency treatment at hospital accident and emergency departments at the onset of a severe acute illness or following injury or accident.

4   Children may have a lifelong condition such as asthma, eczema, diabetes, allergy and problems with sight, hearing or mobility.

5   Children may be admitted to hospital for surgery or treatment of a condition.

6   Children may have life-threatening or life-limiting conditions.

7   Children may have mild to severe physical disabilities.

8   Children may have learning difficulties or developmental delay.

9   Children may need residential or respite care.

10   Children may visit a sick friend or relative in hospital.

11   Children may have a sick or injured relative at home.

12   Children may be bereaved by the death of a close relative or friend.

When we are thinking about children in these particular settings, it is helpful to start from the child's viewpoint and to check that we are really hearing what the children are trying to tell us. Good communication has to be in both directions, since there will be information that health professionals and parents need to tell children, that they need to hear. Empathy – trying to understand how children feel in the situation as they see it – is essential for successful communication and for developing a trusting relationship.

Building a relationship

There are people, sights, smells and sounds in medical settings that are unfamiliar to children. Most of these cannot be changed, so it becomes even more important that the people concerned are able to adapt to the needs of young people. Children and parents remember their first impressions of health professionals, so it is worth paying attention to some details. A few hints would include (not in order of importance):

*   Be friendly and smiling. Welcome children in language appropriate to their age and provide some toys and books in a safe environment.
*   Think about what to wear. Doctors in white coats may appear frightening to some young children; masks and gowns may also give alarming first impressions. Ties showing animals or cartoon characters, small

teddy bears on a stethoscope and attractive jewellery are welcoming for children. They are familiar objects in an unusual setting that help to add some normality.

- Be approachable but allow time for children to observe the people and surroundings before starting an examination or treatment.
- Involve the parents of young children; gain their confidence and trust.
- Offer older children and teenagers the opportunity to ask their own questions, possibly without a parent being present.
- Provide distraction during examination or treatment. Keep a box of toys and books handy.
- Value the opinions and respect the wishes of children and young people.
- Talk to children, sitting at their level. Explain what is to happen, e.g. place a stethoscope on a doll or teddy bear before using it on the child.

Children need information

Most of the protests, refusals to co-operate or crying that children display are a result of their fear in a strange environment. Although it is not easy to prepare children by telling them what to expect, it will be of considerable help in the way they manage these new situations. Many parents have difficulties in preparing their children for visits to the dentist, doctor or hospital, perhaps because of their own fears or because they themselves do not know what to expect or how to tell the children. If children are not told what to expect, they usually imagine it, and their fantasies could be far from the truth. It does not help relationships with parents, or anyone else, if they discover that adults whom they trusted have not been honest with them.

Andrew was 7 years old when he went into hospital to have his tonsils and adenoids removed. When a nurse was taking his temperature he asked her 'Is it true they cut your head off to get out your tonsils?'

Another reason why it is important to be honest with children is that as they grow older their need for information will change, so it is essential that children be told the truth from the beginning. In this way they can build on the information they already know, and it will make sense.

The words used to explain things to children need careful choice. Adults use words quite freely, without always thinking about what they may mean at a child's level of understanding. Euphemisms are common, especially when adults are finding it hard to tell children bad news. When a young child hears that someone has lost a baby, the response could be 'Shall we go and look for the baby?' Children can be very confused when told that someone has 'gone to sleep' or 'gone to Jesus' when they have died; they go to sleep every night and expect to wake every morning, so they might well expect the dead person to wake up again. They may be afraid of going to bed in case they do not wake up, or be scared of the dark, fearing that Jesus could take them away in the night. Information given by adults to children may also sound rather different to them. A 'heart attack' is a phrase in common use, but a child could imagine an attack with weapons. A 'broken' arm could be considered as disposable as broken toys.

Children are usually quite logical, and a simple explanation of a chain of events, giving reasons, helps their understanding. Brenda was very anxious about how she could tell her children that their father was going to have both his legs amputated. It was hard enough for her to think about coping with her husband in a wheelchair and with artificial legs, so she thought the children would be horrified. A nurse planned with her what she could say:

'You know that Daddy had an accident on his motorbike and both his legs were badly damaged. He has been in hospital for a week now and the doctors and nurses have been trying really hard to make his legs better. Unfortunately they cannot be mended and they are very painful, so the special doctors have talked with Mummy and Daddy and they have all agreed it would be best to take off the bad legs. This means that Daddy will not feel them hurting anymore, and some new legs can be made so that he will be able to walk again.'

Brenda was surprised how well the children accepted the news, especially when they started to ask questions about the new legs. Brenda sensed a feeling of relief both in herself, now that the dreaded story had been told, and in the children, who now knew the truth and could move forward in a positive way after all the anxiety and uncertainty of the past week.

Elsegood (1996) offers a useful summary of guidelines for giving factual information to children:

- What has happened.
- What is happening.
- What is going to happen.
- What this is likely to mean for them.
- What is being done to help.

Giving children bad news

Some information that children need to hear may not be welcome; in fact it could be described as 'bad news'. When given in strange surroundings with unfamiliar people around, it will seem worse. In a health setting, 'bad news' could be anything that the child is not pleased to hear, such as having to take some medicines, taking time off school and missing a special event, immobilising a limb, or needing surgery. It could involve someone else, as when a relative or friend is ill. It may have serious consequences for the child and family, particularly if a parent or sibling is likely to die or has died.

These guidelines may help when planning to give bad news:

- *What* does the child need to know or what are they asking to be told? What is known already?
- *How* will the information be given?
- *Who* is the most appropriate person to tell the child?
- *When* is a suitable time to tell them?
- *Who* will support the child afterwards?

Non-verbal communication

The body language that children display may help in understanding their feelings and may offer clues for managing the situation. Children will also pick up clues from their parents' body language. Pay attention to:

- *Actions:* how they came into the room, how they walked, where they sat or stood, whether they played. If they talked. Did they cling to mother?
- *Facial expression:* whether they looked happy or sad, frightened or at ease, smiling or crying. Did they make eye contact?
- *Posture:* did they sit or stand confidently, curl up on a seat, keep head down, hide under the table?

Comments could be made such as 'You looked rather worried about coming in. Let me tell you that nothing terrible is going to happen to you. I need to talk to Mummy and then feel your tummy.'

Specific medical situations

Now that we have considered medical situations from a child's point of view, let us analyse each specific situation in turn.

Children who are relatively healthy

Most children have visits to a health centre at some stage in their development. From birth, a midwife and then a health visitor will see them at home or at the clinic, and routine health checks continue until the child goes to school, when the school nurse makes occasional checks. Some children dread the school medical examination, especially if they have problems that make them seem different from other children in their class. It can be embarrassing to be asked personal questions when their peers can hear, and risk being teased. Even a simple eyesight test will be difficult for children with poor sight who may be teased about being unable to see properly and having to wear glasses.

The first visit to a dentist can be a traumatic occasion, especially if treatment is needed. It is helpful for a child to have watched mother or father sit in the dentist's chair and seen the dentist put instruments in their mouth. The dentist may give a toddler the chance to sit on the parent's lap in the chair, and on a further visit progress to looking in the child's mouth – without any instruments at first. Encouragement for caring for teeth becomes part of the developing relationship between dentist and child, and, hopefully, the child grows to understand the importance of this.

How the rest of the family and other adults behave and discuss visits to health care centres can make a deep impression on children. Over-emphasising fears and making negative comments will not help children to build a trusting relationship with those professionals who are there to treat or prevent health problems.

Children visit hospital outpatient departments

Visiting a busy outpatient department can be a rather daunting experience for children, even though most of them have play areas for children where they can be amused during boring waiting periods. Playing helps them to relax and find the visit less threatening and more enjoyable. A hospital play specialist may be available to help prepare children for certain medical procedures and to work with needle-phobic children before they have a blood test. It often takes time for a child to feel sufficiently at ease to ask important questions such as does their body have enough blood to spare the syringeful. Some children would like to know that happens to their blood after it has been put into the little bottles and why it was necessary to have the sample taken.

It is helpful if thought is given to the way in which the consulting room is arranged, and to the number of people who need to be in the room. A 10-year-old boy said that it was like being in court when he was asked to sit down facing a row of medical and nursing staff!

Children receive emergency treatment at accident and emergency departments

When children need emergency treatment there is little or no time to prepare them for what they might expect. Explanations may not be possible because of a child's poor level of consciousness, the severity of the illness or the intensity of their pain. Parents may not be behaving in their normal manner because they are distressed, and temporarily unable to help their child. Sensing the distress and emotion of parents or other familiar adults may add to a child's own insecurity and fear. Older children may be familiar with television dramas set in hospitals and they may recognise equipment, surroundings and language used by staff. This could be reassuring but it could also cause them to be frightened of what may happen next.

Children who have been involved in an accident may be anxious to learn the fate of anyone else who was there, but could be too scared to enquire. If no one else mentions their names, the child may think they are a 'taboo' subject.

Children with a life-long condition

Some children have a medical condition that is not going to go away, but with good management they are able to have a nearly normal life. Most of these conditions are diagnosed early in childhood, so the child grows up with the problems being part of their way of life. Common conditions would include asthma, eczema, diabetes, allergies, food intolerances, and problems with hearing, eyesight or mobility. Children may need to follow specific guidelines to manage the condition – regular medication, particular diet, use of special equipment and attending the hospital or family doctor regularly. All these requirements make the children different in some way from their 'normal' peers. This often leads to them being teased and even bullied at school. It is very hard for some children to carry an inhaler and use it in the company of their friends, to be forbidden to eat the food at a party, to take medicines to school, to be unable to see reasonably without glasses or to hear clearly without a hearing aid.

As children become more independent of their parents, they take more responsibility for their own care. This might lead to older children and teenagers choosing to ignore medical advice, as they would rather be considered 'normal'. Non-compliance can be a serious problem with this age group and calls for gentle handling and counselling. It is understandable that these young people should go through a period when they rebel against the treatment for a condition they did not want to have.

Children may be admitted to hospital

Admission to hospital as an inpatient may be planned or occur in an emergency. Even if there is not much time to prepare, explanations appropriate to the child's age and understanding are important. Listening for fears that are not expressed openly and inviting the child to share them is usually helpful. Some fears arise from not understanding where certain parts of the body are, or how they work. This could cause difficulties when an operation is needed; children need to be reassured that they can manage without the bit that is being removed, that a bad part is being taken away or something will work better after the operation. Older children sometimes want to talk to the surgeon themselves, and may ask if they could wake up during the operation. Younger children are more likely to need reassurance that Mummy will be there and want to take a favourite toy with them. Good preparation before procedures usually helps children to understand what to expect. This may include looking at pictures of children having treatment, visiting the relevant department in advance, talking to other children who have experienced it themselves and offering plenty of time to talk about their own particular worries.

Children who have been critically ill, involved in an accident, witnessed an unpleasant event or needed to have painful treatment may suffer from some form of post-trauma distress. This could manifest as nightmares, disturbed sleep, or recurring memories. A child may deliberately avoid talking about the event or not be allowed to mention it, but the subject may be brought into their play. The hospital play specialist or paediatric nurse may feel confident to encourage children to use play as a way of externalising the feelings and thoughts inside. Toy cars, ambulances, police and hospital play-people are helpful in allowing a child to act out what is remembered following a road traffic accident.

Older children may benefit from opportunities to talk through what happened with a counsellor or psychologist, and therapy through art, drama or music might be available to help some young people (see Chapters 10, 11 and 12). Parents and other relatives often think it best for a child to try to forget what happened, but experience has shown that following a traumatic occasion, it is important for the victim, adult or child, to describe what was seen, heard, done and felt, rather than 'bottling it up' and suffering repeated nightmares.

Children may have life-threatening or life-limiting conditions

There are many children in this category, who, with the encouragement of positively thinking parents, are able to live their lives as normally as possible. In some families the overriding anxiety is so great that their whole lives centre on the sick child. Such children are often very aware that they are different from some of their friends, so it can be helpful for them to meet others with similar conditions. Their parents will usually find support from the other children's parents. Many make friends with others who have the same problems, usually through meeting with them at the hospital or support organisation. Children with conditions such as cystic fibrosis get to know many others during their frequent hospital stays. Sadly they also have to face the fact that people may die from this and other conditions, and as they get older they will learn that friends have died. This makes them question their own mortality and hopes for the future.

Children may have physical disabilities

There are many children with physical disabilities and their families share many common factors. If the children are able to understand, they realise that they cannot do all the things their peers can and this invariably leads to frustration and anger in the child and the rest of the family. It is very easy for a tired mother to say, in her child's hearing, that she needs a break from all the hard work of constant caring. From the child's view, it may seem unfair to be in a wheelchair and unable to run about. A weary mother's understandable complaints about the unrelenting effort of caring can make a child feel guilty and responsible. A mutual acknowledgement of the pressures on both of them can be therapeutic. Physically disabled children may need regular visits to hospital, perhaps for physiotherapy or corrective surgery.

Children may have learning difficulties or developmental delay

Many of these children have frequent medical assessments and visits to hospitals, specific therapy units and child development centres. Some attend schools for children with special needs, where medication and treatments may be included in the school day. The families of these children are never free from medical care and the effect on family life is profound. It may be hard or even impossible to explain procedures to the children, so painful treatments are also distressing for the families.

Children may need residential or respite care

Residential care might be required as a daily, weekly or permanent arrangement, depending on a child's needs and condition. It can be difficult for brothers and sisters to understand why one of the children in the family is different, and why they have to be looked after somewhere else. They can resent the attention given to the child with disabilities and be pleased when they can be 'sent away'. Conversely, other siblings may be rather possessive of their 'special' brother or sister and want to stay with them.

There are now several hospices for children in Britain that offer respite care. Sometimes whole families choose to stay there together; alternatively, a hospice offers tremendous help to a family by caring for a child's special needs while the parents take a deserved rest.

Children may visit a sick relative or friend in hospital

The question of children visiting people in hospital may be difficult at times. It is only relatively recently that children have been 'allowed' to visit, and some units still maintain restrictions. Some of these may be to prevent the risk of cross infection or because there are no facilities for children, but often they are really there because staff do not feel able to cope with children visiting. Clearly it is not advisable for children suffering from any infections, such as a sore throat, cold sores, cough, diarrhoea, glandular fever or chicken pox, to visit people in hospital.

It could be assumed that there will be no problems for a child visiting someone else, but this assumption avoids thinking about the impact the experience may have on children. I think the first basic question is: has the child asked to visit? If they have not, then do they need to, and how important is it? Much depends on a child's relationship with the person being visited. Children like to visit their brothers and sisters and friends when they are in hospital, and most children enjoy having visitors on the children's wards. If a sick child is in hospital for a long time, younger siblings may get bored and tired. They may prefer to stay at home or play with friends rather than be dragged to the hospital again. They may also resent the attention given to the child in hospital. A memorable visit to hospital might be to see mother and a new brother or sister in the maternity ward, and this can be made a special occasion for children to welcome their baby. Even if the birth was premature and the baby needs to be in the neonatal intensive care unit, the siblings can usually be taken there.

It is helpful for both children and adults to be prepared for what they will see when they go into a hospital. There are excellent books, games and toys available to help set the scene (see suggested reading). Information about the actual room where the patient is, the staff and descriptions of any equipment being used around the bed are important. Photographs are useful to show to children before they see a patient for the first time. A child about to see a parent in the intensive care unit would need to know:

- What has happened – e.g. Dad was in a car accident.
- Why he is here – because he has been badly injured and needs special help.
- Who is looking after him – doctors and nurses who wear special clothes that look like green pyjamas.
- What the machines are for – helping him to breathe because he is not strong enough.
- What the tubes are for – giving him drinks because he cannot drink for himself, and special medicines to stop him feeling the hurt.

When someone close to a child is seriously ill or injured, the question arises amongst the adults as to whether children should visit. Many adults, particularly older members of the family, may try to protect children from seeing the person looking ill and perhaps attached to machines in the intensive care unit. It is with the best of intentions that they want to prevent children getting distressed; but children need to be heard. They do not like being left out of family events, and they too need to be able to share with the adults their feelings of fear, insecurity and sadness. If this significant person in the child's life dies, the death is far more of a shock if the children did not already understand the seriousness of the condition. Children visiting a very sick or dying person need to be well supported. The parents may not be the most suitable source of support if they are very distressed, so other adults who are well known to the child may be better able to help. It is essential that everyone is telling the same story to children, to prevent mistrust and confusion at an already difficult time. Children may ask different people similar questions to check if the story remains the same.

Children may live with a sick or injured relative at home

Many children live in a household with a sick or injured person. This could be a parent who has a chronic illness or disability, such as an amputation of a limb, multiple sclerosis, fits, blindness or breathing difficulties. A brother or sister may be suffering from an illness or condition, perhaps a temporary disability such as a broken leg, or be recovering from an operation. The approach and attitudes of the family would be easier if the problems were not long-lasting, but children do need the chance to discuss not only some information about the condition, but also what it means for them.

The family may have made special alterations to the house to accommodate ramps for a wheelchair, perhaps a bedroom downstairs and/or adapted chairs and table, and space for feeding pumps and medicines. Brothers and sisters often find this hard to live with, especially if they share a bedroom. It may take considerable encouragement for a child to admit to being scared about the strange equipment that has invaded the bedroom. Gentle explanations may be needed to help them understand why it is necessary, and how it works.

Children may be bereaved by the death of a close relative or friend

Although children's understanding of death will depend on their age and any previous experience of loss, it is important for them to be able to share their feelings with adults and to learn how emotions are handled. When someone known to them dies, especially a close relative, children often feel insecure and confused. They may become clingy and not allow parents out of their sight, perhaps afraid to go to bed. Excuses may be used for not wanting to go to school and children may complain of feeling unwell with abdominal pain, headaches and sickness. These are all ways through which children tell us about themselves, but adults need to listen with care to understand the messages they are given. Most of the issues are around fear, so it is important for children to be allowed to ask questions and to be given truthful answers. Bereaved children are often afraid that they too will die, or that their parents or sibling may. This is why they may be afraid to leave them and feel safer staying at home. Older children can develop quite a sense of responsibility for their parents and be very alarmed, to the extent of panic sometimes, when a parent is home later than expected. There may be a great fear that they have been in an accident and would also die.

Anger may be directed at the doctor or the hospital for not making the person well again, or even at the dead person for leaving them; time to talk about what happened and to answer medical questions is important.

Another strong feeling in bereaved children is guilt; children may think that in some way this dreadful event was their fault. It could be desperately important to give a child the opportunity to express this so that reassurance can be given. This again reinforces the need for children to be told the facts so that they are not left to imagine what happened. They need to know that someone was too ill or badly injured to be made better, even though the doctors and nurses did all they could to try and help. Children who witness an accident or death may need specialised help or counselling afterwards. Their guilt could be particularly strong if they think that they should have been able to save the person or prevent the accident from happening.

Children are likely to show different emotions and have different priorities from the adults around them.

Keith

Keith lived with his mother since his parents were divorced and he was happy at the school in the village where they lived. When his mother died suddenly, one of his first questions whilst at the hospital was where would he go to school now? He understood what people had explained to him and was moving on to the reality of this situation. His security had been shattered; he did not know where he would live or who would look after him. Keith's question helped the adult relatives to think about how he was feeling and to listen, not just to what he said, but to the feelings behind the words. They were able to give him the explanations, reassurance and extra love that he needed.

Vicky

Vicky wanted to see her mother after she had died, and her grandmother agreed rather reluctantly after seeking advice from the nursing staff. Vicky told her grandmother that her mother looked different and asked why. Her grandmother, obviously upset because her own daughter had died, tried to 'be strong' and replied 'Oh no, she just hasn't got her make-up on'. Fortunately, a nurse heard this conversation and shortly afterwards had the opportunity to sit with Vicky on her own. She acknowledged with Vicky that she had noticed her mother looked 'different'. Vicky immediately sat upright and asked the nurse 'Why does she look different?' The nurse asked her to say what she was thinking and she answered her sensible questions, explaining that everyone goes cold and pale when they die because the heart has stopped pumping blood around the body. Vicky needed to know that this was normal and she should not be frightened. She also needed to clear the confused messages she was receiving – whether her mother was dead or simply without her make-up, or both.

Conclusion

Medical settings present a range of new experiences for adults and children alike. Many adults feel afraid, apprehensive, overwhelmed or ill-informed, and it is not surprising that children might feel the same. Empathic understanding from adults goes a considerable way towards helping children; we need to remember the importance of listening to what they are telling us.

Reference

Elsegood, J. (1996) Breaking Bad News to Children, in B. Lindsay and J. Elsegood (eds) *Working with Children in Grief and Loss*, ch. 3. London: Baillière Tindall.

Suggested reading

Althea. Books in the 'Talk it over' series by Althea, published by Dinosaur Publications, London: *Going to the doctor*; *Visiting the dentist*; *Having an eye test*; *Having a hearing test*; *I can't hear like you*; *I can't talk like you*; *I have a mental handicap*; *I have diabetes*; *I have epilepsy*; *I have asthma*; *Special care babies*.
Cook, P. (1999) *Supporting Sick Children and their Families*. London: Baillière Tindall.
Devanne-Caveney, C. (1991) *Visit to the Hospital*. Manchester: Little Owl, World International Publishing Ltd.
First Experiences, published by Usborne Publishing Ltd, London: *Going to the hospital*; *Going to the dentist*; *Going to the doctor*; *The new baby*.
Heegaard, M. (1991) Workbooks published by Woodland Press, Minneapolis, MN: *When someone special has a serious illness*; *When something terrible happens, children can learn to cope with grief*; *When someone very special dies*.
Kimpton, D. (1994) *The Hospital Highway Code*, London: Action for Sick Children.
Lansdowne, R. (1996) *Children in Hospital: A guide for family and carers*. Oxford: Oxford University Press.
Mercer, G. (1988) *Inside a Hospital*. London: Kingfisher.
Rayner, C. (1994) *The Body Book*. London: Scholastic.

9

'WORKING WITH HOPE' IN VOLUNTARY ORGANISATIONS

Birgit Carolin

Introduction

The impulse to respond to children's needs is as old as humanity; unfortunately, so is the urge to exploit their helplessness and to corrupt their innocence. Charities providing protection and care, food and shelter for children preceded statutory agencies and political and legal initiatives to promote the welfare of society's youngest, most vulnerable members.

In Britain, such charities are numerous and include: Barnardos (formerly Dr. Barnardo's), National Children's Homes (NCH), the National Society for the Prevention of Cruelty to Children (NSPCC) and the National Children's Bureau (NCB). In addition, there are a large number of organisations founded to meet the specific needs of children with particular disabilities, including autism, multiple sclerosis and cerebral palsy (SCOPE). More recently, agencies like the Children's Legal Centre, Cruse and ChildLine, to name only a few, have established telephone helplines in order to respond directly to children's expressed need for information and support.

Since the British ratification, in 1991, of the UN Convention on the Rights of the Child and the Children Act (1989), well-established national charities, such as Cruse Bereavement Care (Cruse) and the National Association of Family Mediation and Conciliation Services (NAFMCS), have risen to the challenge of providing counselling and support for children suffering from the impact of death and divorce respectively.

In planning this book, we felt, as editors, that the important contribution made by voluntary organisations who listen to children and young people must on no account be overlooked. But how were we to do justice to the value and variety of their work? Our approach and that of our contributors emphasises the personal as well as the professional: each chapter reflects the individual experience of those whose work with children in different settings is firmly based on listening to what they say and also to what they do not or cannot say.

In selecting five child-centred voluntary organisations aimed to serve the needs of those ranging in age from the pre-verbal to the young adult, I have decided to be subjective, for which I make no apologies. My view of each is necessarily limited, although I have made every effort to avoid inaccuracy and misrepresentation. Different as they are from one another, they share a commitment to and enthusiasm for working directly with children of all ages. In order of the chronological age group of the children they serve, they are:

- The Children's Hours Trust (CHT)
- The Children's Service of a Family and Divorce Centre (CFDC)
- The Children's Service of a branch of Cruse Bereavement Care (CRUSE)
- The Rowan Centre (RC)
- Centre 33 (C33)

The Children's Hours Trust (CHT)

A child needs attention most of the time but most children don't get enough. . . . But Rachel Pinney has solved this problem by inventing Children's Hours. What you do is listen to the child while he can play and do anything he likes except dangerous things. . . . It makes the children much happier and they begin to feel wanted. Once they have had 7 or 6 of these the child begins to grow a happier life.

Math (age 7)
Pinney *et al.* (1985 cover)

Background

Rachel Pinney, a doctor who trained with Margaret Lowenfeld, developed the concept of 'creative listening' based upon the principles of non-directive play therapy. This approach differs from those of Melanie Klein and Anna Freud in that it does not interpret but seeks to reflect a child's free activity in a non-judgemental way. To promote the practice of Creative Listening, she founded the Children's Hours Trust in 1983. Since her death in 1995 the Trust continues:

To keep alive the spirit of Children's Hours.
To introduce a training programme.
To include people from any discipline or anyone who can offer a wide range of experience.
To honour experience.
To challenge the prevalent view that only highly trained, qualified and accredited people should be allowed to work with children at a deep level.

(Clarke and Cutler 1997: 14)

What are Children's Hours?

Math's description of 'what you do' serves as an introduction to the booklet describing Children's Hours (Pinney *et al.* 1985) in every detail, quoting examples of good practice and suggesting appropriate play material (such as sand, clay and paint, blankets, bricks and other building equipment, puppets, soft toys and all kinds of miscellaneous objects). Exploring indoors and out is encouraged, but each 'Hour' begins and ends with a simple introductory and farewell ritual, thus giving the child both boundaries and space within which to play freely. Limits are the adult's responsibility in the interests of safety, but there is no embargo on the expression of negative as well as positive feelings, for 'one of the most healing aspects . . . is for the child to discover that the adult allows the natural expression of anger or sadness, as well as happiness and exuberance' (Pinney *et al.* 1985: 7). When Jamie (age 6), fostered many times and about to be adopted, came to say goodbye, he approached his 'Taker' (as the adult is known) with his toy stethoscope, saying:

> 'Let me hear your big heart.' He listened and said, 'Oh dear, it's broken in two.'
> 'And how's your heart, Jamie?'
> 'It's broken in two as well.'
>
> (Clarke and Cutler 1997: 34)

As a method, Children's Hours may be adapted to suit all children from 18 months onwards, including those with special needs or for whom English is not their mother tongue. It may also be used in small groups but is primarily intended to give individual children the benefit of one adult's undivided attention for about one hour at regular times.

Training to become a Taker

A pilot training scheme has been developed by the Trust, supported by the charity Parent Network. Trainees are drawn from a wide range of parents and professionals with an interest in working creatively with children in a variety of settings. At the heart of the programme is the spirit of Rachel Pinney's conviction that freedom is a condition of growth for adult and child alike. Unorthodox herself, she was strongly opposed to the current tendency to confine individual practice within rigid 'professional' limits, and feared that her own ideas would become restricted to one exclusive group. The present trend in statutory and voluntary organisations is, indeed, to tighten up on qualifications. In Britain, the practice of Child (and Family) Therapy requires prolonged and expensive training available to few. In consequence, the vast majority of children (and their families) for whom early intervention might avert later disaster do not receive even minimal attention before it is too late. Another result is that the wisdom and experience of parents and grandparents, as well as professionals, are undermined by the general assumption that only the highly specialised are capable of helping troubled children. By contrast, the Trust believes that any responsible adult willing to devote regular periods of time to a child can enable that child to develop physical and intellectual confidence. Takers in training are urged 'to remind themselves of the energy and activity of childhood, as well as its furies and frustrations' (Pinney *et al.* 1985: 34), to be self-aware and to have their own experience of being heard.

One of the participants on a recent training course writes enthusiastically in her evaluation of the course:

> All the exercises designed to help me contact my inner child were very beneficial. . . . Being the adult to accompany the other person's child was a privilege. . . . I was already using reflective listening in my job . . . to be on the receiving end of this process was new, and it gave me insights into how comforting, affirming and language-stimulating the process is.
>
> (Anon 1997)

Conclusion

The Children's Hours Trust offers adults training in the art of 'creative listening', which helps children, in Math's memorable words, 'to grow a happier life' (Pinney *et al.* 1985).

The Children's Service of a Family and Divorce Centre (CFDC)

Ali (age 8) had been living with his mother after the divorce of his parents four years before, but he had been regularly visiting his father whom he loved. As time went by, however, he had begun to feel increasingly unsafe in his father's care. In the course of one of his visits to him, things came to a head and Ali, young as he was, alerted the police. Her worst fears confirmed, Ali's mother applied to the Court to re-negotiate the terms of her ex-husband's contact with their son. A Court Welfare Officer eventually recommended that supervised access be maintained via the local district Family Contact Agency, while Ali received counselling throughout this difficult period. He was able to express his deeply ambivalent feelings for his father, to resolve his guilt and to articulate his wish that his daddy could behave more like a grown-up and treat him more like the child he is. Ali's story is a dramatic example of the way in which counselling can help children whose parents are separated or divorced.

Background

Since December 1992, the Cambridge Family and Divorce Centre (CFDC), which provides mediation and counselling for people involved in divorce, has also offered help to children. The Children's Service was officially launched in June 1993, financed mainly by a grant from the BBC Children in Need Appeal, and staffed by two part-time counsellors, trained, qualified and experienced in working with young people.

Conceived as a project to meet the needs of an increasing number of children affected by parental separation, the Children's Service aims to prevent long-term difficulties, such as under-achievement, poor self-esteem and serious depression, by providing a timely opportunity to talk in confidence to an impartial listener. Children from 6 to 19 are seen individually at the Centre or are offered group support in schools by the counsellors. A local Health Authority has given money to develop outreach work in support of teachers and pupils in one rural secondary school, and the Joseph Rowntree Foundation has pledged aid to finance a research project evaluating support for children in junior schools experiencing parental separation or divorce. Meanwhile, the BBC Children in Need Appeal continues its substantial grant to the service. Local businesses and volunteers also give vital financial and practical assistance.

Referrals

Children are usually referred by parents and teachers, mediators and solicitors, doctors and social workers, although teenagers over 14 may refer themselves. In view of the Centre's emphasis on fostering co-operation between couples, their policy explicitly states that it is most important that all referrals should be discussed with both parents, who should both consent to their child seeing a counsellor. Only in very exceptional circumstances will a child under 14 be seen without the consent of both parents. Self-referred young people over that age are encouraged, on first meeting the counsellor, to discuss whether to inform their parents. Although this policy of required parental consent does not accord with recent trends towards respecting a child's right to receive guidance and counselling regardless of parents' wishes, in the context of mediation, the centre consider it is in the children's best interests to work even-handedly with both parents. How many potential referrals and self-referrals may be put off by this principle is not, so far, recorded. (In future, more detailed case notes and records will monitor the number of children not seen because of the failure to secure the agreement of both parents.) In the year 1996–7, a total of 46 children (20 girls and 26 boys) received individual counselling, a fraction of the 363 children affected, directly or indirectly, by the divorce or separation of the couples who sought help for themselves from the Centre. Possibly, it is a mark of successful mediation that most of these children do not appear to need help; but it is also possible that the very children who most need to confide in an impartial listener are not given the opportunity to do so. A boy like Ali found comfort and strength in counselling, of which he would have been deprived if either parent had refused consent.

Parents

It is understandable that parents may be reluctant to allow their children to talk to an outsider about intimate family matters, especially if they feel excluded by the confidentiality offered, qualified though it is by current child protection requirements. They may also be unaware of their children's unhappiness, caught up as they are in their own. Even when they do recognise it, they may be unable to accept the anger, confusion and misery of which, in the child's eyes, they themselves are the cause. It is always very hard to listen to passionate emotion, especially when expressed with aggressive words and actions, as it often is by adolescents and younger children.

Play therapy and counselling

Counsellors can offer a younger child a safe and private place, equipped with art and play materials, to help them work through their feelings of sadness, bewilderment and rage. Peter (age 6) found huge release in pounding clay, while Sally (7) devoted much time to re-arranging the doll's house to her own satisfaction.

Older children (the majority referred to the Service are between 8 and 12) may be more able to express their feelings in words, though some, like David (age 10), prefer to find other ways. Coming with his sister (age 14), he would allow her to do most of the talking, while he built a model house for himself with cardboard boxes, which seemed to his counsellor to embody his deep desire to find his own way of dealing independently with his parents' conflicts. Although his house was originally designed for himself alone, his sister was given an attic bedroom and he later added a shop and café, where friends and neighbours could gather.

The counsellors are able to accept whatever thoughts and feelings are expressed, to listen with empathy and yet to remain uninvolved. They have devised a special project for children of 4–8 years in the form of a booklet entitled Me and My Family (CFDC 1996), which includes notes for adults to help children sort out some of their confusions and fears. They suggest that teachers, social workers or health visitors might be better able to help the child with the tasks in the booklet (such as drawing pictures of themselves, their families, pets and homes) than a close family member.

Conclusion

All children, whatever their age or situation, fear abandonment. In the inevitable confusion that occurs when families split up, that fear either bursts into violence or recedes into despair, causing tidal waves of misery that reach well beyond the family and the school to the community at large. Children of divorce may reproduce the cycle of suffering in the lives of their own children, with implications for the well-being of society as a whole. However, there is evidence (Dasgupta and Richards 1997) that, if children's true feelings can be heard and accepted by someone they trust, they may recover their equilibrium and be reconciled to their experience of parental separation and divorce.

The Children's Service of a branch of Cruse Bereavement Care

Death in the family

'They're dead but not buried 'cos they might come alive again.'

Adam (age 6)

'My dad didn't worry about dying; he just worried about leaving us all. Now he'll never see me grow-up – or give me away when I marry. . . . But I *do* worry about dying, it's weird to think that one day I won't be walking on this earth.'

Emma (age 13)

'Now even the good memories are bad, because they make me sad.'

Jim (age 16)

'When your mum dies, you have to decide whether to grow-up as she would have wanted, or to follow your heart and grow up to be yourself.'

Elizabeth (age 14)

(See also Chapters 1, 6 and 8)

When death occurs in a family, it is the children who are most likely to carry the impact of that loss for longest; yet it is also the children whose needs are most likely to be overlooked by the bereaved adults around them. Parents, devastated by the death and distracted by its practical implications, are often unable to attend to their children's demands. They may also find it too upsetting to witness a child's passionate grief as they grapple with their own. They may be shocked by the ways in which children express

145

their feelings or by the blunt questions they ask. Instinctively, adults try to protect the young from the raw reality of death. This is understandable but it is not helpful to children: their fears and worries need to be heard, their questions answered truthfully and their sorrows comforted.

Possible age and gender differences

A very young child, like Adam, may not understand the irreversible nature of death and continue to hope that his dad may 'come alive again' (like the toys in the sand tray), if only he can be good or clever enough to magic him back to life. When being good does not work, he may become furious and frustrated, turning his anger and bewilderment on others. He may dread the dark and resist sleep with fierce determination. Who can convince him that *he* will wake up when his dad did not? If his father was cremated, he may experiment with fire to find out what happens when something burns. Through play, he can express the feelings he is unable to articulate, and so has an opportunity eventually to resolve them, without harm to himself or others.

For a teenager like Emma, who has fully grasped the fact that she will never see her father again 'on this earth', there is profound sadness and a gathering sense of the fatherless years ahead. She grieves for her own loss and also for his. The untimely death of her father has brought her face to face with her own mortality and prompted countless questions, expressed and inexpressible, most of them unanswerable though urgent. She needs to talk to someone who will not be upset by her grief but can empathise and help her to understand her own experience of her father's death.

Jim's attempt to avoid fresh sadness by forgetting even the good times shared with his father is complicated by anger and regret: 'He'd be alive today if he had only stopped smoking. Maybe I could have made him stop if I had tried harder.' By gradually accepting and working through the strength and complexity of his feelings, Jim may come to terms with his father's death.

There are different issues for Elizabeth, whose mother's sudden death means that she is plunged into assuming a quasi-adult role in her family: father's confidante and younger brother's carer. How can she honour her mother's hopes for her and also 'follow her own heart'?

Possible consequences

Although bereavement is a normal and inevitable part of life, it is not nowadays very commonly experienced in childhood. Bereaved children therefore feel 'different', isolated by their misery and unable to convey the depths of their despair to others. The consequences, both in the long and the short term, may be serious: poor physical and mental health, a lack of self-confidence and trust in others, and an unconscious reluctance to become committed to anyone or anything ever again.

Help for children

In recognition of this, and in an attempt to offer help to children, Cruse Bereavement Care, a national organisation founded in 1958 for the benefit of widows and their families, has issued guidelines to its many branches, establishing 'standards of good practice' in working with children and young people. In our local branch, as in many others, initiatives to meet the specific needs of children and young people preceded these 'standards'.

Summer play scheme

For example, since 1990, there has been a summer play scheme, organised annually in August and open to all bereaved children, regardless of their parents' connection with Cruse. The play scheme, which is registered by the Local Authority and caters for up to forty children between 5 and 15, aims to provide them with the opportunity to enjoy themselves with others who have experienced similar losses. It is carefully planned and structured by a team of qualified staff consisting of a co-ordinator and four play-leaders, with the additional assistance of parents, who are encouraged to volunteer their help, especially on the planned outings, such as barbecues, trips to the zoo and a theme park. Thanks to the generosity of a local school, the play scheme is amply accommodated and benefits from the amenities available on site, including a sports centre and swimming pool. Although the emphasis is firmly on the therapeutic nature of play rather than on formal 'counselling', the play scheme offers children many opportunities to confide in one another, as well as in the adults present. Frequently, such encounters occur naturally in the course of an activity such as designing a family shield. For instance, Alan (age 12) talked naturally about his dead mother and grandfather as he drew flowers and a football on his family crest to represent them symbolically.

One-to-one and group support

In addition to the summer play scheme, there is individual help for children living in the local area, appropriate to their ages. For instance, a pre-school child, like Jake, for whom actions speak louder than words, receives the undivided attention of an experienced volunteer, who encourages him to express feelings through play, while his father is offered counselling simultaneously in a separate room by another person. Older children, like Adam, Emma, Jim and Elizabeth, may receive individual (or group) support in school, at home or in a mutually convenient neutral place elsewhere. All these sessions are free, provided by specially trained Cruse volunteers who have had their records checked in accordance with child protection requirements. In view of the difficulty of balancing supply and demand, the number of individual sessions offered is generally limited to six, but no one is ever turned away and everyone is encouraged to renew contact with Cruse if further help is needed.

Conclusion

To speak of 'getting over' the death of a loved one, as if it were a mere obstacle in life's path, is to diminish the importance and ignore the potential for growth that any encounter with death can offer. Children and young people, like Elizabeth, Alan and Jim, Emma, Jake and Adam, may be helped to grow through their early experience of death by the timely support of Cruse workers, who can listen sensitively and so accompany them a short distance along their own way of grieving.

The Rowan Centre: An education service for school-age mothers

Three mothers (still in their teens) recall their feelings when they discovered they were pregnant:

> 'I was happy at first to find out I was pregnant . . . my boyfriend wanted me to get rid of the baby . . . my mum wasn't pleased . . . she got Social Services to talk to me. She wanted me to get rid of it.'

> 'When I first became pregnant I were only 15 and I were confused. I did not know that I could become pregnant at such a young age.'

> 'When I found out I was pregnant, I was really scared. . . .'
> (Rotherham College of Arts and Technology video 1995)

All three might now echo the words of a fourth young woman, who is the proud and bouncy mother of a 6-month-old son: 'I wouldn't have got this far or felt as good about myself without coming here. Everyone's been really encouraging.' 'It's really good that there's a place like this,' is another girl's opinion.

'This place' is the friendly Rowan Centre (RC) in Rotherham, Yorkshire, where school-age mothers are welcomed and supported through the ups and downs of pregnancy and childbirth, and encouraged to continue their education while their babies are cared for in the Centre's crèche. Founded in 1993 as one part of the local Pupil Referral Unit, it is registered with the

DfEE and subject to OFSTED inspection. The creation of the Centre was inspired by the general concern felt by people working in health, education and community settings for the welfare of the unusually high number of pregnant schoolgirls in the Rotherham area. Barnardos, a national charity for children's welfare, owns the purpose-built centre, which accommodates up to twenty mothers and their babies in the course of a school year. Barnardos also pays the salaries of some of the staff, whilst the rest are paid by the Local Education Authority.

Pregnant schoolgirls

The young mothers, aged between 13 and 18, may be referred by schools, social and education welfare workers, health visitors, hospitals or psychiatric and youth services. However, they also refer themselves, for the reputation and success of the Rowan Centre is well-known locally. Everyone is regarded as an individual worthy of respect:

> We consider your protection and well-being to be of paramount importance. We hope that the relationships between staff and students are strong enough such that if you need to gain help or share information you will be able to talk openly and frankly with one of us.
> Above all we must stress that we are deeply committed to your safety and protection and we are always ready to listen to you.
>
> (RC Child Protection Statement 1993–4)

The project embodies the importance of listening, without preconception or prejudice, to the actual experiences and feelings of these young mothers, thereby meeting their overwhelming need for recognition, which was perhaps partly what led them to become pregnant. It seeks to:

> help them to have more confidence in themselves, to believe in wider horizons, to make constructive choices in their lives, and to develop parenting skills in a supported environment. It is part of a conscious attempt to combat the disadvantage that they and their babies experience.
>
> (RC First Annual Report 1993–4)

Education, guidance and support

The Centre provides all this in a variety of ways. Since everyone must continue in education until they are 16, and it is often not possible to remain in school, Rowan enables young mothers to study and have their babies with them by providing group and individual teaching in a range

149

of subjects including English, Maths, Science, Childcare, Technology and IT. It also prepares them for school and public exams, offers links with FE colleges, career guidance, local work experience and part-time placements. 'A nursery nurse is always available to assist with baby care and help in providing a stimulating, developmental, secure environment for the baby' (quotation from 1997 leaflet).

Staff also support young mothers (and fathers) by maintaining contact with home, school and other agencies, by providing ante-natal care, parenting and life-skills, and with counselling. In addition, they offer practical help and advice about babycare and benefits, grant applications, transport and housing. Emphasis is also placed on sex education aimed at encouraging informed and responsible decisions about contraception, HIV and AIDS. The midwife and health visitor are regularly called upon for practical advice and individual emotional support, whilst the parents of these young mothers are also encouraged to become involved.

The Project Worker runs a weekly Thursday support group for former students of the Rowan Centre and their babies, which offers health education, parenting discussion and also outings such as a four-day residential holiday for the mothers and their babies. The group has also participated in a BBC Schools Radio Programme and the making of a video: *Do You Remember the First Time?* (Rotherham College of Arts and Technology 1995). Careers advice and opportunities to discuss mental health issues are other important aspects covered by the Thursday group.

Crèche facilities provide an essential service not only to the mothers and their babies and toddlers, but also to the pregnant girls, who learn by observing and practising childcare under the skilled supervision of trained staff, as well as the other young mums, all of whom help one another.

Sally is one young mother who has not only benefited herself but has also given much to the Rowan. She was 16 and could not bring herself to speak to anyone in the first year when her baby was born, but she attended the weekly support group. Through a traumatic time when her boyfriend's mother was given care of the baby, Sally depended on the staff for support and guidance at various court hearings. After regaining care of her little daughter, she and the father married and have both managed to be employed despite many job changes. She has continued to come to the Thursday group as a volunteer and is very caring towards the younger girls. Through the Opportunities for Volunteers Programme, the Centre has been able to fund her to do a counselling skills course. Her daughter is an affectionate and secure little personality.

Opportunities to be heard

'Listening in' is a well-developed skill amongst all members of staff, who have ample opportunity to tune in to the girls' conversations which, they feel, are intended to be overheard. In this way, they are able to be extra sensitive to the current problems and preoccupations of an individual or group, without necessarily offering formal counselling. However, in cases of particular need when individual counselling is appropriate, sessions are arranged with the Project Worker, a qualified counsellor, although finding space and time in a busy day is never easy. For Mary, however, counselling was especially important. Mary had a very poor school record and became pregnant as a result of rape; she started at the Centre when she was three months pregnant. She has a caring mother but an unstable family: both her parents are mentally ill and separated. Her toddler is nearly 2 and full of life. Mary will finish her schooling this summer and the outlook for her is difficult to imagine. She seeks affection and has a boyfriend; sadly she is also about to have a second termination of pregnancy.

There is an atmosphere of mutual trust at the Rowan that encourages easy communication between the girls and all members of staff: 'I can talk to staff easily'; 'They really listen to me' (RC Annual Report 1996). Young as they are, these mothers handle responsibility for themselves and their babies with confidence, secure in the knowledge that help is at hand whenever they need it.

Conclusion

On the Rowan's notice-board are the words: 'I wanted to go out and change the world but I couldn't find a baby-sitter.' These young mothers may not succeed in changing the world, but their world has certainly been changed for them. 'Working with hope' is a fundamental principle of the Barnardos organisation and is at the heart of the Rowan Centre's work, breaking a common cycle of deprivation by providing not only childcare but also a very special place for young mothers and their babies.

Centre 33: A young people's counselling and information service

Don't call me an adult
and treat me like a child.
Don't call me a child
and give me the responsibility of an adult.

(Centre 33 (1990))

Background

To be an adolescent today can be bewildering in the extreme. Family and community patterns are in flux; religious and educational institutions are beleaguered; medical and legal practices are changing; technology, the media and advertising wield unprecedented power; and political ideologies seem to have lost their way. Add to this complex scenario the confusions of inhabiting a rapidly changing body eager for sexual activity but ignorant of its consequences; capable of energetic action and apathy alike; tending to mysterious ailments and eating disorders but also to robust health and high spirits; inclined to risk life and limb but also anxious; disposed to contemplate and sometimes to commit suicide. At this difficult time, the steady support of understanding people who can offer unconditional respect, confidential counselling and guidance can be enormously helpful to a young person.

A service for young people

Centre 33 was founded in 1981 to provide an independent, free and confidential service for young people aged 25 and under in the Cambridge area. Since then, it has developed a national reputation based on the comprehensive facilities it offers: information and advice; counselling and group work; contraception and pregnancy testing; housing and outreach services, on a drop-in or appointment basis. The Centre's city-centre location (at 33 Clarendon Street) provides a friendly place where young people feel welcome to call in for practical help or just to talk. The reception area, like the counselling rooms, is comfortably and cheerfully furnished. Tea and coffee are on offer and there are staff on hand to help clients, whatever their needs. Not all are in crisis: a substantial number seek information relating to local leisure and social activities, employment and careers, voluntary work and education/training. A full leaflet database system and an e-mail enquiry and Internet service can be accessed by the Centre's users. Funded substantially by Cambridgeshire County and City Councils, BBC Children in Need and the Cambridge Joint Development Team, Centre 33 has well-established links with other agencies and is a source of information to local clubs and organisations on such issues as housing, education and young carers. The Housing Advocacy Service, a lifeline for many clients, co-operates with Social Services, who train volunteers working at Centre 33 to understand official systems and procedures.

Counselling

Clients come with all sorts of problems and fears. There is no 'typical client'. They are all individuals and have unique ways of handling things. Our job is to respond and listen to them with respect and an open heart.

(Centre 33 1996–7)

The growing inclination of young people to seek counselling is matched by an increase in the range and gravity of the problems they bring.

152

Consequently, more long-term work is being done and the Centre is unusual in being able to offer open-ended counselling, unlike the NHS and most other agencies. All clients, whatever their problems, can see a counsellor for immediate assessment and may be offered further sessions, if needed, placed on a waiting list, or referred for appropriate medical or other help. Parental permission is not a prerequisite for counselling, and self-referral is the norm. Confidentiality is maintained, but issues of sexual and other abuse are always talked through first with the young person, so that they can be reported (in accordance with the Children Act 1989) in a way that is safe and acceptable.

To Susan, counselling offered both comfort and strength over a critical period of her life. Her counsellor describes how:

> she came because she needed to talk about her grief. Her mother had died when she was 8 and her father was terminally ill, when she first came at the age of 17. She had never really grieved for her mother because her family found it very difficult to talk about their emotions. Susan had not been told that her mother was dying and was not involved or told what was happening when her mother actually died. Partly as a result of the lack of communication and explanation in the family, Susan was very, very frightened of losing her father and of her own death. She has coped with this by building a kind of false happy persona which was entirely on the surface. At first, she would spend a lot of each session saying that she was fine and only get to how she really felt about ten minutes before the end of the session. I found it important to listen to both the bit of her that said she was really OK and the deep down bit which said she was definitely not OK.
>
> After some time, Susan was able to articulate some of her deepest fears. The imminent death of her father brought up the death of her mother and, by talking through what had happened, she was able to grieve for her for the first time. She also needed to face the reality of her relationship with her father, which was not an easy one. It felt as though, by talking through the problems in their relationship before he died, it would enable her to grieve for him much more easily after he died so that any anger or negative emotion, as she saw it, was acknowledged and did not block her from dealing with his death.
>
> Susan found it particularly hard to find support amongst her friends. Most of them found they did not know what to say to her: the subject of death was too frightening and too much outside their own experience to be able to listen to her as she needed them to listen. This contributed to Susan's difficulties with saying how she felt. Nobody wanted to hear her. It made her feel very split and

it made it very hard for her to acknowledge the validity of her feelings. It also meant that she found making decisions extremely difficult – which bit of herself should she refer to? At her age, her contemporaries were all leaving home, going off to University and so on but Susan was pulled back home to look after her father. It made her feel different from her peers and she just wanted to be one of the crowd.

Susan's self-esteem improved enormously as she started to see that she was working things out for herself. She eventually left home and set out on her own while her father was still alive, which took a great deal of courage, determination and a real understanding of her responsibilities to herself.

(Counsellor's account in personal correspondence 1998)

Training and project work

Both counsellors and information staff at the Centre, many of whom are volunteers, receive regular and compulsory training based on the issues emerging from their work with young clients, such as homelessness. Regular supervision and routine management meetings are integral parts of the support system for all Centre 33 workers. The staff team, management committee and fund-raising 'Friends' are all highly motivated to meet young people's needs. For example, the issue of young men's low achievement and high suicide rate is the focus of a recent Group Work Project aimed at 13–18 year olds. Judging from feedback, this has encouraged boys to 'let off steam' and to 'have a laugh', as well as convincing them that 'not only women have problems.'

Another recent initiative is the publication of a handbook for parents who are splitting up, entitled *Sarah, James and the Giant Change* (1997). The booklet concludes with fifteen pertinent (but not impertinent) tips for parents who are divorcing or separating, for example: 'Give us a voice – Listen to us – Ask us how we feel.'

Clearly, the young people who come in their hundreds each year to Centre 33 do not feel that the staff there need this advice:

> You can come here when you are confused, addicted, upset or angry and Centre 33 will help you.

> I came to Centre 33 with family problems. They helped me with the things I didn't understand. Thank you Centre 33.
>
> (Centre 33 1996–7)

Conclusion

All five of these voluntary services for children and young people have in common a professional level of insistence upon adequate training and supervision for workers, both voluntary and paid. Each is accountable to a committee or governing body and works within clear guidelines that are regularly monitored and revised. In these days of heightened alarm about sexual and other forms of abuse, and the sometimes perceived conflict between the rights of children and those of parents, working with young people has become a minefield. By being aware of the dangers and difficulties, while maintaining a child-centred commitment, voluntary organisations such as these are exemplary.

The Children's Hours Trust

References

Clarke, A. and Cutler, P. (1997) Listening & Learning, in *Counselling News*, March 1997.
Pinney, R., Carr Gomm, P. and Robinson, M. (1985, revised 1990) *Children's Hours: Special times for listening to children*. London: Children's Hours Trust.

Suggested reading

Pinney, R. (1980) *Creative Listening*. London: Spider Web.
Pinney, R. (1983) *Bobby: Breakthrough of an autistic child*. London: Collins/Harvill. (Also published in the US in 1985 by St Martin's Press.)

Further information

Children's Hours Trust
  Anna Clarke
  The Rectory
  East Marden
  Nr. Chichester
  W. Sussex PO18 9JE
  Tel/Fax: 01243 535227
The Parent Network (Reg. Charity no. 327136, Co. no. 2018523)
  44–46 Caversham Road
  London NW5 2DS.

The Children's Service of a Family and Divorce Centre (CFDC)

References

Cambridge Family and Divorce Centre (CFDC) (1996) *Me and my Family: A special project for children 4–8 years of separated or divorced parents*.

Dasgupta, C. and Richards, M. (1997) Support for children of separating parents: developing practice. *Representing Children* 10: 106–16.

Rogers, C. and Pryor, J. (forthcoming) *Review of Research relating to Children of Separating Parents* (Commissioned by the Joseph Rowntree Foundation).

Suggested reading

For adults

Burrett, J. (1993) *To and Fro Children: A guide to successful parenting after divorce.* London: Thorsons.

De'Ath, E. and Slater, D. (1992) *Parents Threads: Caring for children when couples part.* London: Stepfamily Publications.

Garlick, H. (1997) *The Which Guide to Divorce.* London: Consumer Association/ Hodder.

Jewett, C. (1982) *Helping Children Cope with Separation and Loss.* London: Batsford.

Reibstein, J. and Bamber, R. (1997) *The Family Through Divorce.* London: Thorsons.

Tugendhat, J. (1990) *What Teenagers Can Tell Us about Divorce and Stepfamilies.* London: Bloomsbury.

For children

Danziger, P. (1998) *It's an Aardvark-Eat-Turtle World.* London: Pan Piper. Age: 10–13.

Fine, A. (1987) *Madam Doubtfire.* London: Penguin. Age: 9+.

Fine, A. (1990) *Goggle Eyes.* London: Penguin. Age: 10+.

Fine, A. (1995) *Step by Wicked Step.* London: Penguin.

Grunsell, A. (1989) *Let's Talk about Divorce.* London: Aladdin. (Factual) Age: 8–12.

Grunsell, A. (1990) *Let's talk about Stepfamilies.* London: Aladdin. (Factual) Age: 10+.

Lazo, C.E. (1991) *The Facts about Divorce.* London: Simon & Schuster. (Factual) Age: 10+.

McAffe, A. and Brown, A. (1984) *The Visitors who came to Stay.* London: Hamish Hamilton. Age: 5–8.

Stones, R. and Spooner, N. (1991) *Children Don't Divorce.* London: Dinosaur Publications. (Factual) Age: 7+.

The Children's Service of a branch of Cruse Bereavement Care

Suggested reading

For adults

Couldrick, A. *Grief and Bereavement: Understanding children.* Oxford: Sobell Publications, Churchill Hospital, Oxford OX3 7LJ.

CRUSE Bereavement Care (1993) *Supporting Bereaved Children and Families: A training manual.* Richmond: CRUSE.

Dyregrov, A. (1991) *Grief in Children: A handbook for adults.* London: Jessica Kingsley.

Farrant, A. (1998) *Sibling Bereavement: Helping children cope with loss*. London: Cassell.

Lindsay, B. and Elsegood, J. (eds) (1996) *Working with Children in Grief and Loss*. London: Baillière Tindall.

Pennells, M. and Smith, S. (1995) *The Forgotten Mourners: Guidelines for working with bereaved children*. London: Jessica Kingsley.

Pennells, M. and Smith, S. (1996) *Interventions with Bereaved Children*. London: Jessica Kingsley.

Ward, B. *et al*. (1998) *Good Grief 1: Exploring feelings, loss and death with under 11's* 2nd edition. London: Jessica Kingsley.

Ward, B. *et al*. (1993) *Good Grief 2: Exploring feelings, loss and death with over 11's and adults* 2nd edition. London: Jessica Kingsley.

Worden, J. W. (1996) *Children and Grief: When a parent dies*, New York: Guilford Press.

For children and young children

Abrams, R. (1992) *When Parents Die*. London: Letts.

Bo, A. (1996) *I Must Tell you Something*. London: Bloomsbury.

Bryant-Mole, K. (1998) *What do you think about death?* Hove: Wayland.

Burningham, J. (1988) *Granpa*. London: Puffin.

Couldrick, A. (1991) *When your Mum or Dad has died of Cancer*. Oxford: Sobell Publications.

Crossland, C. (1989) *Someone Special has Died*. 'When something terrible happens.' Available from the Department of Social Work, St Christophers Hospice, 51–9 Lawrie Park Road, London SE26 6DZ.

Grollman, E. (1993) *Straight Talk about Death for Teenagers*. USA: Beacon Press.

Haughton, E. (1995) *Dealing with Death*. Hove: Wayland.

Heegaard, M. (1988) *When Someone Very Special Dies*. Minneapolis, MN: Woodland Press.

Heegaard, M. (1991) *When Someone has a Very Serious Illness*. Minneapolis, MN: Woodland Press.

Heegaard, M. (1991) *When Something Terrible Happens*. Minneapolis, MN: Woodland Press.

Krementz, J (1983). *How it Feels when a Parent Dies*. London: Gollancz.

Little, J. (1985) *Mama's Going to Buy you a Mocking Bird*. London: Puffin.

Mellonie, B. and Ingpen, R. (1997) *Beginnings and Endings With Life Times in Between*. London: Belitha Press.

Nystrom, C. (1995) *What Happens when we Die?* London: Scripture Union.

Perkins, C. and Morris, L. (1991) *Remembering Mum*. London: A+C Black.

Varley, S. (1992) *Badger's Parting Gifts*. London: HarperCollins.

The Rowan Centre

Suggested viewing

Rotherham College of Arts and Technology (1995). *Do You Remember the First Time?: A short video highlighting the experiences and views of teenage mothers*.

Enquiries to:

The Rowan Centre,
Broom Lane Clinic,
Rotherham S60 3NW
(Tel: 01709 703418)

Centre 33

References

Centre 33 (1990) *Annual Report: Cambridge C33.*
Centre 33 (1996–7) *Annual Report: Cambridge C33.*
Emma, Christian and Philip (1997) *Sarah, James and the Giant Change: Advice from experienced young people for parents who are divorcing or separating.* Cambridge C33.

Part IV

LISTENING CREATIVELY

Children cannot achieve integration by themselves. They have no choice but to repress the experience, because the pain caused by their fear, isolation, betrayed expectation of receiving love, helplessness, and feelings of shame and guilt is unbearable.

Thou Shalt Not Be Aware: Society's betrayal of the child
(Alice Miller 1995: 313)

10

'I'M GOING TO DO MAGIC . . .'
SAID TRACEY

Working with children using
person-centred art therapy

Heather Giles and Micky Mendelson

I have confidence in the young, from whom
I have continuously learned

(Rogers 1980: 66)

[Person-centred art therapy (PCAT) is an integration of the use of art, and, in particular, images, with the person-centred counselling approach of Carl Rogers. Heather Giles describes its use in an adolescent unit and Micky Mendelson with a group of infant school children. Eds]

Some years ago I [HG] began to notice that the young people whom I was teaching were most ready to talk about their feelings and problems when together in an art group. This realisation coincided with an advertisement for a person-centred art therapy course, and these combined to set me off on a new and formative journey. What followed was the discovery of a fascinating world in which, through using my own images, I experienced an awareness of the great potential for exploration and change that art therapy offers each individual person.

Person-centred art therapy

The use of art as a form of self-expression for those who are disturbed in any way has been accepted since the Second World War when it was first employed in hospitals and convalescent homes. Since those early beginnings, art therapy, in a more developed way, has established itself as a discipline in its own right – used in prisons, homes for disturbed children and adults and under a wide range of community groups. Parallel to these developments was the concept of person-centred therapy developed in the USA by Carl Rogers during the 1940s and 1950s, which was different to the psychoanalytical approach used in art therapy. Rogers' theory holds centrally that the clients know best, and it is the client who knows how and when to move forward. Mearns and Thorne (1989: 14) consider that 'the counsellor's task is to enable the client to make contact with his own resources rather than to guide, advise or in some way influence the direction the client should take'. More recently, Liesl Silverstone has developed a way of combining the images of art with the person-centred approach developed by Rogers. She suggests in *Art Therapy: The person-centred way* that:

> Through art therapy an integration between the thinking and the knowing mode, between conscious and unconscious material, could take place. I brought the person-centred mode of facilitating to the world of art therapy – allowing the client to know what the picture meant. No interpretation. No guess work.
>
> (Silverstone 1997: 1)

In person-centred art therapy we are primarily concerned with what the content of the image a person creates means for them and how to facilitate an understanding of its message. Producing an image on paper can be a release – a safe and visible way to contain and explore feelings perhaps of fear. Images can liberate a person from the initial restrictive confinement of words. The exploration for meaning through words is the next step. Often images symbolise areas and feelings that are suppressed, and being able to express and reveal these is a step towards self-understanding and often towards health.

Through drawing or capturing a spontaneous image, one is tapping into the right-side of the brain and side-stepping the thinking process of the left brain so dominantly pursued in our culture. Right-side brain wisdom, if trusted, can reveal through creativity the inherent wisdom in us all (Edwards 1986). My own symbolic journey has borne fruit in the client group with whom I now work. Adolescents can often be difficult people with whom to communicate. Individually they can find the therapy situation unbearable and eye contact and verbal explanation difficult. The adult in the therapy situation is perceived as too powerful and the young person's experience is often that of not being listened to but being told. Nevertheless, in my experience over the last six years of working in a regional adolescent psychiatric unit, running a weekly art therapy group combined with the person-centred approach can have surprising results.

The person-centred therapist models Rogers' three pillars of wisdom in order to create a climate in which they believe that growth and change can take place. These are:

1   empathic listening, the key to all attempts to engage a client of any age;

2 non-judgemental acceptance; and
3 congruence (being genuine and real).

Set within the therapist's clear boundaries of time and place, these three elements promote the bedrock of the approach (see Appendix 1). There are great benefits to the group situation as the therapist models these values and, if consistent, and prepared to trust the members, sees the participants developing. On many occasions I have stepped back while one group member has supported and accepted another who is upset. There is nothing like peer support for being heard!

Setting up an art therapy group

The art therapy group usually consists of four to eight young people aged 12–18 years, who are admitted to the unit for a wide range of difficulties including serious mental illness, a variety of eating disorders, severe anxiety, obsessional compulsive disorder, chronic school refusal, abuse and depression. The group is self-selected, which illustrates the person-centred approach, allowing choice and independence. The only exception is the exclusion of those with unstabilised mood, who, because they suffer extreme mood swings, can dominate the group, disturbing other group members in an unhelpful way. Once this condition steadies, they too may join the group.

In structuring a series of sessions that we find run naturally with the school terms, the beginnings and endings have significance. The beginning is important in setting the scene by allowing a clear understanding of what art therapy is, in the context of the person-centred approach. The ending is the time of parting and needs to be thoughtfully prepared, allowing time for tying up loose ends and consolidation of all that may have been achieved – a time too of celebration and farewell.

A 'taster' session for all the young people in the Unit during the week prior to starting formally can be helpful. Working with a co-therapist (who may be any member of the Unit's team) is a necessary luxury, allowing for in-built supervision and time for preparation and debriefing afterwards. We begin with a brief explanation of imaging and of the person-centred approach and give people the opportunity to experience this. The group members are asked to close their eyes and allow an image to come to mind: for example an animal, a tree, or an occasion such as Guy Fawkes Night or Christmas; or perhaps a scene: the riverbank, a garden, a room. Simple materials are available: paper in a variety of colours, crayons, chalks, paint and, at times, clay. In the first session we discuss confidentiality and speaking for oneself and not for others. This encourages taking responsibility for what you say and feel. Emphasising that there is no right or wrong way to draw helps those with fears of putting anything down on paper. We talk about 'having a go', being spontaneous and trusting oneself. There is, inevitably, initial embarrassed sniffing and shuffling as they question my state of mind! Experience has armed me with the confidence that they will soon know what I mean. In my experience there is always someone in the group able to do this, and I know that this will be the oil to loosen the more paralysed members.

The four stages of person-centred art therapy

In using art therapy skills it is important initially to incorporate the three stages: to image; to make this image visible in some way; and to speak to your image, if possible. The fourth stage is to work on the issue in counselling, and at this point the client often stops drawing and the talking proceeds. Art therapy is a creative process; the facilitator learns the skills of reflecting back, making a bridge where relevant, to help the picture give up its message: 'My tree has eyes and is weeping. . . . I often cry like the tree.' The client experiences that 'for the first time in my life I feel that who I am is all I need to be' (Rogers 1980: 190).

Anxious children find any expectation of producing something themselves very difficult, so, initially, offering a theme and then visualising it can be very helpful in allowing them to respond more freely. Art therapy expresses itself largely through symbols and metaphors which have their own relevance regardless of the theme. The 'magic' begins with the words 'I can never get started', 'I'm always wrong'. The particular words give the clue as to how the young person feels, and when those words are repeated back to them, a sudden recognition of their message can occur – the link between thinking and knowing: 'I don't like this picture, it's all wrong'; 'You don't like this picture and it is all wrong?'; 'Yes, the family are all wrong'. The use of facilitating skills and 'reflecting back' enables the young person to 'hear' what they have said and make the connection with their feelings, circumstances or behaviour – thus the movement to change begins.

Meeting the group members

Jane

There is usually someone who sits in front of an empty sheet. This can be significant as an image if their fears of starting can be verbalised. I remember Jane, a depressed young girl known to self-harm, who sat with head in hands in front of an empty white page for six sessions but turned up on time each week. The group supported her and made her welcome and she gradually began to draw boxes chained and barred with herself inside. Finally we saw a bleeding seal on a rock in the middle of a turbulent sea, 'I will die if I stay there yet I am too afraid to move and where will I go?' pleaded Jane. At this point I offered Jane individual art therapy sessions, feeling I could now take the risk to do so. Jane accepted and several sessions later she admitted to being abused. She continued to draw and paint through the horrors of joint police interviews and being taken into care. On the page she faced her past experiences. Her black paintings eventually changed to colour and she finally gave up painting and talked and talked. We had reached the fourth stage of working through the issues.

Working in a group is often the first step in communication and, there-fore, has many advantages. There are always one or two responsive children who will take the risk to make connections out loud. This gives permission to others, more fearful, who may never speak but who may have their feelings validated through others; and this, combined with their images, is an internal process that will inevitably have its effect in its own time. They begin, over the weeks, and in their own time, to speak for themselves.

Sue

Sue, an emaciated 15-year-old girl with an eating disorder, was shaken by her pictures of creatures with voracious mouths and the strength of feeling of her inner conflict. She went on individually to explore the potential of a sand tray in the classic way of play therapy. She would choose from an array of small toys and produce her own world in the sand tray. She felt more in control of solid objects she could move around. This highlights the interface between play therapy and art therapy which can often be used interchangeably, depending upon the individual and perhaps their age. Play therapy is a creative, often non-verbal, spontaneous experience that I believe can be used successfully with adults too.

John

John, a 14 year old, locked in the strange, unfamiliar world of Tourette's Syndrome (a condition of severe and multiple tics and involuntary obscene speech), and unable to communicate other than in a very concrete and often abusive way, was able to show us through his image of being buried in the ground with a cement block bolted on top of him, what it felt like to live with this condition. His peers, who had previously felt cross and dismis-sive of his angry outbursts, had new insight into his experience.

Alice

Alice, a 15-year-old girl with a debilitating eating disorder, found the group too difficult and would draw for fifteen minutes each day in a corner of the schoolroom. Over the months she began to talk more and more, and five years later she is in the art world herself as a book illustrator and restorer.

This has involved a long journey through foundation course, degree and subsequent specialisation.

The acceptance and support of the group at times is moving to watch, and Carl Rogers' person-centred approach is a central factor in empowering and giving permission to the members to explore within a climate of trust. If they can take the risk to reveal the horrors of their inner world, surely I can trust them as a group 'to be treated as doing their best to grow and to preserve themselves given their current internal and external circumstances' (Appendix 1). At times we are confronted by awkward situations – the member who always comes late, the one who tries to distract – but group agreements in the first session create a structure within which the group can tackle these problems, e.g. if you are more than five minutes late do not come into the session. At times they surprise me by their firmness; at other times they make greater allowance – I trust them to decide.

Endings need to be addressed soon after the mid-session point, and the last two sessions marked in a special way. The intensity of the mid-sessions necessitates a gradual move towards a gentle ending – perhaps an exercise in looking ahead (e.g. an image of a crossroads or pathway) or a review of expectations that were discussed in the first session. In the final session, a celebration is called for. This may be linked with an annual celebration of Christmas or spring, or a 'giving of gifts' to each other on paper which is symbolic of the sharing that has taken place in the group over the weeks. A carefully planned ending validates the journey the young person has travelled and the value of self-exploration, and is a preparation for leaving and moving on. It emphasises 'change' as a normal and expected pattern in life.

Outside the group, we are experimenting with other possibilities. One morning each term given over to creative activities is proving successful and may combine art, music and drama. We encourage staff and young people to participate together, as this experience of mutual fun can benefit children who have been deprived of it. It can also broaden their experience of adults as being accessible and supportive.

Working with younger children

Art therapy and play therapy

Working individually with younger children raises the question of where play therapy ends and art therapy begins. Younger children move very easily between concrete objects and drawing. I was well taught by Neil, an 8-year-old boy who attended for individual weekly sessions for over a year. He was locked inside a polite, neat exterior by the anxieties of separating parents, emerging learning difficulties and unrealistic parental expectations. At this stage, with little more than paper, paint, crayons, scissors and glue, he produced tight little pictures and polite responses. Then, as the sessions progressed, Neil began to move around the room, cut out shapes and breathe life into them. With each move forward he would revert to a maze drawing, in which we both got lost. The crayons became soldiers, and the brushes guns, before I produced a bag of assorted objects (baby's bottle, soldiers, animals, monsters, cars) which he seized with relief. Over the months I watched in awe as he moved from tight control, through uncontrollable rage and sadness, slowly incorporating appropriate internal controls, and finally emerged as a chirpy 9 year old better able to address the threatening world. I felt confirmed in the person-centred therapists' creed, which states: 'It is not that this approach gives power to the person, it is that it never takes it away.' When we succeed in freeing a child from inhibitions, depression and denial through the art therapy process, we are rewarded with increasing energy and activity.

'I'm going to do magic . . . ' said Tracey (the story of four young children and their group experience of person-centred art therapy)

Once Upon a Time . . .

. . . there was a deep concern amongst Headteachers of infant schools for a group of children who did not seem to be thriving socially and emotionally or reaching their intellectual potential. These children were very young – between the ages of 4 and 7 – and seemed disquieted, having difficulty in concentrating or absorbing information. Importantly, they did not present any extreme deviant behaviour, although their histories suggested trauma and/or deep loss. So they did not fit into any formal, established support structures. (The process of statementing, for example, was lengthy, addressed extremes, and recommendations were dictated by limited resources.)

As a teacher I [MM] felt helpless and unskilled in enabling these children to grow in self-esteem and discover their natural abilities within the demands of the classroom. Following my own discoveries of the power of images and the messages they carried, when drawing and painting, I trained in person-centred art therapy (PCAT) and began to work with small groups of children in schools.

Through discussion with the Headteachers, I clarified boundaries to maximise trust and safety for the children and myself. This required the same room at the same time every week for one hour, when interruptions were severely discouraged. We agreed to a block of twelve sessions. Confidentiality was thoroughly discussed and clearly defined by myself, in supervision, with the staff and (if the opportunity arose) with parents and, of course, the children. It was agreed that I would share nothing of the details or content of the PCAT sessions with anyone other than my supervisor. I could, however, discuss the process and issues in general terms with parents and named staff.

In working with children it seems a delicate balance to achieve a private space for safe, free expression rather than a secret, collusive experience that burdens and inhibits. I respected the children's ability to choose freely with whom they wished to share their experience of PCAT outside the group. This is an empowering aspect of the process of change and growth. I explained my position that I would need to speak to other people if I thought they were in danger of being hurt.

A great deal of time and thought was spent composing letters to parents and carers (see Appendices 2 and 3). I have never felt that any letter was adequate. Usually the emphasis was on using art expressively to develop confidence, and making myself available at several different times in and outside school hours for any queries, further information or discussion. This process was repeated at the end of every term. No parent ever refused their child PCAT, and one in four responded to the invitation to meet.

. . . there were four children

Jack was the youngest – barely 5 – and quite small for his age. He seemed detached from the hubbub of the classroom and chose to play on his own, rarely speaking to the other children.

Tracey was 7. Her limbs, head and eyes moved involuntarily while she manoeuvred her wheelchair. Her intellectual capacities were known to be far beyond her age.

Lara and Jason were both 6 but from different, parallel, classes. Lara's efforts to please and get everything right were disproportionate to the results. Jason's concentration span was extremely short which meant that he was often wandering about the classroom unable to settle to any one thing.

(For the purpose of this chapter I have changed names, identifying features and as many details as possible to protect the anonymity and confidentiality of the children, their families and schools. Much of the work took place several years ago.)

. . . and into the woods we go

It's the first session. I collect the children from their classrooms. They sit on the carpet of the quiet area (Tracey is in her wheelchair) in a typical infant classroom – sand, water, paints, home corner and much else. I explain: 'I am going to be here every week for one hour. This hour is for you. You can choose whatever you like to play with or make when you come . . . would you like to find out what is in the room or would you like me to show you?'

168

Lara and Jason immediately go to explore. Jason beckons to Tracey to look around. Jack is more diffident. Tracey stays where she is, playing with some large wooden bricks on top of a bookcase. Jason joins her.

The children move from one activity to the other in quick succession, calling to each other. Jason assumes the role of testing out for the group. He begins to paint without an overall. He also discovers the stock cupboard and later begins to splash paint onto Lara. We negotiate and establish 'agreements'. We agree to wear overalls (including me) and not hurt anyone. This becomes an on-going process.

The whole group listens whenever I draw attention to agreements. Lara and Jason spend some time mixing paints and discovering the colours. They look at me sideways to gauge my response. I acknowledge these glances by saying, 'I notice you are looking at me sometimes – maybe you are wondering what is allowed here.' And again with Jack – 'You seem to be watching, Jack.'

These are reflections and observations. They are spoken with deep empathy, genuine positive regard and without judgement, while being totally accepting of the children. I take my cue from their play, actions and words. I make no interpretations or links. The children communicate directly through what they do. This develops their understanding of the world around them, including feelings and relationships. In the group they can safely try out different ways of being. The safety arises from confidence in firm, non-punitively held boundaries. This can lead to the expression of the 'unspeakable' – that which has been taboo – or that which the child has learnt to recognise is unbearable to the adult. In the room there is no collusion to protect the child or the adult.

At the end of the first session I say, 'We just have a little time left today – five minutes.' Jason begins to play with the brown clay. Lara joins him. He turns to her and says, 'Don't do a plop-plop.' They both giggle. I say, 'You laugh when you talk about plop-plop.' Tracey and Jack watch and listen. They also laugh, but cautiously.

During the next two or three sessions, the children continue to explore, challenge and test their physical environment and myself. Tracey begins to throw bricks around the carpeted area. She seems in a world of her own. Occasionally she says an isolated word like 'come' and 'go'. Lara picks the bricks up and puts on a soft voice, saying, 'Tracey, you mustn't do that.' Tracey responds by pretending to be a baby and throwing more bricks. Lara becomes more and more like a mother – she tidies, chides and affectionately pampers. Jack watches and begins to paint. His face is set in a frown. He paints a baby giraffe behind black bars. He says, 'The baby wants to get out', but he doesn't want to speak. He is still watching the others.

In PCAT, the image or action reflects an aspect of the self, whether it be in the past, present or future. Young children may not need to verbalise, as the act of doing and expressing is a process of internal communication as well as one of emotional relief.

Jason makes several things during these sessions, all of which he breaks, squashes or tears. On several occasions, he has pulled everything down in the home corner. It is not until the fifth session that he is able to speak directly to me. He tells me of a family trip while he is building a train track, then he breaks it up. I say, 'You've broken up the track.' 'I break all my toys at home.' He has made his own link between a family trip and the breaking of the track. I say, 'You break all your toys at home and you broke up the track.' He laughs. I reflect this also, thus acknowledging his pleasure and confusion at what is happening at home.

Lost in the woods and finding the clues . . .

Issues are beginning to crystallise. Jason seems to be more frenetic. His attendance at school is erratic and he misses a few sessions. He refers constantly to defecating, either verbally or through his play in the clay, sand and water. He also begins to attack Tracey verbally, while Lara's attempts at making order become more exaggerated. She tidies, cleans, organises, comforts and looks to me to make some sense of the 'mess'.

Tracey reverts to being a baby by sucking on a bottle and speaking in a baby voice. She says, 'Lacy-Tracey. She doesn't seem to know when she will bump into things.' Later she comes up to me after more taunts from Jason calling her a 'baby', which she has fended off by spitting 'I hate this, one day I will be the one that wins.' With determination and conviction she outlines her plans to be a lawyer, based on her manifest intellectual abilities.

Jack looks on. He plays, saying little, but over the weeks the frown has deepened.

Lara becomes engrossed by the theme of marriage. She creates a king and princess out of the puppets and has them getting married. She asks me to take care of them. 'You would like me to take care of the married King and princess?' Lara's parents are separated. She is struggling to make sense of this now that one of them is remarrying. Lara repeats this play with another marrying couple, again asking me to take care of them. 'You want me to take care of these two who are getting married?' 'Can you?' she asks. I reply 'Do you think I can?' She does not give me the couple. She rolls around all over the room with Jason. Is this relief? Can she also now begin not to 'take care'?

The sessions are active and dynamic. Each one is repeating known, tried and tested modes of being. PCAT in a group setting is an opportunity to make changes as a realisation grows that the familiar may not be effective or growth enhancing.

At the end of the eighth session, Tracey begins to laugh uncontrollably while throwing bricks. Jason runs around and around, pushing everything over, while Jack looks on, seemingly withdrawing into an imaginary shell.

Lara tries to mollify Tracey but, seeing that this doesn't have any effect, gets drawn to Jack. Tracey shouts, 'You are such a baby, Jack.' Jack's face turns very red and his eyes gleam. I reflect, 'Tracey, you are shouting at Jack because you think he is a baby and you say you don't like anyone to shout or make you feel small.' Tracey glares at me. This is a wider reflection of feelings expressed in earlier sessions. The session ends.

The following week, Jack refuses to come to the session. He comes to tell me that he doesn't like Tracey. Tracey hears what he says. She grins broadly. On the tenth session, Jack decides to return. Tracey calls him a baby and laughs at him for not coming the week before. Jack's colour rises. He suddenly says to Tracey, 'You can't walk.' Tracey begins to rock her wheelchair from side to side. 'I can walk, I can walk.' Jack repeats several times, 'You can't walk.' The unspeakable has been spoken. I say, 'Tracey has been laughing at Jack for not coming last week and Jack is saying to Tracey that she can't walk, and you are both shouting at each other.' Tracey shouts, 'I just can't walk like everyone else.' Jack keeps saying, 'You can't walk and I'm not a baby.'

Lara has been playing in the sand with her back to Tracey and Jack. She says, 'I think Tracey can't walk and Jack is the baby here. He's only five and little.' Tracey sinks in the chair. Jack gets up and walks to the pile of boxes and junk. I say, 'Jack, you are the youngest and smallest and you don't like being called a "baby". You can do things that babies can't do, like decide not to come one week because you didn't like how Tracey was to you. Tracey, you can't get around by walking, and you also don't like being called a baby. You can do things that babies don't do, like make up rhymes and decide what you can do, like be a lawyer.'

Lara begins to sing a little song under her breath and pushes play-people deep into the sand. Jason rolls on a bean bag. It feels calm in the room.

. . . and in the end . . .

. . . there are two sessions left. The children know there are twelve sessions from the start. Every week I tell them how many more are left. They know that when Christmas comes we have our last session. This is still difficult for them to understand. By missing sessions, Jason doesn't seem to have a sense of belonging in the group. Jack is talking more. Lara sometimes dances in the room. She doesn't stop anyone from making a mess, and on one or two occasions joins Jason when he mixes the clay with paint and water while talking about 'poos'.

They choose to spend part of the last session walking in the garden. Tracey thinks of the idea. Jason, Lara and Jack run around, calling to each other, making discoveries. Tracey holds my hand and cries a little. In the group process she seems to hold the sad feelings for the others. Back in the room, Jason runs around, pulling things down as quickly as he can.

This seems to be his way of saying goodbye. Lara tries to tidy everything up. Jack is very quiet.

Outside the group, the teachers and I notice significant changes in the children. They are subjective and difficult to evaluate. Tracey says during one of the sessions. 'I'm going to do magic – I will win one day.' All the children display a natural determination to grow and survive. Jack has become assertive and determined in the classroom. Lara's intellectual abilities begin to develop noticeably. Her teacher reports that she no longer offers to help so frequently. Jason's concentration is still very limited. The PCAT sessions may have allowed him to express his feelings without a resolution. He has, however, communicated a great deal about his circumstances at home and how he is affected by them. The Headteacher and staff pursue further support for him. Tracey continues to excel intellectually. She has begun to explain to others how and why she cannot walk.

Conclusion

The experience of working with PCAT for several years has convinced us that, by listening and using facilitative skills in art therapy, we may be privileged to see with the eyes of a child – to visit their worlds of fantasy, hopes, dreams and fears. For each of us – child and adult – journeys of the mind can begin and continue through the fascinating and often mysterious world of recorded images, which unlock our self-understanding and foster our sense of identity (Kramer 1971).

References

Edwards, B. (1986) *Drawing on the Right Side of the Brain*. London: Fontana.
Kramer, E. (1971) *Art as Therapy with Children*. New York: Schocken Books.
Mearns, D. and Thorne, B. (1989) *Person-Centred Counselling in Action*. London: Sage.
Miller, A. (1995) *Thou Shalt Not be Aware: Society's betrayal of the child*. London: Pluto Press.
Rogers, C. R. (1980) *A Way of Being*. Boston: Houghton Mifflin.
Silverstone, L. (1997) *Art Therapy: The person-centred way*. 2nd ed. London: Jessica Kingsley.

Further reading

Axline, V. M. (1989) *Play Therapy*. Edinburgh: Churchill Livingstone.
Axline, V. M. (1990) *Dibs: In Search of Self*. London: Penguin.
Judd, D. (1989) *Give Sorrow Words: Working with a dying child*. London: Free Association Books.
Rogers, C. R. (1961) *On Becoming a Person*. London: Constable.
Rogers, C. R. (1986) *Freedom to Learn for the Eighties*. Colombus, Ohio: Charles Merrill.
Rogers, C. R. (1989) *Carl Rogers on Personal Power*. London: Constable.

Sinason, V. (1991) Interpretations that feel horrible to make and a theoretical unicorn. *Journal of Child Psychotherapy* 17 (1): 11–23
Wadeson, H. (1995) *The Dynamics of Art Psychotherapy*. Chichester: John Wiley.
Winnicott, D.W. (1971) *Playing and Reality*. London: Tavistock.
Yalom, I.D. (1970) *The Theory and Practice of Group Psychotherapy*. New York: Basic Books.

Appendix 1: The Person-Centred Counsellor's Creed

The person-centred counsellor believes:

that every individual has the internal resources for growth;

that when a counsellor offers the core conditions of congruence, unconditional positive regard and empathy, therapeutic movement will take place;

that human nature is essentially constructive;

that human nature is essentially social;

that self-regard is a basic human need;

that persons are motivated to seek the truth;

that perceptions determine experience and behaviour;

that the individual should be the primary reference point in any helping activity;

that individuals should be related to as whole persons who are in the process of becoming;

that persons should be treated as doing their best to grow and to preserve themselves given their current internal and external circumstances;

that it is important to reject the pursuit of authority or control over others and to seek to share power.

(Mearns and Thorne 1989: 18)

Appendix 2: Sample letter to parents

Sample letter A

Dear (Parent's or Carer's name/s)

From September 19— the school is starting a small Person-Centred Art Therapy group.

The group will be run by myself, whom the children know as a support teacher, for an hour a week for twelve weeks. I am trained in Person-Centred Art Therapy which allows for expression using paints, clay, sand, toys and water without making any judgements or interpretations.

The aim of the group is to allow the children to gain confidence in school and to realise their potential.

I would like to offer (name of child) a place in the group. Please could you give your permission in writing for (name of child) to attend the group on the form below.

I would be happy to meet with you to answer any queries you may have and discuss the group in more detail. I will be available on (date) from 8.30am to 10.30am and on (date) from 6.30pm to 8.00pm. Please contact the school to make an appointment. If these times are not convenient, other arrangements can be made.

I look forward to meeting you.

Signed by Practitioner and Headteacher

....

I give/do not give permission for my child to attend the Person-Centred Art Therapy group starting in September.

Name of Child: ....

Name of Parent/s or Carer/s: ....

Signed: .... Date: ....

Please return by: ....

Appendix 3: Sample letter to parents

Sample letter B

Dear (Parent's/Carer's name/s)

Since September I have been meeting with (name of child) in the Person-Centred Art Therapy group. The sessions are now coming to a close on (date).

I would be happy to meet with you if you wish to talk about (name of child) or discuss issues that may have arisen. I will be available from 8.30am to 10.00am on (date) and from 6.00pm to 7.30pm on (date). If these times are not convenient, other arrangements can be made.

Please contact the school to make an appointment.

I look forward to meeting you.

Yours sincerely,

Signed by Practitioner and Headteacher

....

11

LISTENING TO CHILDREN
THROUGH PLAY

Carol Dasgupta

Nuts and bolts

As a therapist, it is not enough to attend only to the words a child might use to describe their emotional responses to life; indeed, most young children do not yet have the appropriate vocabulary or verbal sophistication to be able to describe their world adequately. As with adults, a child's body language and relationship style will provide important and revealing clues and information. But by providing children with the opportunity to play, and by observing and interpreting their play, we can add another dimension to our understanding of what it is to listen to children.

As a play therapist in private practice, I work with children from the age of about 3 until that time when they no longer wish to express themselves through play, generally about the age of 10 or 11. The length of therapy varies, but unless I am trying to help with a very specific, well-defined problem, I would expect to work with a child on an open-ended basis, with sessions continuing for anything between a few months to several years. The sessions last fifty minutes and take place in the same room at the same time each week. I mention only two boundaries at the beginning of the work: neither of us is allowed to hurt the other, and neither of us is allowed intentionally to break or smash up the toys or equipment in the room. A child may, on occasion, decide to end a session before the fifty-minute limit, but I would usually make a verbal recognition of this. The room is equipped with standard play therapy equipment: a doll's house with dolls and furniture, a play house or corner with tables, chairs, pots, pans, cutlery, crockery, etc., puppets, toy animals, cars, dolls, paints, paper, pencils, hammer and peg set, two toy telephones, two sets of toy soldiers and army equipment, nursing bottles, bricks, Lego-type construction toys and a sand tray.

Referrals come through GPs, health visitors, social services, schools and parents. After the initial contact (usually by telephone), I generally arrange a consultation with one or preferably both parents before meeting the child. This enables me both to take a history of the child and to get a sense of how the parent(s) define or present their child. A child's difficulties can sometimes be the outward manifestation of a marital conflict or other parental issue, in which case some other intervention (such as family or couples therapy) might be more helpful. I would then arrange to have two meetings with the child alone, during which the following kinds of questions will be hovering in my mind:

• What kind of relationship style does this child come with?
• Does it seem likely that a therapeutic relationship will be possible?
• Does this child want to come here enough, or is it predominantly the parental need that is being satisfied?

These preliminary sessions would typically be somewhat more directive than ongoing therapy sessions, and I might engage a child in specific tasks such as drawing a picture of a person, or drawing everyone in their family doing something. I often use Winnicott's 'squiggle game' at this point. This game, in which therapist and child take it in turns to make a simple line-drawing and invite the other to turn it into something, can help to establish a therapeutic relationship in which play can occur. It is also used as a projective tool – what does the child make the squiggle into? After these two assessment sessions, I meet with the parent(s) again. If there is agreement on both sides that play therapy may be helpful, I spend some time explaining the nature of the work, the fact that the content of sessions will be confidential (apart from any statutory obligations), and practical arrangements such as appointment times, payments, cancellations and holidays. It is my belief that therapy will be more helpful if such management issues have been discussed and agreed upon before the work commences. When working with children in a private practice, it is probably important to make some arrangement to meet with the parent(s) at regular intervals (maybe every four to six weeks) to discuss the therapy in general terms and within the bounds of confidentiality. These meetings help to 'hold' the parent(s) who may be experiencing feelings of anxiety, guilt, envy and ambivalence. (In a clinic setting, other workers can often provide this support for parents.) If, for whatever reason, it is decided not to proceed with therapy, I think it is important to encourage parent(s) to think about the reasons behind this and help them with a referral to another source of support if appropriate.

So the therapy starts. I am non-directive, waiting to observe, then follow and respond to, a child's play. In this, I am adhering not only to the principles behind Axline's (1996, 1969) theory of non-directive play therapy, but also to the basic tenets of psychodynamic therapy and counselling. As the sessions unfold, I try to be aware of the transference and countertransference issues around – who is the child making me into? What is it in their internal or external world that is making them behave with me in their particular manner? What feelings is this child arousing in me that cannot be explained obviously or rationally? In order for these kinds of questions to be relevant and helpful, I have, of course, to be as consistent as possible in my behaviour and attitudes, aware of my personal strengths and weaknesses, and careful not to become too drawn into a child's world, although the temptation or desire to be so may be very strong. I believe the urge in adults to 'make things better' for children, to help them, and rescue them from pain is strong, but that has to be resisted here. The ability to stay with hurt, suffering and sadness is essential. It is the consistent offering of time, space, holding and attention that is helpful, rather than the premature offer of the release from pain, sadness or anger. This is sometimes terribly hard. I worked with one child over a period of several years. The individual sessions and the overall treatment were intense, and involved close attention to sad, painful, probably unresolvable issues. Session followed session; I wrote my notes, discussed the case with my supervisor, and generally proceeded in a professional manner. Very shortly after therapy ended, however, I found myself crying unexpectedly and uncontrollably. I believe I had managed to 'hold' the terrible pain and sadness during my professional involvement, only allowing myself to feel the sheer misery after therapy had finished. This emphasises the importance of adequate, ongoing supervision and support when working therapeutically with children. I make interpretations, always expressing them directly to the child through the toys being played with or through the relationship between the child and me. I try to establish a warm, positive relationship (but not cloyingly or smotheringly affectionate) with the child as quickly as possible.

What is play?

Definitions of 'play' are complex and varied. Erikson (1950) attributed great importance to play as a means of enabling a child to build up a sense of self-awareness and self-knowledge. Schaefer and O'Connor (1983) provide a useful review of the literature on play and identify certain aspects of it. Play is driven by pleasure and fun, rather than purpose or function, and it does not occur in new or frightening situations. A child's attention becomes increasingly focused on the action or fantasy and less on his or her own body state or situation. It is the unconscious aspect of a child's play that has induced therapists and counsellors to use play in their work. In the child-centred and psychodynamic models of working with children, play provides a communication function – the 'play cure' being somewhat analagous to Freud's 'talking cure'. Play provides not only the means to communicate, but also the possibility of a relationship developing between child and counsellor, so that in the therapeutic context, the potential space between therapist and child may be provided through play. Donald Winnicott (1971) emphasises the importance of seeing play as therapeutic in its own right, as a creative experience, and as a basic component of a child's growth process.

A brief history of play therapy

Although Freud (1909) attempted psychotherapy with a child (conducted indirectly through the child's father), the first direct use of play in the therapy of children was undertaken in 1919 by a Viennese psychoanalyst, Hug-Hellmuth, who considered it to be an essential part of child analysis. Subsequently, both Anna Freud and Melanie Klein incorporated play into their otherwise traditional psychoanalytic sessions. Anna Freud used play as a way of encouraging children into analysis, by enabling the formation of the therapeutic alliance, or strong positive relationship between child and therapist. Klein (1961) believed that play was the child's natural medium of expression, and therefore a direct substitute for verbalisation. A child's verbal skills were, she thought, insufficiently developed to express the complicated thoughts and feelings they were experiencing, and she was of the opinion that any child, from the normal to the most disturbed, could benefit from 'play analysis'.

Winnicott (1971) developed further ideas on the therapeutic use of play with children. A leading exponent of the developing object relations school, his ideas concentrated on the individual's very early relationships, typically with the mother. He saw the therapist/child relationship as echoing the earlier mother/child relationship, and he hoped the therapeutic relationship would be able to repair what was lacking, or wrong, in the earlier one. He argued that therapeutic work could occur in the space and relationship that develops when two people can play with each other:

> Psychotherapy takes place in the overlap of two areas of playing, that of the patient and that of the therapist. Psychotherapy has to do with two people playing together. The corollary of this is that where playing is not possible then the work done by the therapist is directed towards bringing the patient from a state of not being able to play into a state of being able to play.
>
> Winnicott (1971: 44)

Winnicott argued that playing is essential, as it is in playing that we are being creative, and it is only in being creative that we discover ourselves. To be really creative, a person needs an experience of a non-purposive or relaxed state, and relaxation is possible if 'the child patient among the toys on the floor be allowed to communicate a succession of ideas, thoughts, impulses, sensations that are not linked except in some way that is neurological or psychological and perhaps beyond detection'. There must be 'room for the idea of unrelated thought sequences which the analyst will do well to accept as such, not assuming the existence of a significant thread' (Winnicott 1971: 65).

Margaret Lowenfeld (1979), also a paediatrician by training, recognised the significance of children's play, and the importance of non-verbal forms of thought and communication. In the 1920s she developed the World Technique, in which children used a sand tray to make 'worlds' with small real-life and fantasy objects. This allowed for the exploration of a child's inner world, and the nature of the child's relationship to a particular social or environmental reality.

Virginia Axline's model of play therapy

Virginia Axline's (1969) model of client-centred, non-directive play therapy was made widely accessible through the moving description of her work in awakening the mute child, Dibs. Non-directive play therapy allows the child to be him or herself without facing evaluation or pressure to change. The child is the source of his or her own growth and therapeutic change: 'the therapist may leave responsibility and direction to the child' (Axline 1969: 9). During non-directive play therapy, a child can experience growth under the most favourable conditions: by playing out feelings, the child faces them, learns to control them or abandons them. The child 'begins to realize the power within himself to be an individual in his own right, to think for himself, to make his own decisions, to become psychologically more mature, and, by so doing, to realize selfhood' (Axline 1969: 16). Children will experience being accepted as they are and will be given the empathic understanding, warmth and security they are unlikely to experience in other relationships.

The role of the play therapist is to facilitate this growth, using an approach in which Axline identifies eight basic principles through which the therapist:

1 develops a warm, friendly relationship with a child, in which a good rapport is established as soon as possible;
2 accepts a child exactly as he or she is, in as non-judgemental a manner as possible;
3 establishes a feeling of permissiveness in the relationship so that a child feels free to express his or her feelings completely;
4 is alert to recognise the feelings a child is expressing and reflects back those feelings in order to help that child to gain insight into his or her own behaviour;
5 maintains a deep respect for a child's ability to solve his or her own problems if given an opportunity. The responsibility to make choices and to institute change is the individual child's;

6   does not attempt to direct a child's actions or conversation in any manner. The child leads the way. The therapist follows;

7   does not attempt to hurry the therapy along. It is a gradual process and is recognised as such by the therapist;

8   needs to find ways (such as time limitation, or the establishment of commonsensical boundaries) to anchor the therapy to the world of reality.

Case material

(All identifying features have been changed or omitted.)

I worked once a week for seven months with Philip, a boy of 6 years. He was referred to me by his GP because teachers, health visitors and social workers were concerned about his out-of-control behaviour at school and in the neighbourhood. There was also concern over his mother's parenting skills. Philip's mother and father had separated shortly after his younger sister's birth four years earlier, after a stormy relationship, and contact between Philip and his father was minimal. (In fact, Philip's father died suddenly and violently during the course of our therapy.) Both children were frequently found roaming the neighbourhood on their own, engaging in aggressive and threatening behaviour; they were badly clothed and often hungry. Philip in particular was felt to be in need of help: he appeared to have no sense of his personal safety, and he was already so disruptive and out of control at school that it was hard to contain him there. The therapy was to be jointly funded by social services and the health authority for twenty-two sessions. Some family therapy was set up at another agency, and Philip's mother was offered counselling to assist her to regain some measure of control over herself and her family. Early on in the course of Philip's treatment, it became clear that his mother had a serious drug addiction. Within a few months, her condition deteriorated so badly that she was unable to care for the family, and Philip and his sister were placed in foster care. Philip continued to attend his therapy sessions with me. Extracts from my ongoing notes are denoted by quotation marks.

1st session

Philip demonstrates an ease and independence in the playroom and in his relations with me – there is both a comfortable interaction with me, as well as an ability to play independently. He places his hand gently on my knee at one point, suggesting a need for some physical relationship. I noticed in this first session a wide variation in his moods – he ranges from a soft gentleness to expressions of intense anger.

2nd session

Philip arrives happily and goes immediately into the playhouse, which he calls 'my house'. He tells me I can do whatever I like in the sessions (an echo of my words to him last week), and it feels to me that he has taken charge of me and the sessions. In the house he cleans up the floor with the dustpan and brush, and he says he is going to do things his Mum doesn't allow. The session continues with some sand play and drawing. Philip plays with some puppets and makes the owl bang so hard on the walls of the playhouse that I have to remind him of our boundaries in the playroom. He buries another puppet in the sand, pours water around him, unburies him and announces that the puppet is messy. He washes the puppet, then hurls him onto the floor of the playhouse. At this point, I tell him that there are five minutes left until the end of the session. Philip shouts 'I'm not leaving', then starts just smashing and throwing the contents of the playhouse, and pushes the walls over. He goes berserk, and seems really amazed that I am not stopping him. He is furious about leaving. I am left feeling exhausted and drained by the session, and also fed up, because it takes me so long to get the room ready again. But I am aware that I am already drawn to this child, and feel a strong commitment to him. I think I have begun to understand him, and am reminded that Freud wrote in *'Little Hans'* that no moment of time was so favourable for the understanding of a case as its initial stage. Philip is concerned about the mess in his life, and indicates ambiguous feelings about clearing it up. He has, I think, already indicated a wish for attention and a maternal relationship, and is possessed by an anger when that attention is threatened (as it was at the end of the session). The strength of his wish for attention and relationship is suggested by the quickly established level of my commitment to, and strong maternal feelings for, him and by my feeling of being so drained by the intensity of the session.

3rd session

'Philip makes a terrible mess (of sand, water, and paint) . . . he was aware of the mess he was making, and couldn't quite believe he was getting away with it.' He hurls the playhouse furniture around, 'systematically destroying what he had previously been so pleased to call "my house"'. Almost immediately afterwards, he picks up the feeding bottle, sits on my lap and sucks it with gusto. 'He says he's a baby, and I say that it seems he's a very hungry baby. He repeats this – "I'm a very hungry baby" – several times.' It feels to me that he is quite intensely in touch with his need for mothering here, and angry, also, with his lack of it. 'As we leave the room at the end of the session, he leaves the tap full on, and I let him do this, and he puts his hand marks all over the wall. Philip seems to me to be extremely needy, greedy for attention. He is *very* angry and hurt and shows signs of regression – the mess and the bottle. I am left exhausted, overwhelmed. It is an intense experience.

4th session

Again, Philip's chief activity is the smashing around of the playhouse and its contents, alongside periods of lying in my lap, drinking from the feeding bottle.

5th session

Aware of my growing frustration at the length of time it takes to clear up after his sessions, I tell Philip that when he makes a mess, it has to be within the sink and draining board area of the room. He can make as much mess as he likes there. He continues to want to be in my lap, being fed water through the bottle.

6th session

(Earlier in the week, Philip was told that his father had died.) Philip plays in the sand, and asks me to join in the play. He wants to add lots of water to the already wet sand. I set a limit of two bowls. He gets another bowl to put in the sand, and prepares to put it in. I remind him of the limits, so he puts the bowl on the chair, and says it's to wash his hands in. Although he tries to stick to the limits as laid down last week and this week, the playroom is amazingly messy – there is sand all over the floor, on the walls, clothes buried in the sand, paint on the floor, in the sink, on the walls. It feels to me that he is showing me the whole mess in his life, and I reflect this by saying what a big mess he is showing me today. He shows me a hurt on his finger, covered by a plaster. He wonders if the hurt will be too much for me. I ask him if he thinks it will be too much for me, and he thinks it will. I feel it is important for me to tell him that I don't mind seeing things that are painful (for I think that was his concern – that I just would not be able to stand his pain). We play in the house. Philip climbs in and out over the top, which alarms me. We discuss how I should get in the house – he says I must climb in through the window, because all the doors are broken – his Dad has broken them all. He gets a doll and asks me if I like it. At this moment, I am uncertain how to respond, and I hesitate, and before I reply, he hurls the doll angrily onto the floor (I suspect he was wanting me to tell him how much I liked the doll [him]). Here, I was left feeling intensely inadequate, as if I could do nothing but fail him, however I responded. Again, I think that here I am reacting to his enormous, insatiable need for care, attention and love. He finds the toy stethoscope. I explain how delicate it is, and we take turns listening to each other's hearts, very gently, as well as the hearts of the toys to see if they're alive. He plays with a soft bee toy, then gets out the emergency vehicles (police car, fire-engine, ambulance: typically used by children when acting out concerns about traumas, safety, rescue). He puts no people in the emergency vehicles, but takes the vehicles to the scene of a bad accident. This seems to be a fire, and the vehicles enter the house. I suspected that he was playing out fantasies to do with his father's death and the fact that it seemed that no one could ultimately help him, and I responded by saying that sometimes the help that people can give is just not enough. At this point, it is time to warn about the end of the session. Philip becomes very angry about this, throws the vehicles around, with the intention of breaking them, and the session ends chaotically and violently, with me removing him physically from the room. My notes end: 'Philip seems a very frightened, sad, defended, vulnerable little boy.'

7th session

Philip makes a dreadful mess, with toys all over the playroom. He plays with playdough, mixes it up with paints, so it's all brown. He asks me what it reminds me of. I pick up the hint, and tell him it reminds me of poo. He looks relieved, as if he can now *really* enjoy it. He tells me that his mother never let him make a mess at home, and how he used to do poos all over her floor. I don't know whether this is real or fantasy, but it *is* real that he is talking about how far his mother could tolerate mess.

8th session

(After two-week gap) Constant testing of boundaries. Anger at end of session.

9th session

Testing of boundaries. Sits on my lap to drink from feeding bottle. At one point asks me how long it is till end of session. When I reply ten minutes, he responds by saying it's ten years – 'it feels as if he is aware of how much he needs'. He is agitated and angry at the end of the session, and he pushes the session beyond its time limit. I recognise that I seem to allow myself to get forced into inconsistent behaviour with Philip. 'I find I'm letting him get away with extending the period far too much.'

10th session

Philip seems stronger today. He removes furniture gently from the house, cleans and replaces it. Feeds himself from feeding bottle – says he's very big and strong.

11th session

Mess again. Hard for him to accept end of session, but no physical anger.

12th session

Philip expresses his desire to make a mess with sand, water, paint. I remind him of the limits involved with this – the mess has to be kept in one area, but it can be as messy as he likes there. He *does* make a terrible mess, but it is contained. Hard for him to end session. I make an interpretation now: I tell him that I've noticed how angry he gets when I tell him that a session is ending, and that maybe he wants to have me all the time, and is frightened that when a session ends, we might never have another one. He looks at me and listens, says nothing, but I feel he is grateful that at least I am *trying*.

13th session

Philip says he's very angry as he comes into the room, and he throws furniture out of the playhouse violently. He tests me on my boundaries incessantly, and I feel cruel as I maintain them. I remind him about the Christmas break (three weeks), and he tells me he'll be glad not to see me for three weeks. But he is furious at the end of the session and throws things around.

14th session

(After three-week break) A quiet session, which he starts off by telling me he wants to marry me. But terrible anger at end of session – smashes Lego and throws things.

15th session

Spends session making a globby mess with sand and water in a plastic bowl, which looks like faeces. He seems to be trying hard to contain his mess and (anger). It feels a bit as if he is frightened of his mess bursting out all over.

16th session

(Gap of one week – Philip is ill) Philip seems to be indicating that he wants lots of help. We spend much time in the playhouse, but several times he 'collapses' outside the house, and asks me to carry him in. He tells me I'm his mother. He fills sink with water, and spends about ten minutes

184

slurping up/sucking water through the plastic piping. 'He makes loud panting/heaving/slurping sounds, and I'm left feeling very elemental – as if, somehow, I'm feeding him, allowing him to be nourished. He blows down the piping, it sounds like farting and he likes it. It feels very intense, elemental play. Philip tries to prolong the session by asking incessantly and in a hard-to-refuse way to play with one last thing. It's difficult to get him out of the room, and I think I just don't know how to get him out without destroying him. He feels *very* needy/greedy, and I'm aware that he is expressing his anger at not getting enough.'

17th session

Philip pours water onto the floor – more than I can reasonably be asked to allow. Then he starts to fill the wooden baby bed with water, says he wants it to overflow, so I say we can only do that over the sink (*always* trying to maintain boundaries with him). He spends much time filling the bed with water, and it upsets, so there is a mess, anyway! and I am not really surprised. I think to myself that he is indicating his great, over-whelming need for lots of attention and love. 'As always, an exhausting session – he is loving and terrible; wants to be nursed, then wants to smash things; always pushing to the limit.'

18th session

I am about two minutes late, and Philip is waiting for me – looking angry. He tries to shut me out of the room. He plays at the sink, but makes me sit on a chair at the other side of the room. I am being punished for my tardiness. He fills the sink with water, saying he wants to have just a little flood. Here, he seems to be expressing the continual dynamic between us – he has enormous, 'flooding' needs that might result in awful mess, but he also wants to please me, keep me happy, not frighten me away. This feels so difficult, perilous even, walking a tightrope between us drowning in an endless flood of water or mess, and me being judgemental, restricting, unaccepting. As it is, we settle for a rather unsteady, but just about main-tainable, limit of water in the basin – just lapping over the top, but not a deluge. During this session, Philip makes probably the worst mess ever – paint, water, paper, sand, paper towels all churned up together, then smeared over his T-shirt. Terrible anger at end of session.

19th session

Again, Philip tries to shut me out of the room. I tell him we have four more sessions before we end. Philip denies this – says we have eighty-eight more sessions. I remind him that we have four more sessions, to which he replies that he has another friend called Carol, who looks just like me. I say that it sounds as if he is going to miss me, and that maybe he is going to feel very sad about our sessions ending. He plays in sand, in a way that feels very angry. When I tell him that I sense that he is angry, he tells me that he *is* angry. We talk about some of our previous sessions. He asks me to feed him from the bottle. Anger at the end of session.

20th session

I mention ending of sessions, and sense that Philip is in a rage about that. This session is characterised by a pretty systematic destruction of the room during the last ten minutes – almost everything movable is tipped out, thrown about, messed up. I make an interpretation: this anger is to do with the hurt he is feeling at the prospect of losing his time with me. I am angry as I tidy up the room – it takes me about thirty minutes. I know that I don't want to be angry during our last two sessions. I am aware of wanting the sessions to end well, so that Philip can leave the relationship without destroying it (I very nearly had to end this session) or me. I determine to define the boundaries again, at the beginning of the next two (last) sessions.

21st session

I start the session by reminding Philip of the two boundaries. He immediately upset the toy dresser in the playhouse, but then we played that it was due to a burglary. We talk about our last session next week, and I tell him that he can choose what we do. He asks if we can have a cake – just for us two. We play we are married and take turns sleeping and working. Then, a theme of being equal develops – we have the same number of toy cars, we do the same things in the sand. At five minutes before the end, I ask him if he wants to end the session himself. He says he does, and does actually manage to decide when to leave the room, having walked to the sink to wash his hands. He walks out of the room confidently, having kissed me first.

22nd (last) session

Philip talks about the cake as we walk to the room, and it feels tense until he sees there is actually a cake. He is delighted, grinning from ear to ear. He wants to eat it straight away, and I think he may devour it, totally, on the spot. He cuts two pieces – a large piece for him, a small one for me. He eats cake ravenously, and I tell him that it is *his* cake, and he doesn't need to have it all now. We play in the playhouse, and he starts a game with me whereby he climbs over the wall, then hangs, upside down, as if falling, and asks me to save him. I catch him, lower him to the floor, and tell him I've 'saved' him. We repeat this three times, and I tell him that it must feel good to be 'saved', and that if he played the game again, there would be other people to play the saving game with him. We play with water in the sink, testing which things float and sink. No flooding today – Philip seems to be withdrawing from our intense relationship. I sense that he wants to say goodbye calmly. At the five-minute warning, he sits on my lap, and we hug each other. I tell him I shall miss our sessions, and he says he will, as well. We calmly leave the tidy room.

I think this fairly short-term work helped Philip to feel that his 'mess' had been listened to, and was containable and acceptable, and this acceptance facilitated some ego development. Longer-term therapy would have to wait until Philip's circumstances settled down – a situation not uncommonly encountered, and of necessity tolerated, by play therapists.

References

Axline, V. (1966) *Dibs: In search of self.* London: Victor Gollanz.

Axline, V. (1969) *Play Therapy.* New York: Ballantine Books.

Erikson, E. (1950) *Childhood and Society.* New York: Norton.

Freud, S. (1909, reprinted 1990) *Analysis of a Phobia in a Five-Year-Old Boy ('Little Hans').* Harmondsworth: Penguin.

Klein, M. (1961, reissued 1989) *Narrative of a Child Analysis.* London: Virago.

Lowenfeld, M. (1979) *The World Technique.* London: Allen & Unwin.

Schaefer, C. E. and O'Connor, K. J. (1983) *Handbook of Play Therapy.* New York: John Wiley.

Winnicott, D. W. (1971) *Playing and Reality.* London: Tavistock.

12

LISTENING

The first step toward communicating through music

Amelia Oldfield

Introduction

For me, 'listening to a child' conjures up an ideal of a child sitting on a parent's lap sharing a difficult experience. The child wishes to communicate and the parent is ready to listen. In most of my work, the children have great difficulties in communicating and often don't appear to want to do so. The parents are often frustrated, feel isolated from their children and some have lost the ability to listen to them.

As a qualified music therapist, I can offer children and their families a new way of establishing communication through playful musical interactions. Thus children may become less isolated and more willing to communicate and parents will rediscover some of the ways of listening to their child.

In this chapter, I focus particularly on my work as a music therapist at a Child Development Centre and at a Unit for Child and Family Psychiatry. All the names of the children and the adults I have worked with have been changed.

The Child Development Centre, Addenbrookes, Cambridge

The Child Development Centre (CDC) in Cambridge is an outpatient centre attached to Addenbrookes Hospital. Children are usually referred by their GP or school doctor for an initial appointment with one of the Centre's specialist doctors, who may suggest further assessment and/or ongoing treatment by one or several of the specialists attached to the Centre. Children of all ages, with a wide range of difficulties, may be referred. Most children will first be seen at the CDC as babies or toddlers, but some children's difficulties become apparent only in later years, often after they start school.

188

Staffing at the Centre includes specialist doctors, physiotherapists, speech therapists, occupational therapists, a clinical psychologist, a music therapist, a health visitor and a social worker. As well as treating children at the Centre itself, staff liaise and run sessions at various schools that cater for children with special needs. Children are treated individually and in groups, and efforts are made to give parents as much support and help as possible. Staff meet regularly to discuss their work and a number of groups are run jointly by multiprofessional teams. As therapists, we all have different skills and can learn a great deal from one another. I have been lucky enough to work closely with speech therapists, physiotherapists and occupational therapists (Oldfield and Parry 1985; Oldfield and Peirson 1985; Oldfield and Feuerhahn 1986).

Music therapy at the Child Development Centre

I attend the Centre six hours a week and try to work with those children whom I feel will particularly benefit from music therapy sessions. These tend to be pre-school children with communication difficulties who may not have developed speech or may be choosing not to use language. Children often have no fixed diagnoses at this stage, but many of the children I see are in the process of being diagnosed as having childhood autism or Asperger Syndrome. Asperger Syndrome is related to autism; children with this condition often have a high level of intelligence but struggle to form meaningful relationships and have many obsessive behaviours. This frequently leads to a high level of frustration that can sometimes be addressed in music therapy sessions. Other children may have specific language disorders, emotional difficulties or developmental delay.

Thus children are usually referred to music therapy by one of the other specialists working at the Centre, after initial consultations and general investigations have taken place. I generally offer two music therapy assessment sessions to determine whether or not music therapy will be a particularly effective means of helping a child and/or a family. I then discuss the children's needs with the family and other specialists working with them and we agree on some aims and directions for the work. We might, for example, decide to focus on helping to motivate a child to be interested in interacting with me or helping a child to remain focused on any one activity for longer. At this stage, we will also set a time (usually six to twelve weeks later) to review progress. However, music therapy work can sometimes continue over a period of two years (Oldfield 1991).

I always find it hard to refer to one standard therapeutic model when talking about my music therapy approach. Developmental, behaviourist and psychodynamic approaches all influence my way of working. If I had to describe my work in one sentence, I would say that I have an interactive approach that involves live and mostly improvised music making. Most of the children I work with (but not the parents) are unaware of the therapy process. Progress occurs through the children's involvement in music making. The relationship with a child (and the family) grows out of this musical interaction, and the style of approach is influenced by the nature of this relationship.

Martin

Martin was 4 when I first started seeing him and he had a tentative diagnosis of childhood autism. His parents were anxious for me to see him as they felt that Martin was a very creative child who needed help to focus on what he was doing and also needed to develop social skills such as turn taking and listening.

When I have worked with young autistic children in the past, I have often found that it was more useful to see them on their own rather than with a parent in the room. Usually, the children are so isolated that I have to work very hard to establish any communication such as eye contact, anticipating a response or basic turn taking. Having a parent in the room seems to confuse children, who then isolate themselves from both of us. Sometimes I find it more difficult to concentrate on listening to small musical changes or allowing myself to give the child enough time to respond, when I feel under pressure to show meaningful communication to an anxious parent. Of course, the situation is different if children are very anxious about separating from their mother or father. Then I either have to work with the parent and the child together or start off in this way and then work towards an eventual harmonious separation.

Martin was happy to come into the room on his own and was very excited by the musical instruments. He would play noisily, shouting and waving his arms and legs around and eventually throwing the beaters around the room. His music sounded out of control and wild as though it was too much for him to cope with. I did not feel he was being deliberately naughty, so I introduced a clear structure to the session: a 'hello' song to start with and a 'goodbye' activity to close the session. I also made sure that each piece of work we did together had a clear beginning and an end which I would emphasise by saying something like 'Do you think we've finished on the drum?' If this was agreed upon the instrument would be moved away. Martin was greatly reassured by this familiar structure. Sometimes, he would say 'Put drum away?' when we wanted to move on, and in this way he could play a constructive part in the organisation of the session, rather than us getting stuck in the pattern of my having to end things because he was getting too boisterous or too loud.

As Martin felt more settled in our sessions, he became better at accepting my direction as well as enjoying the omnipotence of being in control himself. After two terms of weekly individual sessions, our musical improvisations became much more equal. Martin would initiate musical ideas (on the drum and cymbal, for example) and I would pick up his rhythms and weave harmonies around them on the piano. But, unlike at the beginning of our work together, Martin also began to respond to my change in dynamics or speeding up of the tune. We both learnt to trust one another sufficiently to listen before initiating further ideas of our own. Some of our later improvisations were very exciting and exhilarating. Martin would lose himself in the music, chattering away to himself and clearly talking about the past week's events or about a video he had seen while accompanying himself on the instruments. I could not understand what he was saying but I could hear and feel the intensity of his involvement. However, I knew he was not cut off from me, as he continued to listen and respond to my musical suggestions. I did not feel it was important to analyse or interpret the verbal contents of these improvisations. The experience in itself seemed to be beneficial to Martin. He was always calm after these intense musical exchanges and found it easier to concentrate for longer in subsequent activities.

There were other signs of progress outside the music therapy sessions. Martin's speech improved and he found it easier to listen to verbal instructions. His concentration span grew longer and he became more tolerant of change. Although it is always impossible to know how great a part music therapy has played in a child's progress, I do feel that our sessions contributed to Martin's realisation that he can trust people enough to listen to them and can give and take in a way previously very difficult for him. At the same time, I would not have been able to help Martin had I not been listening carefully to the way in which his playing initially appeared chaotic rather than naughty, and had I not been constantly listening to the subtle changes in his musical improvisations. This maintenance of a balance between following and initiating is crucial in working with isolated children (Oldfield 1995).

The mothers and toddlers group

This group is for pre-school children with a variety of difficulties, varying from cerebral palsy to more general developmental delays and behaviour problems. Parents and siblings (who are not at school) also take part. The aims of the group are to help individual children to work on two to three especially difficult areas, such as learning to listen and take turns or becoming more tolerant of other children's needs, and to provide encouragement, support and guidance for the parents.

I work with a loose structure. The group starts with a greeting song which is repeated every week. This song serves as a theme tune reminding everyone that the group is about to start. I then welcome each of the children and improvise around the children's and parents' names. I watch and listen very closely, trying to pick up small signals from each of the children. A child might glance in the direction of another child and I will pick this up by singing 'Does John want to say hello to Mary?' Another child might vocalise softly and I will try to match the quiet nature of that vocalising by picking out a tune on the guitar. A parent might seem embarrassed or ill at ease and I will make sure I don't focus directly on them and make a mental note to try to talk to them after the group. Another parent might be struggling with a handicapped toddler as well as a noisy baby. I will make a reassuring remark, try to distract the baby with a new sound and perhaps set up a situation where the baby can be briefly held by another parent.

In most groups, there are times when the whole group is playing together and times when we listen to one another. In the group playing, I usually lead from the piano but turn to face the group as I am playing so that I can watch as well as listen to what everyone is doing. Although I may start off with a clear rhythmic structure, I quickly, and if possible unobtrusively, modify my rhythm to follow a child's or a parent's playing. I might notice that a child is getting frustrated because their quiet instrument is being overshadowed by louder banging on drums. I could then suddenly become quieter and match my playing to that of the softer instrument. I might also notice that a child has stopped playing. In some cases I will support this child by singing 'Mathew is choosing not to play'; in others I might encourage the child to play by singing 'Wouldn't it be nice if Mathew played.'

All these thoughts and many more go through my head as I am improvising from the piano, using stops and starts strategically depending on the spontaneous reactions from the group. An outsider looking through the door might think we were just having a noisy play together, but each change of key, harmonic structure and rhythm change is being used in response to my listening and watching the children. The music engages the families and motivates them to take part. But in order for music therapy to take place, the music has to ebb and flow to meet the individual needs of each of the people in the group.

I will usually close the group sessions by introducing a new tone colour such as the clarinet, the wind chimes, or two chime bells. The novelty of the sounds will initially attract the children's and the parents' attention and, if I listen and watch carefully, I can hold the group's attention by alternating my playing with singing. The singing will match the mood, tonality, rhythm and colour of the instrument I am playing and it will also allow me to incorporate the children's names, particularly if I notice I am losing a particular child's interest. Here again musical improvisation is created to meet the needs of the children and the families in the group through listening and watching the children's and parents' reactions as I am playing and singing. Music therapy at the CDC has been recorded on video (Oldfield 1992).

The Croft Children's Unit

The Croft Children's Unit is a residential unit that aims to assess and in some cases treat children (up to 12 years old) and families who are troubled by emotional and behavioural disturbance and disturbance related to the ability to learn. In the last couple of years the most common diagnoses of children seen at the Unit have been: Attention Deficit Disorder (with or without hyperactivity), Asperger Syndrome, Giles de la Tourette Syndrome (a psychiatric disorder characterised by tics, obsessive and disinhibited behaviours and inappropriate language), developmental delay and specific language disorders. Although some families are admitted residentially, other children attend on a daily basis and regular meetings are arranged with the parents. Children are generally admitted only if their parents agree to work closely with staff on the Unit. Assessments may last from two to six weeks and some children will attend for a longer specific treatment (twelve weeks to a year).

Staff on the Unit include psychiatrists, specialist nurses, a teacher, an occupational therapist, a clinical psychologist and a music therapist. Social workers, health visitors and the teachers involved with the children work closely with staff on the Unit.

Music therapy at the Croft

I work at the Croft two days a week and try to work very closely with the rest of the team. I rely on individual children's keyworkers to advise me on whether or not they feel a particular child or family will benefit from one or two individual music therapy sessions during their initial assessment period. I see all the children on the Unit (usually no more than eight at the most) for a weekly group session and take part in team discussions about the children on a weekly basis. These meetings allow me to contribute to the assessment of the children's difficulties and also to discuss which children and which families I should take on for music therapy treatment. Quite a lot of my work at the Croft is short term, varying from four weeks to a year depending on the individual needs of children and families.

Unlike my work at the CDC, which is mostly with young and often non-verbal children, many of the children at the Croft already have an idea of what a music session might be like. This idea is obviously determined by their previous musical experiences and could vary from an expectation that they are going to be made to sing, to the idea that I might be about to teach them to play the violin. Many of the children we see have been emotionally, physically or sexually abused, and have, understandably, become quite wary and distrustful of adults. My first sessions are therefore aimed partly at reassuring the children and partly at showing that we are

193

going to improvise music together on equal terms rather than the emphasis being on teaching or performing. A general overview of my work with families at the Croft can be found in Oldfield 1993.

Assessment sessions

Lee

Lee was admitted to the Unit when he was 7. He had been previously diagnosed as having Attention Deficit Disorder and was on regular medication for this condition. He was referred to the Unit by his GP who was concerned that he might be depressed and that his medication might need to be changed. He comes from a large family who were struggling financially and who had little time or patience for Lee.

When I saw Lee for his first individual music therapy assessment session, he appeared outwardly confident and chatty. He was happy playing a variety of instruments and enjoyed and was competent at singing. However, he seemed to find it hard to relax, wanting to move fairly quickly from one activity to the next. At times, he seemed to want the next instrument before he had even had time to try the first one he had chosen, almost as though if he paused to take a breath the opportunity would disappear.

In our free improvisations, he showed considerable skill, following and watching what I was doing and also initiating his own ideas. But I did not feel that he was thoroughly involved either in his own playing or in our dialogue. His playing was competent but didn't come from deep inside himself, and seemed more of an effort to impress me than free play. This impression was reinforced by questions such as 'Did you like what I was doing?' or 'Did I do all right?' He seemed desperately to want adult attention and approval, but when it was offered to him he was unable to enjoy it or gain anything from it.

Thus, although Lee appeared bright, cheerful and motivated at first, the way he played the instruments and improvised with me told another story. I was left with the impression of a very sad little boy.

Sam

Sam was 9 years old and had a mild learning disability. He was admitted to the Unit to assess whether or not he was suffering from Attention Deficit Disorder. His parents were caring and warm towards him, but his difficulties had been slightly overlooked because his younger sister suffered from cerebral palsy and had far greater difficulties than he did.

Sam appeared quiet and slightly diffident when he first came into the music therapy room. He wanted me to choose which instruments we should play and lacked spontaneity. I was therefore a little surprised when he played the drum and the cymbal I had offered him extremely loudly and energetically. His whole body posture changed and he beamed excitedly. I felt that part of his excitement came from the thought that he might be doing something daring and naughty. But he continued to play with vigour and enthusiasm, even after I gave him permission to continue playing loudly by answering with equal energy and volume on the piano.

In our second assessment session, I suggested that we make up a story together using the instruments to accompany the text. Sam told a tale of a boy who was very naughty and in spite of multiple attempts by parents and later the police, defied all authority and in the end stole and drove away a police car. Each time the boy escaped authority, Sam accompanied himself by loud, emphatic drum and cymbal crashes and laughed wildly. Again, some of Sam's excitement came from the feeling that this child was being naughty. But he still continued to be loud and expressive even after he was able to acknowledge that a real child would be unlikely to defy authority in this way. This indicated to me that he realised the story was made up but could still use it with the instruments as a way to express his feelings.

When I discussed Sam at our weekly team meeting, I found that although he often told violent stories, this was the only time in the week when he was so expressive and loud. We decided that individual music therapy sessions would give Sam an opportunity to express pent-up emotions and feelings and that these sessions should continue. In this case it was impossible not to hear and listen to Sam's very loud playing, but it was understanding how he wanted to be heard and what the music was allowing him to do that was a little harder.

Music therapy in the parenting project

The aim of the parenting project at the Croft Children's Unit is to provide support, advice and help for families who are either having, or felt to be at risk of having, a wide range of difficulties in their parenting skills. Families might be referred for a combination of the following: post-natal depression, very young single mothers, mothers having experienced physical, emotional or sexual abuse as a child, or extreme financial hardship. It is hoped that by helping families who might be at risk, future difficulties may be avoided.

A group of up to six mothers (and/or fathers) who are either expecting a baby or have a young child up to 2 years old are invited to the Unit with their children to take part in a day's work, once a week, for six to twelve consecutive weeks. In each of the six week blocks, I provide one group music therapy session. The session will be watched on videotape by parents, the staff present at the session and myself the following week. I meet with staff from the project before and after both sessions so that families' progress can be discussed.

Clare and Cathy

Clare was a strong-willed 18 month old who liked to be in control. Her mother Cathy, felt she spent her entire life fighting with her daughter and found life very tiring. In the music therapy group, Clare clearly loved music and was the first to make choices. She was confident and happy to perform to the group. Although I had noticed Cathy struggling to hold on to Clare when we were playing instruments on the floor, I also noticed her gleam of pride when her daughter was enjoying playing for the others. The best moment came when Clare led the group from the drum and controlled everyone's playing. When Clare played, we all joined in. When she stopped, we all stopped. Here Clare was in control in a positive way and she was obviously delighted. When reviewing the video, Cathy was able to see her daughter's need to control in a positive light for the first time. It was through watching and listening to Clare that I was able to determine that she liked and needed to feel in control of situations. However, I did not feel that she was always seeking confrontation or being deliberately naughty. I was, therefore, quite easily able to set up a situation where her strength and confidence were shown up in a positive light.

Tom and Lizzie

Lizzie was a 16-year-old mother with a 7-month-old baby boy, Tom. She was reluctant to come to the group and showed adolescent embarrassment about playing any instruments herself. She did, however, agree to come for Tom's sake. Tom was very interested in my guitar playing and watched me intently. When I started playing the piano, he started swaying to the music, and I noticed how Lizzie was so focused on her son that she was swaying with him. Later on, she forgot herself again and started playing some bells with him, clearly enjoying the music making herself. I did not comment on her involvement in the music making during the next week's video review, as I felt she wasn't yet ready to acknowledge this. But she was more positive about the session, saying she wanted to come again . . . because Tom enjoyed it so much.

In this example, it is the child's natural ability to respond to music that draws the mother back into a forgotten (or in some cases never experienced) playful mode. The mother cannot resist listening and feeling her baby's reactions to the music. Her own new or re-found ability to be playful will make it easier for her to play with her son and thus enhance their relationship.

Other music therapists in this country have worked with mothers and children (Levinge 1993 and Warwick 1995) and this fairly specialised area of music therapy has been explored further (Oldfield 1996).

Reflections

It is interesting to wonder why it is that music can have such a powerful effect on both children and parents. Of course this question has been asked before and leads to another question of why music or art ever evolved in the first place. Many people, ranging from scientists to philosophers, have attempted to find explanations. Physiological explanations for different types of reactions to music are explored by Critchley and Henson (1977). Cook looks at the ways in which composers have conveyed moods (Cook 1989); and finally Gilroy and Lee (1995) investigate recent research by art and music therapists.

For me, some new thoughts on this topic emerged a few years ago when my twin daughters, Laura and Claire, were 8 to 16 months old. At the time, I was working with Timothy. Timothy was a little boy of 4 who was diagnosed as having Asperger Syndrome. The main emphasis of my work with Timothy was on motivating him to communicate with me and helping him to develop language. I felt that Timothy had missed out on the babbling stage as a baby, and I therefore used sound exchanges and musical improvisations to re-create this type of communication. Gradually he became more spontaneous vocally and started using some simple phrases in a communicative way. For a long time, however, all our exchanges had to be on his terms and he needed to control the situation. He would be quite happy for me to imitate his sounds but would quickly lose interest if I initiated my own sounds.

At home, Laura, at 8 months, would giggle every time I made a 'pa' sound. This reminded me of Timothy, in our initial tapping exchanges on the drum. At 11 months, Claire enjoyed passing an object back and forth to me, very like Timothy waiting for me to imitate his vocal sounds. Timothy was too old to enjoy passing an object back and forth but I could re-create this type of exchange through musical improvisation. At 13 months, Laura thoroughly enjoyed refusing to let me have a toy she pretended to pass me. Like Timothy, she delighted in the control she had over me. Obviously, my relationship with my children is different to my relationship with Timothy: in one case I am a mother and in the other I am a therapist. But it is the type of humorous, non-verbal exchange that I think is similar in both cases, rather than other aspects of the relationship, and I compare these in a music therapy training video (Oldfield 1994).

Thus I would suggest that one of the reasons why music therapy can be so effective when working with children and their parents is that it can allow a non-verbal and/or non-communicating older child to go back to a pre-verbal stage, in order to recreate basic sound responses and exchanges. It can also provide an opportunity for the parent and the child to re-experience (or experience for the first time) the early mother–baby types of playful interactions.

When I heard Daniel Stern's keynote talk at a recent music therapy conference about the timing involved in early mother/baby babbling exchanges, I was struck not only by how similar these exchanges were to those in music therapy improvisation, but also by how carefully both the mother and the therapist had to listen to their child or client (Stern 1996).

The music therapist Heal-Hughes (1995) also made the parallel between mother–infant interactions and the client–therapist relationship. She uses this comparison to suggest a model of thinking about the unconscious meanings that adults with learning difficulties are communicating. For the purpose of this chapter, however, I think it is the similarity in the listening processes in the mother–baby relationship and the client–therapist relationship that is both relevant and important.

Conclusion

These examples show that music therapy can help both children and parents to listen to one another. For the music therapist, listening is the first step towards communication. In my case, I have learnt to listen not only because of my experience as a music therapist but also through raising my own four children. I developed slightly different systems of non-verbal communication with each baby. In each case, we had to get to know each other's special ways. As in the therapeutic relationship, the experience is often frustrating and difficult, but the thrill of learning to listen to one another and communicating is so great that it makes all the efforts and struggles well worthwhile.

References

Cook, D. (1989) *The Language of Music*. Oxford: Oxford University Press.

Critchley, M. and Henson, M. (1977) *Music and the Brain*. London: Heinemann.

Gilroy, A. and Lee, C. (1995) *Art and Music Therapy Research*. London: Routledge.

Heal-Hughes, M. (1995) A comparison of mother and infant interactions and the client–therapist relationship in music therapy, in T. Wigram, R. West and B. Saperston (eds) *The Art and Science of Music Therapy: A handbook*. Chur, Switzerland: Harwood Academic Publishers, pp. 296–306.

Levinge, A. (1993) The Nursing Couple. Unpublished paper presented at the 1993 World Music Therapy Conference in Vitoria, Spain.

Oldfield, A. (1991) Preverbal communication through music to overcome a language disorder, in K. E. Bruscia (ed.) *Case Studies in Music Therapy*. Phoenixville, PA: Barcelona Publishers, pp. 163–74

Oldfield, A. (1993) Music therapy with families in M. Heal and T. Wigram (eds) *Music Therapy in Health and Education*. London: Jessica Kingsley, pp. 46–54.

Oldfield, A. (1995) Communicating through music: the balance between following and initiating, in T. Wigram, R. West and B. Saperston (eds) *The Art and Science of Music Therapy: A handbook*. Chur, Switzerland. Harwood Academic Publishers, pp. 226–37.

Oldfield, A. (1996) Music Therapy with Parents and Young Children: Restoring and improving relationships. Sub-keynote paper presented at the 8th World Music Therapy Conference in Hamburg, Germany, 1996 (forthcoming).

Oldfield, A. and Feuerhahn, C. (1986) Using music in mental handicap: 3 – Helping young children with handicaps and providing support for their parents. *Mental Handicap* 14, March: 10–14.

Oldfield, A. and Parry, C. (1985) Using music in mental handicap: 1 – Overcoming communication difficulties. *Mental Handicap* 13, Sept: 117–19.

Oldfield, A. and Peirson, J. (1985) Using music in mental handicap: 2 – Facilitating movement. *Mental Handicap* 13, Dec: 156–8.

Stern, D. (1996) The Temporal Structure of Interactions between Parents and Infants: The Earliest Music? Keynote paper presented at the World Music Therapy Conference in Hamburg, Germany, 1996 (forthcoming).

Warwick, A. (1995) Music Therapy in the Education Service: Research with autistic children, in T. Wigram, R. West and B. Saperston (eds) *The Art and Science of Music Therapy: A handbook*. Phoenixville, PA: Harwood Academic Publishers, pp. 209–25.

Training videos

Oldfield, A. (1992) *Music Therapy at the Child Development Centre*. Training video produced at Addenbrookes Hospital, available from the British Society for Music Therapy. Price £16.

Oldfield, A. (1994) *Timothy – Music Therapy with a Little Boy who has Asperger Syndrome*. Training video produced at Addenbrookes Hospital, available from the British Society for Music Therapy, 25 Rosslyn Avenue, East Barnet, Herts EN4 8DH. Price £16.

Part V

CHILDREN, RESEARCH AND THE LAW

Childhood must no longer be left to chance.
Children First: The story of UNICEF, past and present
(Maggie Black 1996)

13

'IT'S COOL . . . 'COS YOU CAN'T GIVE US DETENTIONS AND THINGS, CAN YOU?!'

Reflections on research with children

Virginia Morrow

This chapter provides a researcher's account of some of the methodological and ethical issues raised in listening to children in an on-going, school-based, qualitative research project, 'Attending to the Child's Voice: Children's accounts of family and kinship', funded by the Joseph Rowntree Foundation. The project aims to establish how a sample of children (not necessarily seen by adult agencies as having problems) define and make sense of the concept of 'family', from a sociological perspective. The notion that children's voices should be heard on matters that affect them is a relatively new development for practitioners (and indeed researchers), and the project attempts to assess how, methodologically, children's views can be elicited in an appropriate and satisfactory manner. At the time of writing, research has been carried out in two Cambridgeshire village schools, with a sample of ninety-nine children aged between 8 and 14 years. This chapter describes and reflects upon the research process as an important source of data in itself (it does not attempt any analysis of data at this stage), and also alludes to previous experiences of research with children in an earlier project on children's work (Morrow 1994). There are a number of issues raised: one is that of carrying out research with an age group that is potentially vulnerable by virtue of social status and the differential power relationship between adults and children; another is that of researching a sensitive topic with that age group, and a third is that of carrying out social research in schools.

The chapter first describes the background to the study, and then explores the theoretical underpinning and discusses how different standpoints or ways of seeing children influence social research with children. It then describes the methods used and discusses some of the ethical considerations that arise, focusing on issues of informed consent. The chapter concludes with a brief reflection on the researcher's role in research with children.

Background

There have been recent legislative changes that require that children's voices be heard and their opinions sought in matters that affect them. The England and Wales Children Act 1989 represented a move from parental rights to parental responsibilities, and stipulated that courts shall have particular regard to 'the ascertainable wishes and feelings of the child concerned (considered in the light of his [sic] age and understanding)' (Section 1(3)(a)). In 1991, the UK government ratified the UN Convention on the Rights of the Child, which not only provides a framework addressing rights relating to children's need for care, protection and adequate provision, but also has important clauses on children's rights to participation (Article 12). This set of principles acknowledges that children have rights to be consulted and taken account of, to have access to information, to freedom of speech and opinion, and to challenge decisions made on their behalf. If this set of principles were respected, it would clearly represent a shift in the recognition of children as participants in society (Lansdown 1994). Further, there have been legal changes in how children's 'competence' to make decisions for themselves is regarded. Correspondingly, in some areas of social research there has been a growing recognition that children's views and perspectives can and should be sought on a range of issues that affect them.

To date, however, the idea of attending to 'the child's voice' occurs only in specific and limited settings, for example at divorce via court welfare officers only in certain disputed cases, and within some divorce mediation. The effect of attempts to ascertain children's opinions in matters of law has yet to be evaluated (Trinder 1997). There is no legal requirement to take account of children's views in a range of other settings, such as education, health matters, and within families (Lansdown 1994).

In UK social policy research, and in sociology more generally, the focus of attention has been on 'problem children and children's problems' (Qvortrup 1987), but relatively few studies have been based on children's accounts of their experiences. Indeed, sociology as a discipline has tended to ignore children, and left them to psychologists to study. However, tucked away in research reports one often finds encouraging evidence of children's abilities both to provide spontaneous and rich accounts of their lives and to be actively engaged in the research process itself (James 1993; Ennew and Morrow 1994; Middleton et al. 1994; Morrow 1994; Prendergast 1994; Mayall 1996). Contemporary children are increasingly likely to experience a variety of family settings as they pass through childhood and adolescence, but there is remarkably little social policy research into how children make sense of contemporary patterns of family life and kinship (O'Brien et al. 1996). This lack of basic social research means that it is difficult to articulate notions of listening to children's voices in policy terms.

Theoretical underpinning

Research with children from a sociological perspective raises the same methodological and ethical issues that all researchers face, at least implicitly, when collecting people's stories: issues of appropriate and honest ways of collecting, analysing and interpreting data and of disseminating findings, as well as issues of protection of research participants. At the same time, researchers have also found it helpful to consider the differences between adults and children, because while ethical considerations that apply to adult research participants can and must also apply to child research participants, there are some added provisos. There are four key considerations.

1 Children's competencies, perceptions and frameworks of reference may be different at different ages, and this has implications for the consent process as well as data collection methods and interpretations.
2 Children are potentially vulnerable to exploitation in interactions with adults, and thus day-to-day adult responsibilities to children must be fulfilled.
3 The differential power relationships between adult researcher and child participant become highly problematic at the point of interpretation and presentation of research findings. However much a researcher may intend the research to be participatory, 'the presentation . . . is likely to require analyses and interpretations, at least for some purposes, which do demand different knowledge than that generally available [to children], in order to explicate children's social status and structural positioning' (Mayall 1994: 11) (though again, the same may be true of research carried out with adults).
4 Access to children has to be mediated via adult gate-keepers, and this has implications for the consent process.

James has recently identified four ways of 'seeing children'. She explores four 'ideal types' of 'the child', and what she calls the *social child* is the model I have used in this and previous research (Morrow 1994). This model envisages 'children as research subjects comparable with adults, but understands children to possess different competencies, a conceptual modification which . . . permits researchers to engage more effectively with the diversity of childhood' (James 1995: 14). James suggests that this has implications for the methods used in studying children: children have different abilities, and are encouraged to be skilled and confident in different mediums of communication (drawings, stories, written work, and so on) that researchers might usefully draw upon. Such approaches need qualification because, for example, children's willingness to join in participatory research techniques may vary from age to age, drawings may be appropriate at younger ages

205

whilst older children may be willing to talk freely (this is certainly borne out by the current research). Using methods that are non-invasive and non-confrontational might be one step towards diminishing the ethical problems of imbalanced power relationships between researcher and researched at the point of data collection. It involves seeing children as 'nothing special but simply as actors in the social world' (Waksler 1991: 62), whose accounts have the same veracity as those of adults. Any researcher working with children is likely to be asked if they can 'really believe' children's accounts of their experiences and themselves. My intention in the current project is to take children's accounts of themselves very much at face value and to try to avoid projecting my own interpretation on to what they say, write or draw.

Description of the process of research: research setting

To date, research has been carried out with four classes of children in two Cambridgeshire village schools: a village secondary school (village college), and one of its feeder Church of England junior schools nearby. At first sight, school may seem an ideal place to work with children. Schools may be seen as providing access to a large and (depending on the school) fairly representative sample of children in a particular locality. A researcher can usually fit data collection activities into the rhythm of the school day without causing too much disruption to the children concerned. However, there may be problems associated with research with children in school and these are worth mentioning.

1 Schools are currently under pressure from National Curriculum demands and funding shortages, and pressures may be greater at different points of the year and for different ages of children.
2 As discussed below, a researcher has to negotiate with a range of adult gate-keepers and gain the trust of the adults concerned before access can be obtained.
3 Of course some schools (and teachers and parents) will not welcome the disruption that a researcher inevitably causes to the school routine. A flexible approach about how to do the research, which age groups to work with, and when to collect data has been helpful in the current project.
4 A researcher has to be able to develop a rapport not only with a range of adults, but obviously and most crucially, with the children themselves (see also Hill et al. 1996).
5 A researcher may have to work with children with the teacher present, and this may affect the data. In practice I have worked in a range of settings, from having the teacher present (but busy marking pupils' work, and this has been helpful in whole-class activities where children

206

are drawing or writing on their own) to having teachers or learning assistants in the next room. It is quite difficult to be completely private in schools. It may finally be the case that children see the researcher as a teacher (they often refer to the researcher as 'Miss', for example) and I discuss this in more detail below.

Methods

In my current project I have used multiple methods (see Brannen 1992) to explore and cross-check the issues raised by the research questions, thus building up a picture of how children perceive and define 'family'. A further aim of the project is to evaluate these methods. In particular, it has been helpful to use methods that children are comfortable and familiar with, such as drawing and written work. (This may reinforce the researcher-as-teacher role, but I always emphasise that there are no 'right answers' to my questions.) Individual interviews have not been used, because the aim is to explore norms, values and representations rather than focus on individual experiences. To date, the 'group' method has worked well and does not put pressure on children who may be unwilling to speak. My previous experience suggests that children are not necessarily comfortable with being asked a range of rather open-ended questions by an adult wielding a tape-recorder (Morrow 1994). Moreover, the children in the current project said that they preferred being with their friends rather than being interviewed individually, if they had a choice. This is not to say that individual interviews are not a useful way of collecting data from children, but it is worth bearing in mind that adults do not generally seek out children's views, opinions and ideas, and similarly children themselves are not used to being asked to relate their experiences to unknown adults.

I now want to describe the three main methods I have used (drawing and writing, sentence completion, group discussions) and discuss some of the pros and cons of each.

Drawing and writing

In the junior school, I helped in the classroom in each of the classes in the sample, with the aim of getting to know the children by name, and for a brief period I was a familiar person in the school. The first task the children undertook was a whole-class activity. They drew or wrote about 'who is important to me?' This is an exercise that (junior) school children are familiar with, and it gives not only some insight into their family composition, but also an indication of how important other people, and their own pets, are to them at different ages. The children chose how they wanted to express themselves. Generally, the younger children (i.e. 8 to 11 year olds) preferred to draw, and older children, especially girls, chose to write. The style of drawings varied considerably – some drew elaborate cartoons, some used diagrams, and others drew straightforward pictures; some commented that they 'couldn't draw all the people who were important to them', and added handwritten lists. Virtually all of the junior schoolchildren had drawn, written about or listed their pets as important, and at one session the groups discussed their pets and why they were important (they could talk forever about this topic).

There is a good deal of psychological literature on children's drawings (Andersson 1994; Goodnow 1977) and a growing body of work on the use of children's drawings in health research (Pridmore and Bendelow 1995). The draw-and-write technique was developed for a Health Education Authority study of primary schoolchildren, and involves asking children to draw pictures and write about health and ill-health issues (Williams *et al.* 1989). Developmental psychological research has tended to use children's drawings as ways of emphasising different competencies in perception and pictorial representation at certain stages of development; psychoanalytic approaches have tended to use children's drawings as ways of projectively interpreting children's inner emotional states. However, 'children's drawings have not traditionally been used to facilitate empowerment, but rather the opposite' (Pridmore and Bendelow 1995: 475; but see Chapter 10 this volume).

One of the main benefits of the draw-and-write technique is that it enables all children to participate, including young children; the drawbacks are essentially ethical ones, to do with consent, ownership of drawings (in this study, younger children, 8 and 9 year olds, were keen to have copies of their drawings) and, most importantly, interpretation (Pridmore and Bendelow 1995). Both developmental psychological and psychoanalytic approaches are problematic, from a sociological point of view, because unless a researcher is prepared to sit and listen to a child talking about and explaining their drawing, then the dangers of misrepresentation and over-interpretation are very great indeed (Pridmore and Bendelow 1995; Morrow 1997). My intention is to use children's drawings (and the lists they provided) to count the people they mentioned as important, using a method that children are familiar with and often enjoy using. So, for example, if an 11-year-old boy chose to illustrate the people who are important to him as a cartoon-style drawing, then all he intends to convey to me is that these are the important people in his life, no more or less.

Sentence completion and writing

I made ten visits to the junior school over a period of five weeks. At the subsequent visits, the children were arranged in smaller groups, in which they completed a kind of 'worksheet' (again, something that children in school are familiar with). These sheets asked them to complete two sentences: 'What is a family? A family is . . .' and 'What are families for? Families are for . . .'; it also asked them to write yes/no answers under five one-sentence stories (described below). This task was completed first as an individual exercise (though in reality there was a good deal of looking over shoulders, checking answers, and general banter that went on while they read and answered the questions). In previous research (Morrow 1994), I have used secondary schoolchildren's written accounts of their everyday lives outside school as a source of data, and again essay writing is a method that works well because children are used to this kind of activity.

Focus group discussions

Having completed their 'worksheets', the groups discussed the five one-sentence stories (vignettes). These describe a particular configuration of people, and the children were asked whether this configuration constitutes 'a family'. This method was previously used by O'Brien et al. (1996):

1   John and Susan are a married couple without any children. Are they a family?
2   Janet and Dave are a married couple with a 6-year-old son called Ben. Are they a family?
3   Jim and Sue live together with their 6-year-old son called Paul. They are not married. Are they a family?
4   Sally is divorced with a 10-year-old daughter, Karin. Karin lives with Sally. Are these two a family?
5   Karin's father, Tom, lives at the other end of the town. Are Karin and Tom a family?

I had shown these to the class teachers beforehand, and discussed potential difficulties that these vignettes might cause for any individual children. There was only one situation where a teacher suggested that it might be appropriate to move on to talk about the other items for discussion, and this was in the older age group, where the vignettes did not give rise to much discussion anyway. The point here was to use the vignettes as a way of generating a group discussion. The groups then moved on to discuss what they read, what they watched on TV, and images of families they saw, issues of children's rights and 'being listened to' and, finally, how they felt about being involved in research.

Focus group discussions are intended to explore a specific set of issues based around a collective activity (Kitzinger 1994). They are essentially artificial situations that are used to encourage people to engage with one another and verbally formulate their ideas. The interaction between participants is a useful and illuminating source of data, and this is confirmed in the current research (Kitzinger 1994: 106). The vignettes gave rise to some very lively debate, particularly amongst the younger children. Some of the discussions raised some personal issues, but did not appear to cause any distress. The children seemed to be describing situations that were well-known to other members of the group, and the children appeared to know each other very well. For example, with the older children (11–14 years), the vignettes mostly (but not always) gave rise to very little discussion at all, just straight yes/no answers or occasionally a single-sentence comment in disagreement. In contrast, discussions about media images of families, and children's rights and being listened to, tended to be much livelier and fuller in the older groups.

The groups were mostly arranged by the teachers, and were virtually all mixed gender, which led to some predictable exchanges between boys and girls, particularly when it came to discussions about what they watched on TV and what they read. Younger boys often played around and took some time to settle to the tasks at hand. On the other hand, boys did not tend to dominate the discussions. Children were mainly with their friends, and this worked in both positive and negative ways. For example, one group of 13–14 year olds were clearly used to debating and discussing things with each other, while another group of the same age (all girls) obviously knew each other so well that they kept referring to their own disputes and quarrels, frequently trying to silence one member of their group to the extent that I had to insist that the others 'let her speak'. Prendergast and Forrest (1997) also discuss the way in which groups function in secondary schools.

It was only possible to see the secondary schoolchildren on two occasions, due to pressure of timetabling at the school, though a large amount of data was produced. The children wrote (nearly all wrote, only a small number of boys drew and wrote) 'Who is important to me?', and some did their sentence completions, as a whole-class activity. As any teacher will be aware, children work at tremendously different rates, some finishing in five minutes, some taking thirty minutes to write about who is important, so it was helpful to have a range of tasks. I then took away and read what they had written before I went back to do the group discussions.

At the end of each term, I carried out a preliminary analysis of the data for each group, and returned to give feedback to the children in a very general way. On two occasions, I was given a round of applause, together with a hail of requests to 'see the report'.

Ethical considerations: the consent process

Obtaining informed consent from children to participate in research is a relatively new issue for researchers (Morrow and Richards 1996). Previous writers have noted the careful measures that researchers have to take in order to be able to carry out research with children, which usually involve lengthy negotiations with adult gate-keepers, particularly so in the case of school-based research, where consent has to be obtained from a series of adults before one can embark on obtaining it from children themselves (James 1993; Prendergast 1994; Mayall 1996).

Consent from adults

In the case of the current research, the project received ethical approval by the University Psychology Research Ethics Committee (interestingly, and perhaps predictably, the concern here was with the written information being given to *parents*). However, each school dealt with the consent process in different ways (Headteachers are technically *in loco parentis* and assume responsibility while children are in school, and a researcher has to be guided by the Head, though in every case a letter was provided for parents inviting them to withdraw their child).

Consent from children

Parental consent was the first stage before verbal consent was sought from the children themselves. This was negotiated as follows. I began by introducing myself and asked if they knew what 'research' was. I told them I was undertaking a 'project' (a very familiar idea to children, thanks to the National Curriculum) and described briefly what the research was about: (how children think about 'family', and what images they get of families from the media they encounter, such as books, comics, magazines and TV and video). I explained to them that, by working with me, they'd be helping me to find out what children say and their opinions and views. This would be written into a report that would hopefully be useful to people working with children in circumstances where children's views need to be sought. I subsequently described the tasks I'd be asking them to do. I asked them for their agreement, and talked about confidentiality, anonymity and privacy – how I phrased this depended on the age of the children. For example, I explained that they were doing the tasks for me; I'd be the only person who'd see all their work, though, if they agreed, bits of what they said/wrote/drew would be used in the report. I told them that what they said/wrote/drew would be confidential to me, though I had a responsibility to help if they told me that they had some kind of problem. They also chose their own pseudonyms on the last visit (usually a source of great hilarity) and I told them that the village would be disguised. Finally, I said several times 'Is this OK? Are you happy to do this? If you'd rather not do [task], we can ask [teacher] for a different task, or you can do something else for me', and I asked permission each time to tape discussions. I concluded by telling them that, at the end of term, I would come back and spend five to ten minutes giving them my first impressions of what we had produced. At the end of the project, a copy of the book or report is sent to each school. I also return drawings and written work, if the children want them, and, when time allows, the group hear the tapes of the discussions played back.

Is this really informed consent?

In all school-based research, there is an uneasy sense that because the tasks the children participate in take place in school, because they have taken letters home, and because their schools and teachers have agreed, this is to a large extent a 'captive sample'. To this extent, and because children are the 'objects' of schooling, it is possible to argue that they are similarly the objects of the research. As other researchers have suggested, 'the voluntary nature of any student participation in a school-based study may be doubted at a general level' (Wallace *et al.* 1994: 177; see also Mayall 1996).

Children have responded with varying degrees of enthusiasm to tasks, and, as I have already mentioned, some of the topics for discussion engaged the children more than others, and this varied between groups and with different ages. Some groups discussed volubly and fully, while with others the group dynamic hardly developed at all.

My impression is that if you ask children for their agreement, they all tend to say yes, but a minority of them will simply not participate at all, will write minimally, and say virtually nothing in discussion. However, they all wrote or drew *something*, even if they did not necessarily speak. Of course, there are many issues to consider when doing research in a school setting. First, there is the possibility that the children see the tasks as some kind of test, so each time I see the children, I emphasise that it is their opinions and ideas that I'm interested in, and that there are no right answers to the questions. Further, the discussions may raise issues that the children have never considered or articulated before, and which may always veer towards the highly personal and unsettling. I try to steer the discussions away from very personal accounts (though some children seem to relate their experiences with enthusiasm, and often it appears that the rest of the group are familiar with the stories). What the children say is not *necessarily* contextualised in their current household structure, though their family composition often emerges in their accounts of who is important to them. But for some (like one 13-year-old boy who wrote 'I am important to me because you've got to look after No. 1') it is not possible to say what their family circumstances are, because they chose not to describe them. All of these issues are explored more fully in the final report of the project (Morrow 1998).

Reflecting on the researcher's role

Wallace *et al.* (1994), writing about educational research, distinguish between two roles for the researcher, as 'observers' and as 'participants'. In reality, there are multiple roles that a researcher assumes in a school setting, and this will be influenced by the age, gender, ethnicity and personal style of the researcher and, indeed, any previous experience of being a research participant (see also James 1993; Mayall 1996). Broadly speaking, the following come to mind:

1 confidant(e)/counsellor/friend (particularly by girls);
2 authority-figure/teacher, to be tested (especially by boys): hence the title of this chapter. Would I allow them to chew gum in the discussions? Would I allow them to wear hats? Both of these are presumably against the school rules;
3 an interesting and sometimes entertaining diversion from the school routine;
4 as a person in my own right: occasionally the children asked me about my own children, or complimented me on my haircut.

The time of year in the school calendar also has an effect on how a researcher fits into the rhythm of the school day. In the junior school, I felt I got to know the children well. This was the last half of the summer term and the atmosphere was relaxed. Some of the girls went to some lengths to be able to talk to me on my own, to ask my advice or relate their problems. This raises interesting questions about whether the children saw me as a 'mother figure', and highlights the fact that children do not necessarily have ready access to objective unconnected adults in the normal course of events. Children are always in a structural relationship to the adults around them: a child is a child of the family, somebody's son or daughter, or a 'schoolchild'. A schoolchild is in a particular working relationship with his or her teachers, and this relationship may be purely professional. Moreover, there is often simply not time for teachers and children to talk on a one-to-one basis. Gender, both of the researcher and the children, is likely to be crucial here: had I been a male researcher, would the boys have seen me in a similar way as a source of advice and 'someone to talk to'?

Conclusion

Research with children from a sociological perspective in a school-based setting raises a range of methodological questions that have needed to be addressed in this research. There are inherent difficulties in research not only with the age group concerned, but also with the topic. This chapter has drawn attention to the importance of the researcher's standpoint in research with children. It has also argued for seeing children as research subjects who are essentially social actors in their own right, but with the added proviso that children may possess different competences and may be more skilled in other forms of communication than one-to-one interviews.

It has been helpful to draw on these skills in various ways using the range of methods described above. The chapter has discussed some of the problems around issues that are often taken for granted in research with adults, such as obtaining informed consent, and finally it has reflected on the researcher's role in school, as perceived by participants. Research with children involves particular problems, because of the way in which society tends to discount their words and opinions. If we are going to listen to children (which is innovative in itself), then we are going to have to be innovative about doing so in a way that is appropriate and satisfactory and, hopefully, meaningful to the research participants themselves.

Acknowledgements

I am immensely grateful to the children who participated in this research, and to their teachers and schools for enabling the research to take place. I would also like to thank Gill Dunne, Nina Hallowell, Shirley Prendergast, Frances Price and Martin Richards for helpful comments on earlier drafts of this chapter.

References

Andersson, S. (1994) *Social Scaling and Children's Graphic Strategies: A comparative study of children's drawings in three cultures.* Institute of Tema Research, Linkoping University, Sweden.

Brannen, J. (ed.) (1992) *Mixing Methods: Qualitative and quantative research.* Aldershot: Avebury.

Ennew, J. and Morrow, V. (1994) Out of the mouths of babes, in E. Verhellen and F. Spiesschaert (eds) *Children's Rights: Monitoring issues.* Gent, Belgium: Mys & Breesch.

Goodnow, J. (1997) *Children's Drawings.* London: Fontana.

Hill, M., Laybourn, A. and Borland, M. (1996) Engaging with primary-aged children about their emotions and well-being: methodological considerations. *Children and Society* 10 (2) 129–44.

James, A. (1993) *Childhood Identities: Self and social relationships in the experience of the child.* Edinburgh: Edinburgh University Press.

James, A. (1995) Methodologies of competence for a competent methodology? Paper prepared for Children and Social Competence Conference, Guildford, Surrey, July 1995.

Kitzinger, J. (1994) The methodology of Focus Groups: The importance of interaction between research participants. *Sociology of Health and Illness* 16 (1), pp. 103–21.

Lansdown, G. (1994) Children's rights, in B. Mayall (ed.) *Children's Childhoods: Observed and experienced.* London: Falmer Press.

Mayall, B. (1994) *Children's Childhoods: Observed and experienced.* London: Falmer Press.

Mayall, B. (1996) *Children, Health and the Social Order.* Buckingham: Open University Press.

Middleton, S., Ashworth, K. and Walker, R. (1994) *Family Fortunes: Pressure on parents and children in the 1990s*. London: Child Poverty Action Group.

Morrow, V. (1994) Responsible children? Aspects of children's work and employment outside school in contemporary UK, in B. Mayall (ed.) *Children's Childhoods: Observed and experienced*. London: Falmer Press.

Morrow, V. (1997) Methods, ethics and children: preliminary thoughts from a research project on children's definitions of family. Paper presented to Urban Childhood Conference. Trondheim, Norway, June 1997.

Morrow, V. (1998) *Understanding Families: Children's perspectives*. London: National Children's Bureau.

Morrow, V. and Richards, M. P. M. (1996) The ethics of social research with children: an overview, in *Children and Society* 10: 90–105

O'Brien, M., Alldred, P. and Jones, D. (1996) Children's constructions of family and kinship, in J. Brannen and M. O'Brien (eds) *Children in Families: Research and policy*. London: Falmer Press.

Prendergast, S. (1994 [1992]) *'This is the Time to Grow Up': Girls' experiences of menstruation in school*, 2nd edition. London: Family Planning Association.

Prendergast, S. and Forrest, S. (1997) 'Hieroglyphs of the Heterosexual': Learning about gender in school, in L. Segal (ed.) *New Sexual Agendas*. London: Macmillan.

Pridmore, P. and Bendelow, G. (1995) Images of health: Exploring beliefs of children using the 'draw-and-write' technique, *Health Education Journal*. 54: 473–88.

Qvortrup, J. (1987) Introduction. *International Journal of Sociology*, Special issue, 'The sociology of childhood': 17(3): 3–37.

Trinder, L. (1998) Competing constructions of childhood: Children's rights and children's wishes in divorce. *Journal of Social Welfare and Family Law* 19 (3): 291–305.

Waksler, F.C. (1991) *Studying the Social Worlds of Children: Sociological readings*. London: Falmer Press.

Wallace, G., Rudduck, J. and Harris, S. (1994) Students' secondary school careers: research in a climate of moving perspectives, in D. Halpin and B. Troyna, *Researching Education Policy: Ethical and methodological issues*. London: Falmer Press.

Williams, T., Wetton, N. and Moon, A. (1989) *Health for Life 1: A teacher's planning guide to health education in the primary school*. Walton-on-Thames: Thomas Nelson and Sons.

14

CHILDREN AND THE LAW

Pat Monro

Introduction

The recommendations of a report of the Inquiry into Child Abuse in Cleveland (1988), with the emphasis on listening to children, and the implementation of the Children Act 1989 (which consolidated legislation concerning the welfare of children) have had a significant impact on lawyers working in the field, and there has been an enormous increase in the numbers of lawyers interested in work involving young people, with a corresponding increase in the attention paid to how we work with them.

The solicitor's firm in which I work was set up in 1975 to act for children. It was established as a result of concern about the poor quality of representation of children who appeared before what was then the juvenile court. The principles on which the firm was established were, first, to take on only cases in which the main element involved was children and young people; second, it would undertake mainly legal aid work, as opposed to privately funded work (85 per cent of the work remains publicly funded). The other two principles were, third, that the firm's approach would not be over legislative, and, wherever possible, non-lawyers with relevant social services skills would be used, and fourth, work permitting, that time would be devoted to advancing the law relating to children and undertaking test cases.

Twenty-three years later, a review of our work shows that the firm has maintained the first two principles, and has no intention of changing them. However the third concept, having lawyers and non-lawyers with social science qualifications working together on cases, proved difficult to maintain, because of the limitations of legal aid to strictly legal work. There is no public money available to pay people whose professional skills and understanding would support children in their difficult encounters with the legal world.

Our fourth ideal has been difficult to put into effect within the firm, because of pressures on time and finances; however, in 1979, funding was obtained through the UK Committee of UNICEF at the start of the United

Nations Year of the Child, to establish a Children's Legal Centre to undertake the advancement of the law relating to children. The centre continues in existence, now based at the University of Essex, offering an advice line, publishing the journal *Childright* as well as information sheets and pushing for reform in child law (see Useful Addresses).

Our legal team includes five full-time, one part-time and three trainee solicitors. We regularly take a student on placement from Brunel University. Public and private law cases form the bulk of our current work, together with a smaller amount of adoption, immigration and asylum, housing, education and welfare issues. Complaints and actions against local authorities and criminal injuries compensation claims are also undertaken.

The context in which we work

The Children Act 1989 aimed to strike a balance between the rights of children to express their views on decisions made about their lives, the rights of parents to exercise their responsibilities towards the child, and the duty of the state to intervene where the child's welfare requires it. 'There will be a greater emphasis on representing the views, feelings and needs of the child in these proceedings' (Guidance and Regulations to the Act: Court Orders).

Article 12 of the UN Convention on the Rights of the Child holds that:

> States parties shall assure to the child who is capable of forming his or her own views the right to express those views freely in all matters affecting the child, the views of the child being given weight in accordance with the age and maturity of the child. . . .
>
> For this purpose, the child shall in particular be provided the opportunity to be heard in any judicial and administrative proceedings affecting the child, either directly, or through a representative or an appropriate body, in a manner consistent with the procedural rules of national law.

In more everyday language, Gerison Lansdown has commented that:

> consulting with children means more than just asking them what they think. It means ensuring that they have adequate information appropriate to their age with which to form opinions. It means being provided with meaningful opportunities to express their views and explore options open to them, and it means having those views listened to, respected and considered seriously.[1]

The legislation deals with children's wishes in the following way

Section 3 of the Adoption Act states:

> in reaching any decision relating to the adoption of a child, a court
> or an adoption agency shall have regard to all circumstances, first
> consideration being the need to safeguard and promote the welfare
> of the child throughout his childhood; and as far as practicable
> ascertain the wishes and feelings regarding the decision and give
> due consideration to them, having regard to his age and under-
> standing.

Section 1 (3) of the Children Act 1989 (known as the welfare checklist[2]
requires that on any contested application for an order under s8,[3] or any
application under Part IV of the Act,[4] a court shall have regard in particular to . . . the ascertainable wishes and feelings of the child concerned
(considered in the light of his age and understanding). (Applications for
child assessment orders and emergency protection orders are to be found in
Part V of the Act, and it is not required that the welfare checklist is considered prior to the making of an order, although in practice this usually
happens.) In the Children Act, a child is defined as a person under the age
of 18 years.

The Family Law Act 1996 is not yet fully implemented. However, there
is provision in s11 (4) (a) placing a duty on the court to 'have particular
regard' to 'the child's wishes and feelings'. Other sections of the same Act
(not yet implemented) require that professionals encourage parents to
consider the child's wishes and feelings: at the information stage (s8 (9)
(b)), in mediation (s27 (8) (a)) and in consultation with legal representa-
tives (s12 (2) (a)). Some children will be directly consulted in mediation
sessions, (s27 (8) (b)). In addition, s64 enables the Lord Chancellor to
make regulations providing for children to be separately represented (s64),
although it is not yet clear how many children in private law proceedings
will be permitted to do this or following what criteria.[5]

The child's views are relevant in the following situations

1 The court must have regard to 'the ascertainable wishes and feelings of
   the child concerned, considered in the light of his age and understanding' (s1 (3) (a)) before it makes, varies or discharges an order under either
   Part IV Children Act 1989, or on opposed applications for s8 orders.
2 Where there is a conflict between the wishes of children and the instructions of the guardian *ad litem* appointed to safeguard their interests,

the solicitor must consider whether to take instruction directly from a child client.[6]

3 Where there is no guardian *ad litem* appointed, children may directly instruct their own solicitor, who will have to be satisfied that the child client is competent to give instructions.

4 Where there is a question as to whether the appointment of the guardian *ad litem* should be terminated, the views of the parties to the case will be obtained, and this will include the views of the child.

5 When a medical or psychiatric examination, or any other assessment, is directed (on the making of a Child Assessment Order s43, or under s38 (6)), a child who is of sufficient understanding to make an informed decision may refuse to submit to the examination or other assessment. In practice, this means that whatever order a court may make about assessments or examination of a child, it will be difficult if not impossible to carry out the terms of the order without co-operation. This means that the guardian *ad litem* and solicitor will have to be very careful to discuss the proposals with a child before the hearing at which the order is requested.

6 A child may wish to apply for the variation or discharge of an order already made, such as an emergency protection order, supervision or care order, or may wish to apply for a contact order.

7 When the making of a contact order is being considered, the views of the child must be considered.

8 Children who are accommodated or the subject of a care order must be consulted by the local authority before any decision is taken concerning them (s23).

9 When children are in care to a local authority, as part of each statutory review, they must be informed of the steps they may take themselves, which include applying for the discharge of the order, applying for a contact order, or variation of an existing order or for leave to apply for a residence order (Guidance Vol.3 para 3.57).

10 Where the local authority is considering appointing a visitor for a child (Sched 2 para 17), if the child has sufficient understanding to object to the appointment, or an appointment continuing, the local authority must abide by the child's view.

Children may apply for the following orders

1 if they have sufficient understanding
   • an s8 order (for contact, residence, prohibited steps, specific issues)
   • a variation or discharge of an s8 order
   • an order bringing parental responsibility to an end
2 whether or not they have sufficient understanding

- the discharge of a care order, or variation of a supervision order (s39)
- when they are in care, for a contact order, or to vary or discharge that order, or to authorise the local authority to refuse contact (s34)
- for the appointment of a testamentary guardian to be brought to an end (s6) (with the prior leave of the court). This means that where a parent of a child dies, and a guardian has been appointed either by will, or by the court, to care for the children, they may apply to bring that person's appointment to an end.

Through whom are the child's wishes obtained?

A court welfare officer

all children should be seen by the court welfare officer unless there are strong grounds for not doing so . . . . Wherever their age and maturity permit it children should be offered the opportunity to express their wishes and feelings . . . . Children should never be forced to express a view.[7]

There are occasions when it may be inappropriate for children to be interviewed in connection with a court application; for instance, they may be receiving treatment from a therapist or psychiatrist who advises that an interview may cause great distress or disturbance. In those circumstances, the court may be asked to make a ruling as to whether or not the interview should take place.

The future of the court welfare service is presently under review by a government working party. However, the Home Secretary has indicated that the services of the court welfare officer, guardian *ad litem*, and Official Solicitor are likely to be merged, and a new unified service will be established, independent of the present agencies that manage them.

The Official Solicitor

The Official Solicitor is a department of the Civil Service attached to the Court service, under the Lord Chancellor's Department. The Official Solicitor employs a number of investigative officers to deal with cases involving people under a disability, who cannot represent themselves in court cases, whether because of mental illness or because they are children, and deemed to be under a disability for that reason. The Official Solicitor will act in the interest of the client, and instruct a barrister to present the case in court. He will usually act only in the most complex of cases, for instance those involving complex medical evidence, conflict between experts, and cases where children come from outside the UK or where there may be a possibility of them going to live outside this country.

Guardian ad litem

Following the death of Maria Colwell in 1973, when a care order was discharged without the court having the opportunity to hear from any social worker independent of the local authority and parents, the law was changed to provide for such representation, through a guardian *ad litem*. In 1984, the government brought into force a system of panels of guardians *ad litem* to represent children in cases involving local authorities, and the Children Act 1989 extended these provisions, so that at present, children are represented in nearly all cases involving local authorities (cases known as specified proceedings, under s41). The court appoints guardians, and their task is to safeguard the welfare of children throughout the proceedings. They will instruct a solicitor to act, interview anyone connected with the children, and the children themselves, and will write reports for the court, and give evidence in court.

Through the parties themselves

Anyone who makes a statement for the court proceedings, whether in writing, or by giving evidence, will be able to put forward what they understand of the views of the children involved in the case. The court will attach what weight it considers appropriate to this evidence, depending on how close the witness is to the child, and whether they might have any reason for distorting the views in an attempt to achieve what they want; (for instance the parent who says the child alleges abuse by an absent parent, in order to stop contact taking place).

Through their own solicitor

Some children are permitted to instruct their own solicitors, without having a guardian *ad litem*. They can do this only when they are of sufficient age and understanding to have an appreciation of the nature of, and reason for, the proceedings. If there is a dispute about the level of understanding, the court will make a ruling.

Children may give evidence in court

The child may give sworn evidence if they understand the nature of the oath. The dividing line is regarded as being somewhere between 8 and 10 years.[8] A child whom the court considers able to understand what is happening in court, and the importance of telling the truth, can be compelled to give evidence as a witness.[9]

Children seeing the judge

This is rare: judges take the view that although it may be beneficial for children to see the judge, they may give information or a view that they do not want revealed to their parents; and the judges take the view that 'to treat evidence as confidential and not to be disclosed to the parties creates ... major difficulties for the parties in the conduct of their cases'. Dame Margaret Booth, formerly a judge of the Family Division, and Court of Appeal, has said that

> Many children may wish to see the judge. . . . This may be very beneficial for the child. . . . But a child may impart some new information to a judge which that judge is bound to pass on to the other parties. . . . To the child that may well be seen as a breach of confidence. . . . It also is quite an uncomfortable thing for a judge to have to do.

Situations in which lawyers must listen to children in order to ascertain their views

Whether or not a lawyer will have to seek out directly the views of children whose welfare is being considered by a court, will depend on the children's status in the proceedings. If the child is a party, then they will be represented either directly by a lawyer, or indirectly through a guardian *ad litem*. In either case, if a solicitor is instructed, they will have to see the child.

Adoption/freeing for adoption cases

In the High Court, a child is always a party (which means that they can participate fully in the proceedings) and must be represented through a guardian *ad litem*, who must, under the court rules, appoint a solicitor. In the Magistrates Court and County Court, the court rules do not permit a child to be made a party, but often the guardian *ad litem* will be joined as a party instead, and will then be represented by a solicitor.

Public law cases (those proceedings set out in s41 Children Act 1989)

A child is always a party, and the court must appoint a guardian *ad litem* unless satisfied that it is not necessary to do so to safeguard the interests of the child. The guardian must instruct a solicitor for the child, unless the child has sufficient understanding to instruct a solicitor and wishes to do so.

Where the solicitor is instructed by the guardian *ad litem* and there is a conflict between those instructions and instructions from the child, the solicitor must consider whether he or she should take instructions directly from the child, and not through the guardian *ad litem*: the child must be able 'having regard to his understanding, to give instructions on his own behalf'.[10]

Private law cases (those between individuals)

A child is always a party where he or she may wish to make an application themselves, or to be joined as a party. The court rules permit a child to be involved in family proceedings only through a guardian *ad litem* or next friend. There is an exception to this rule, where the court gives permission, or where a solicitor has accepted a child's instructions, having considered in the light of the child's age and understanding that they are able to give instructions.

The Children Act entitles a child to ask the court for leave to apply for a s8 order. However, the court rules provide that the court may grant leave only if it is satisfied that a child has sufficient understanding to make the application.

These applications must be heard by the High Court,[11] and not only must a child convince the court that they have the necessary understanding to make the application, but in addition, they must show that the application concerns an issue that it is proper for the court to determine and that it has a reasonable chance of success.

The definition of 'sufficient understanding'

The decision as to whether or not children are competent, and therefore can give instructions, is difficult, and is one in which objectivity and precision are not easily achieved. The courts have considered on a number of occasions in what circumstances children can instruct their solicitor directly. It has been held that, ultimately, it is a matter for the court whether children have sufficient understanding, but once it is decided that they do, then the court cannot impose a guardian *ad litem* on them. The court retains the ultimate right to decide whether a child has the necessary ability, having regard to their understanding, to instruct their solicitor.

A challenge to a solicitor's assessment will be rare, and in borderline cases the solicitor's view will be given the benefit of the doubt. It has been emphasised that the test is not one of age but of understanding, and that where issues raised by the case require insight that only maturity could bring, then the court would be less likely to allow a child to conduct the proceedings without a guardian *ad litem*.[12]

The following quotations from cases indicate the thinking amongst the judiciary on this complex issue:

223

a child, is after all, a child. . . . they are likely to be vulnerable
and impressionable. . . . The judge has to do his best, on the evidence
before him, to assess the understanding of the individual child in
the context of the proceedings in which he seeks to participate.

[whilst] it is no doubt true (at least of children) that understanding
increases with the passage of time there can be no line of demar-
cation based on age, and wisely so.

different children have different levels of understanding at the same
age.

understanding is not absolute. It has to be assessed relatively to
the issues in the proceedings.

where any sound judgement on these issues calls for insight and
imagination which only maturity and experience can bring, both
the Court and the solicitor will be slow to conclude that the child's
understanding is sufficient.

the reason why the law is particularly solicitous in protecting the
interests of children is because they are liable to be vulnerable and
impressionable, lacking the maturity to weigh the longer term
against the shorter, lacking the insight to know how they will react
and the imagination to know how others will react in situations,
lacking the experience to measure the probable against the
possible.[13]

the assessment (of understanding) must be in the context of the
proceedings in which she seeks to participate.

I would hold as a matter of law the parental right to determine
whether or not their minor child below the age of 16 will
have medical treatment terminated if and when the child achieves
a sufficient level of understanding and intelligence to enable him
or her to understand fully what is proposed. It will a question of
fact . . . a minor's capacity . . . is not to be determined by reference to any judicially fixed age limited.[14]

The solicitor's relationship with the child

Central to the solicitor's relationship with a child client is the need to make
a decision as to whether or not that child is capable of giving instructions
to the solicitor, as opposed to the solicitor listening to the child, but taking
instructions from the guardian *ad litem*.

When to obtain a child's wishes

These wishes have to be kept under constant review, as they may well change during the course of the case; there are particular points in the case when they should be obtained, and these are:

- at the start of the proceedings;
- at the time of any court hearings;
- when a major change in the child's living situation is likely to take place;
- before the final hearing; and
- when the report of the guardian *ad litem* is available.

How to ascertain a child's wishes

1 Know sufficient about a child before the meeting.
2 Discuss with the guardian *ad litem* whether it is preferable to go together for the first meeting.
3 Consider where to see a child: in their home, foster home, children's home, school, office, McDonalds.
4 Consider the appropriate dress to wear.
5 Be sensitive to the issues of race, gender, religion and culture; e.g. a young Asian woman may not be happy about being seen in public with any white solicitor, whether man or woman.
6 Be sensitive to the fact that a child may not want to discuss details of abuse, and may express a wish to return to their parents' home from a foster home, in spite of the possible danger, and lack of protection.
7 Consider whether or not to take what a child says at face value, or to interpret it, and act on the interpretation. There is a difference of opinion amongst childcare lawyers about this issue; some take the view that it is for the guardian *ad litem* and other social work professionals to interpret what a child says, and that a lawyer has no competence or training to do so. Others suggest that it is perfectly proper and sensible not to take what a child says at face value, but to decide whether what is said is what is really meant.
8 Make sure not to make promises you cannot keep.
9 Consider whether or not a child should attend the court building for the hearing, and whether or not he or she should give evidence.
10 Consider how much information to provide to a child, and what documents to disclose.

Confidentiality

Solicitors have a duty to keep confidential the affairs of clients, and to ensure that their staff do the same. However, there may be exceptional circumstances involving children where a solicitor should consider revealing confidential information to an appropriate authority; this may be where a child is the client and reveals information that indicates continuing sexual or other physical abuse, but refuses to allow disclosure of such information.

A solicitor has two duties to a child client: the duty to act in the child's best interest, and the duty of confidentiality. When considering the duty to act in the best interests of a client, the solicitor has to decide whether or not the child client is competent to give instructions. If they are competent, then they must be represented in accordance with those instructions. If they are not competent, then the solicitor must act in their best interests.

The decision as to whether or not a child is competent has other consequences. The solicitor's entitlement to breach the duty of confidentiality will depend on this.

Where a mature child (whether defined by age or understanding) tells the solicitor that they are or have been abused, there is an absolute duty of confidentiality, although efforts would be made to persuade the child to report this or to allow the solicitor to do so. However, if a solicitor is told, or believes, that younger siblings (or possibly other children outside the family) are being abused, or that a child is in fear of their life or serious injury, then the solicitor may have a discretion to breach confidentiality.

Where a child is immature, then the solicitor must do his or her best for them and try to persuade the child to disclose the abuse. If they will not do so, the solicitor should consider reporting this, if it is in the public interest, and if there is no other way of dealing with the situation, such as telling the guardian *ad litem*. In those circumstances, the solicitor will also have to consider whether the child's parent, if he or she is the alleged abuser, should be given the information. It may be preferable for the social services department and/or police to decide at what point the disclosure should be notified.

Any client, whether an adult or child, has the right to be made aware of when and in what circumstances the solicitor's duty of confidentiality may be breached. It is not easy to decide when and how to make a child client aware of this possibility. It is preferable to tell a child at the first interview, although this may well result in them being unwilling to disclose abuse to the solicitor. Not surprisingly, the *Guide to the Professional Conduct of Solicitors* states:

> in the end it is for the solicitor to exercise his or her professional judgement about when and how to explain the duty of confidentiality to any client; it is impossible to formulate a rule that can be applied in all circumstances.

Editor's note

The Children's Legal Centre information sheet *Offering Children Confidentiality: Law and Guidance*, also sets out the legal position on confidentiality in an understanding and helpful way.[15]

Notes

In references to Law Reports: WLR = Weekly Law Reports; FLR = Family Law Reports.

1 Lansdown, G. 1992 in *Childright* 1991 (November: 4)
2 Section 1 (3) Children Act 1989 provides that in contested applications under s8, or on any application under Part IV, a court shall have regard in particular to:

- the ascertainable wishes and feelings of the child concerned (considered in the light of his age and understanding);
- his physical, emotional and educational needs;
- the likely effect on him of any change in his circumstances;
- his age, sex, background and any characteristics of his which the court considers relevant;
- any harm which he has suffered or is at risk of suffering;
- how capable each of his parents, and any other person in relation to whom the court considers the question to be relevant, is of meeting his needs;
- the range of powers available to the court under this Act in the proceedings in question.

3 Section 8 Children Act 1989 defines orders that can be made in family proceedings. They are:

- a contact order: an order requiring the person with whom a child lives, or is to live, to allow the child to visit or stay with the person named in the order;
- a prohibited steps order: an order which prohibits a person with parental responsibility from exercising all or part of it;
- a residence order: which settles the arrangements to be made as to the person with whom a child is to live;
- a specific issues order: which gives directions as to how a person may exercise their parental responsibility.

4 Part IV of the Children Act 1989 provides for applications by Local Authorities or the NSPCC for care or supervision orders.
5 Section 8 (9) (b) Family Law Act 1996 provides that regulations must make provision with respect to the giving of information about, amongst other things, 'the importance to be attached to the welfare, wishes and feelings of children'. In relation to the provision of legal aid for mediation in family matters, section 27 (8) (a) provides that:

where there are one or more children of the family, the code (of practice for mediators) must also require the mediator to have arrangements designed to ensure that the parties are encouraged to consider – the welfare, wishes and feelings of each child, and whether and to what extent each child should be given the opportunity to express his or her wishes and feelings in the mediation.

Section 12 (2) (a) permits the Lord Chancellor to make rules, which will require the lawyer for a party proposing to commence divorce proceedings to inform their client that in relation to the arrangements to be made for a child, the parties should consider the child's welfare, wishes and feelings.

6 The Family Proceedings Courts (Children Act) Rules 1991 r12 (1) (a) require that a solicitor should represent a child in accordance with instructions received from the guardian *ad litem*, unless the solicitor considers, having taken into account the views of the guardian *ad litem*, that the child wishes to give instructions that conflict with those views, and that they are able, having regard to their understanding, to give such instructions on their own behalf (FPC (CA 1989) R 1991 r12 (1) (a) and FPR 1991 r4.12 (1) (a).

7 *National Standards for Probation Service Family Court Welfare Work*, Home Office 1994.

8 R v Hayes (1977) 1 WLR 234.

9 R v B County Council ex parte P (1991) 1 FLR 470.

10 See note 6 above.

11 Practice Direction (1993) 1 FLR 668.

12 Re CT (A Minor) (Wardship: Representation) (1993) 2 FLR 278.

13 Sir Thomas Bingham in Re S (a minor) (independent representation) (1993) 2 FLR 437.

14 Gillick v West Norfolk and Wisbech A.H.A. (1986) AC 112: Lord Scarman.

15 Children's Legal Centre (1997) *Offering Children Confidentiality: Law and Guidance*. Colchester: Children's Legal Centre, University of Essex.

AFTERWORD

This book was conceived in the conviction that actively listening to children is an important key to their healthy development as people. That conviction has grown steadily with the book, and it is our hope that the wealth of evidence within these pages will help to convince readers that time given to listen to children is time well spent.

Writing the book has been a labour of love in which many have had a hand. Contributors have given willingly of their time and talents, despite the heavy demands of their personal and professional lives. But the vital energy and enthusiasm, without which the book would never have been possible, has come from young people. We hope that they will inspire you, as they have inspired us, to listen with open hearts and minds to what children have to say.

Pat Milner and Birgit Carolin

USEFUL ADDRESSES

Association for Child Psychology and Psychiatry (ACPP)   70 Borough
  High Street, London Bridge, London SE1 1XF.
Association for Professionals in Service for Adolescents (APSA)
  Buckham Hall House, Uckfield, East Sussex TN22 5XZ.
Association of Lawyers for Children   PO Box 2029, Buckhurst Hill,
  Essex IG9 6EQ
Association of Professional Music Therapists (APMT)   38 Pierre Lane,
  Fulbourn, Cambridgeshire CB1 5DL.
Barnardos   Tanners Lane, Barkingside, Ilford, Essex IG6 1QG.
British Society for Counselling (BAC)   1 Regent Place, Rugby,
  Warwickshire CV21 2PJ.
British Society for Music Therapy (BSMT)   25 Rosslyn Avenue, East
  Barnet, Herts EN4 8DH.
Brook Advisory Services   165 Grays Inn Road, London WC1X 8UD.
Cambridge Family and Divorce Centre   1 Brooklands Avenue,
  Cambridge CB2 2BB.
Centre 33   33 Clarendon Street, Cambridge CB1 1JX
Child Bereavement Trust   Harleyford Estate, Henley Road, Marlow,
  Buckinghamshire SL7 2DX.
ChildLine   Royal Mail Building, Studd Street, London N1 0QW.
Children's Hours Trust   The Old Rectory, East Marden, Nr Chichester,
  West Sussex PO18 9JE.
Children's Legal Centre   University of Essex, Wivenhoe Park, Colchester,
  Essex CO4 3SQ.
Counselling in Education Division, BAC   See BAC.
Cruse Bereavement Care   Cruse House, 126 Sheen Road, Richmond,
  Surrey TW9 1UR.
Cambridge Cruse   Victoria Road Community Centre, Cambridge
  CB4 3DZ.
End Child Prostitution, Pornography and Trafficking (ECPAT)   Thomas
  Clarkson House, The Stable Yard, Broomgrove Road, London SW9
  2TL.

Foundation for the Study of Infant Deaths   14 Halkin Street, London SW1X 7DP.

Kidscape   152 Buckingham Palace Road, London SW1W 9TR.

Mental Health Foundation   37 Mortimer Street, London W1N 7RJ.

National Association for Family Mediation and Conciliation Services 9 Tavistock Place, London WC1H 9SN.

NAFSIYAT Intercultural Therapy Centre   278 Seven Sisters Road, Finsbury Park, London N4 2HY.

National Children's Bureau   8 Wakley Street, London EC1.

National Children's Homes   85 Highbury Park, London N5 1UD

National Pyramid Trust   12 Brierly Court, Church Road, London W7 3BN.

National Society for the Prevention of Cruelty to Children (NSPCC) 42 Curtain Road, London EC2A 3NH.

Newpin   Sutherland House, 25 Sutherland Square, London SE17 3EE.

Parentline   Westbury House, 57 Hart Road, Thundersley, Essex SS7 3DP.

Person Centred Art Therapy Centre (PCAT)   17 Cranbourne Gardens, London NW11 OHN.

The Place to Be   Liningstone House, 11 Carteret Street, London SW1H 9DL.

Resource Network for Adolescents   DLI, Mill Lane, Warford, Alderley Edge, Cheshire SK9 7UD.

Rowan Centre   Broom Lane, Rotherham S60 3NW.

Samaritans   10 The Grove, Slough, Berkshire SL1 1QP.

Trust for Study of Adolescence   23 New Road, Brighton, East Sussex BN1 1WZ.

UNICEF   Unit 3, Rignals Lane, Galleywood, Chelmsford, Essex CM2 8TU.

Volunteer Reading Help   (Inner London), Ebury Bridge Centre, Sutherland Street, London SW1V 4LH.

Winston's Wish   Gloucestershire Royal Hospital, Great Western Road, Gloucestershire GL1 3NN.

Young Minds   22a Boston Place, London NW1 6ER.

INDEX